CW01657593

asian 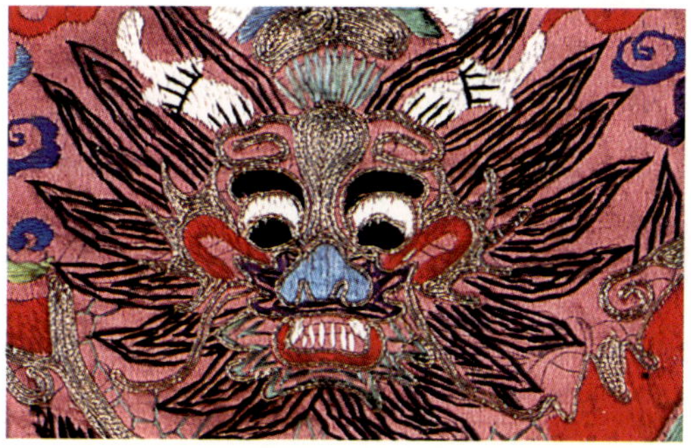

style source book

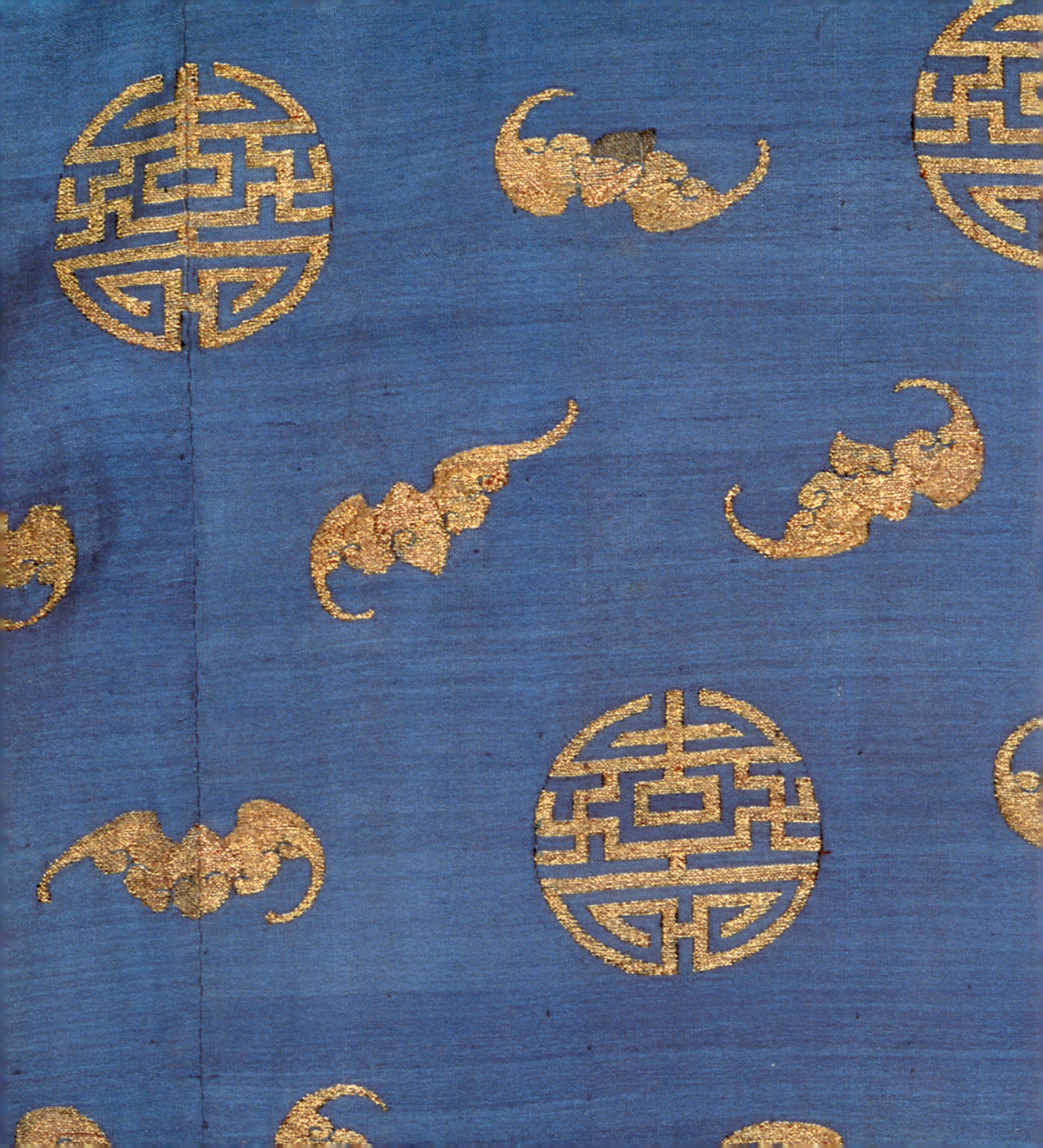

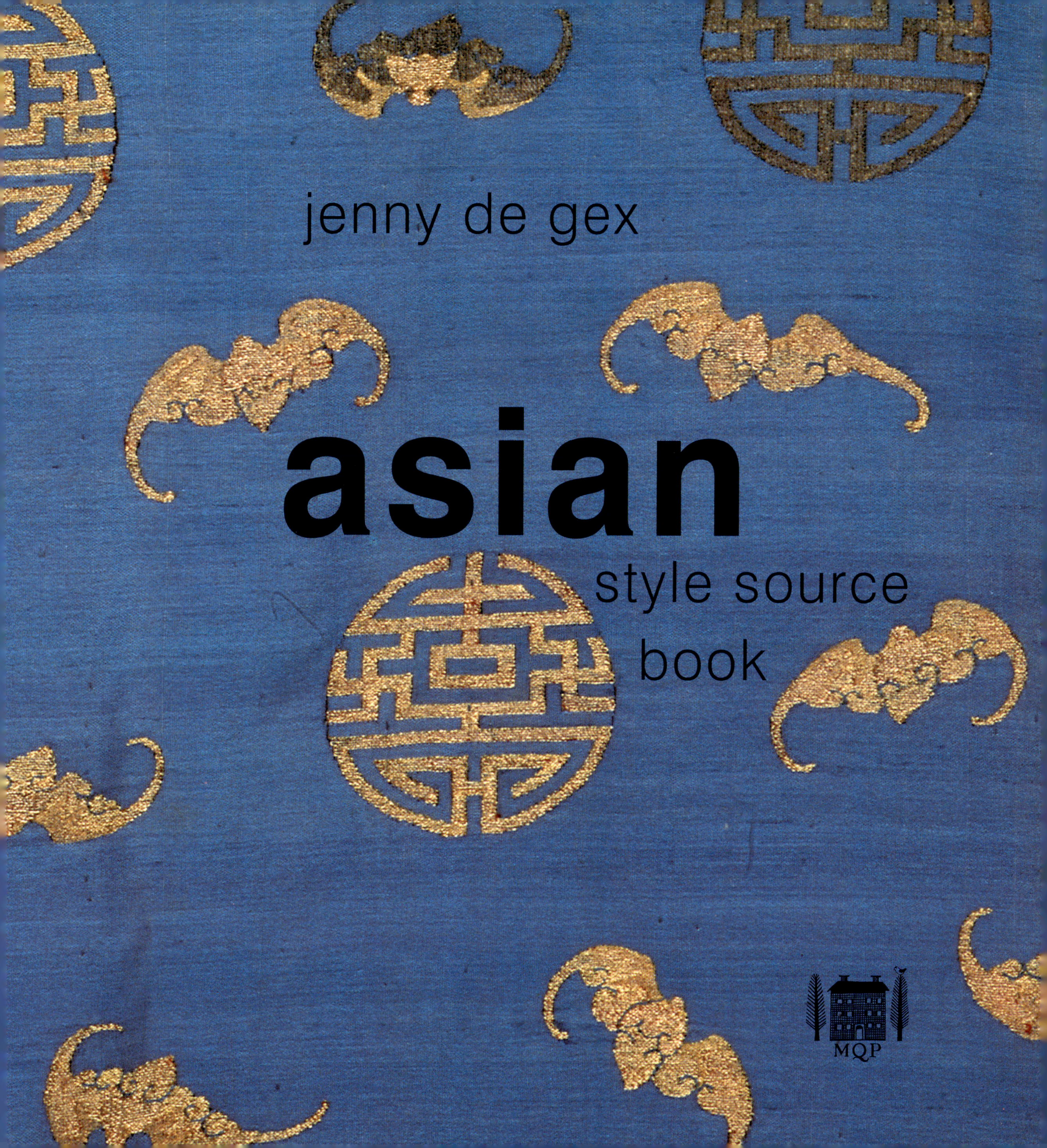

jenny de gex

asian

style source book

MQP

Published by MQ Publications
254–258 Goswell Road
London EC1V 7RL

Copyright © MQ Publications Ltd, 2000
Text copyright © Jenny de Gex, 2000

All rights reserved. No part of this publication may be reproduced or transmitted in any form or by any means, electronic or mechanical, including photocopy, recording, or any retrieval system now known or to be invented without permission in writing from the publishers.

A CIP catalogue record for this book is available from the British Library

ISBN: 1 84072 090 5

1 2 3 4 5 6 7 8 9

Printed in Italy

Series editor: Ljiljana Ortolja-Baird
Project editor: Nicola Birtwisle
Text editor: Eric Chaline
Designer: Bet Ayer

contents

introduction 6

color 12

pattern 36

texture and materials 54

architecture 84

furniture 102

gardens 122

time line 140

acknowledgments 141

credits 142

index 143

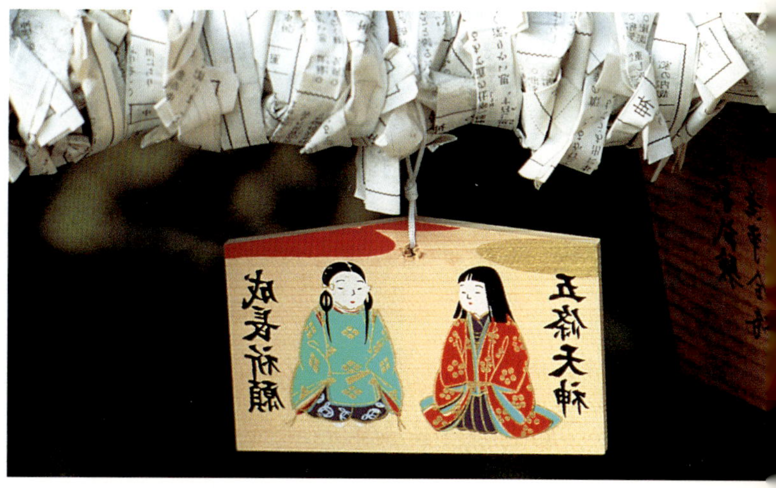

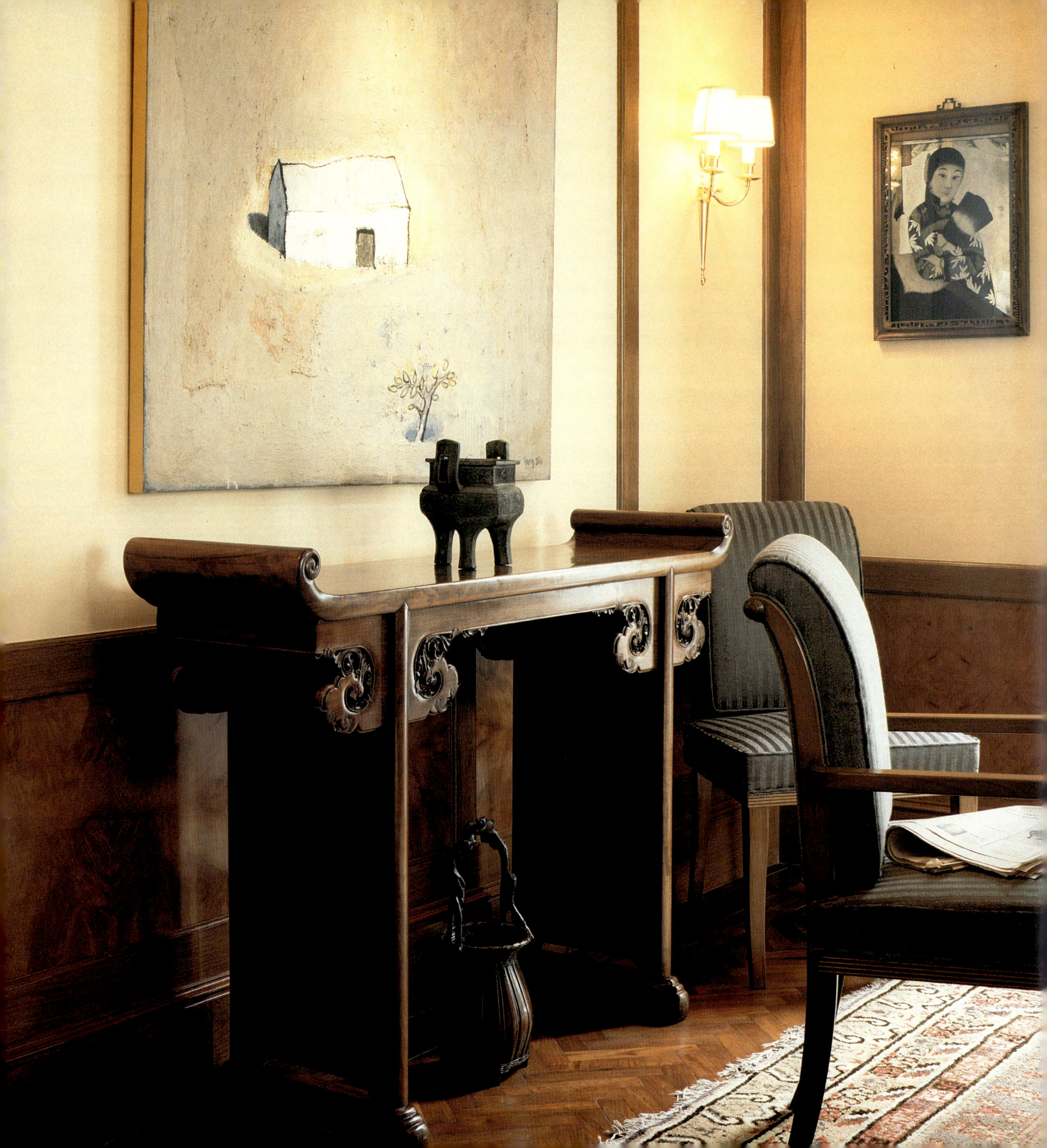

introduction

In writing this book, I have tried to show how the traditional arts and crafts of China and Japan have influenced Western taste and design over the past three centuries. The task of sifting through the treasure house of East Asian style to distill its principles and order them in the simple framework of a book has been a task both inspiring and daunting. The wealth of artistry and craftsmanship that can be glimpsed on every page represents a tiny fraction of the creative genius of these two great cultures.

China and the West

The "Middle Kingdom," China, is one of the cradles of world civilization. As the first people to smelt iron, make paper and gunpowder, drink tea, and weave silk, the Chinese led the world in technology until the fifteenth century. Unlike the Romans, who used their technological superiority to create a vast empire in the West, the Chinese exerted their influence on their near neighbors Korea and Japan primarily through the peaceful means of trade, art, and religion.

China has traded with the West since Roman times, when silks and ceramics were carried along the Silk Route through Central Asia to the Levantine ports for redistribution in Western Europe. The rise of Islam in the seventh century A.D. interrupted the overland trade route, and direct contact with the West was so infrequent that China became a land shrouded in myth and mystery. Medieval chroniclers amazed their readers with colorful tales of China's fierce monsters and one-legged, one-eyed inhabitants who hopped from place to place. There were rare visitors, such as Marco Polo, who traveled to the court of the Mongol emperor Kublai Khan in 1271—but even his sober account was considered by many of his contemporaries to be too fantastic to be true.

left A small incense burner stands on an antique Chinese side table with elegantly curved ends and intricate carvings, blending classical eastern tastes into an elegant Western-style interior.

After the collapse of the Mongol Yuan dynasty (1260–1368), and the rise to power of the native Ming dynasty (1368–1644), China turned in upon itself and forbade all contacts with the outside world. Many art historians and connoisseurs consider that the culture of the Ming dynasty represents the zenith of Chinese artistic achievement. However, although the early stages of China's isolation provided the fertile ground for the rebirth of the native tradition, over time, the lack of interaction with the rest of the world sapped innovation, replacing it with the stale replication of established models. Denied the wealthy foreign trade that would make it rich, the Ming state became mired in social problems and political corruption. As the empire sank into chaos, the Europeans were opening the maritime trade routes to Asia. Under external pressure, the Chinese government lifted the ban on foreigners in 1533, and established trading links with the Portuguese, Dutch, and British.

Although the West was already familiar with Chinese ornamentation and design from imported ceramics, lacquerwork, and textiles, the first illustrations of Chinese architecture and gardens to reach the West in the late sixteenth century had an instantaneous and far-reaching impact on the decorative arts, textiles, and furniture design, giving birth to a new style known as *chinoiserie*, which, literally translated from the French, means, "Chinese things."

Japan and the West

Westerners did not reach Japan—the fabled isles of Xipangu of medieval cartographers—until the late sixteenth century. This initial period of contact, although fruitful for both sides, was to be short-lived. In the early seventeenth century, the first Tokugawa *shogun*, Ieyasu (1543–1616), fearful of invasion, banned Christianity, and his successor closed the country to foreigners altogether. Only one port remained open to external trade, Nagasaki in Western Japan, whose tiny community of Dutch and Chinese merchants were Japan's only window on the wider world until the mid-nineteenth century, when the United States was granted full trading rights by a crumbling shogunal government in 1858, ending two and a half centuries of isolation.

The first foreign visitors to Japan, whose tastes had been formed by the highly ornamented Victorian style, were shocked by the spare, minimal interiors they saw there. A full appreciation of Japanese aesthetics, which although unchanged for centuries, were a century ahead of their time in Western terms, required the development of a more refined artistic sensibility. Among the first Westerners to "discover" Japanese art were the French Impressionists. They became avid collectors of *ukiyo-e* woodblock prints, which had first made their way to Europe in the late nineteenth century as packaging for export ceramics. At the beginning of the twentieth century, the revolution in design begun by the Arts and Crafts Movement sought to reinvigorate the Western decorative arts by delving deep into its own past and borrowing from other traditions. In the early twentieth century, Scottish architect and designer Charles Rennie Mackintosh, especially, employed the clean lines and graphic, sweeping shapes of Japanese design as one source of inspiration for his strikingly modern interiors.

Symbolism in East Asian style

In the Taoist world view, social harmony, personal health, and good fortune are attained by the balancing of the two elemental principles of *yin* and *yang*, represented by the paired opposites of light and dark, male and female, sun and moon, and hard and yielding, and depicted in the familiar circular symbol, which often appears as a decorative device itself. Applying this theory to the material world, the Chinese developed the complex art of geomancy known as *feng shui* (wind and water), whose purpose was to channel the energies of the cosmos to attract propitious influences and dispel evil. The principles of *feng shui* were applied in the choice of materials, color, symbolic patterns, and to the physical layout of rooms, buildings, and gardens.

Although Japan borrowed much of its material culture, religion, and early political institutions from China during the sixth and seventh centuries, it also underwent long periods of isolation from the mainland, during which it transformed imported forms and ideas, combining them with pre-existing native elements to create uniquely Japanese cultural forms.

Zen style

Stripped of all ritual and theology, Zen Buddhism is not a religion in the conventional sense of the word, its only devotions being the practice of *zazen* meditation and the solving of *koan* riddles. It was instrumental in the development of Japan's decorative arts and architecture.

The transcendent Zen world view and the aristocratic appreciation of beauty of the Heian period (794–1185) were combined in the sixteenth century to create the Way of Tea, or *Sado.* The tea ceremony (*chanoyu*) is the supreme expression of the philosophy of *wabi-sabi.* These two elusive principles, which are both moral and aesthetic, celebrate poverty and solitude, and advocate a tranquil life far from the world, devoted to discovering beauty in simplicity. In the decorative arts, this was expressed by a preference for natural materials, such as unfinished wood, natural fibers, and roughly plastered walls, and for unadorned, "rustic" furnishings and ceramic wares.

Modern influences

In their native countries, traditional Chinese and Japanese arts and crafts continue to be practiced. China, which earlier this century was persecuting its artists and traditional craftsmen, is now encouraging them to work and pass on their skills to a new generation. Temples, gardens, and palaces, neglected or damaged during the excesses of the Cultural Revolution, are being restored and reopened for the growing tourist industry, as well as to rebuild links with China's imperial past. Japan has preserved much of its traditional culture and way of life. The cutting-edge technology and culture that we so admire today is deeply rooted in aesthetic concepts of balance and simplicity that are a thousand years old. In the modern period, the artistic and craft heritage of both China and Japan continues to attract and inspire Western artists, architects, and designers.

right A *tsukubai* or bamboo and stone water fountain, echoing an old ritual of purification, one of the tea masters' contributions to garden design. After drinking or washing, the "clack" of the bamboo resonates and fades, symbolizing the movement of time.

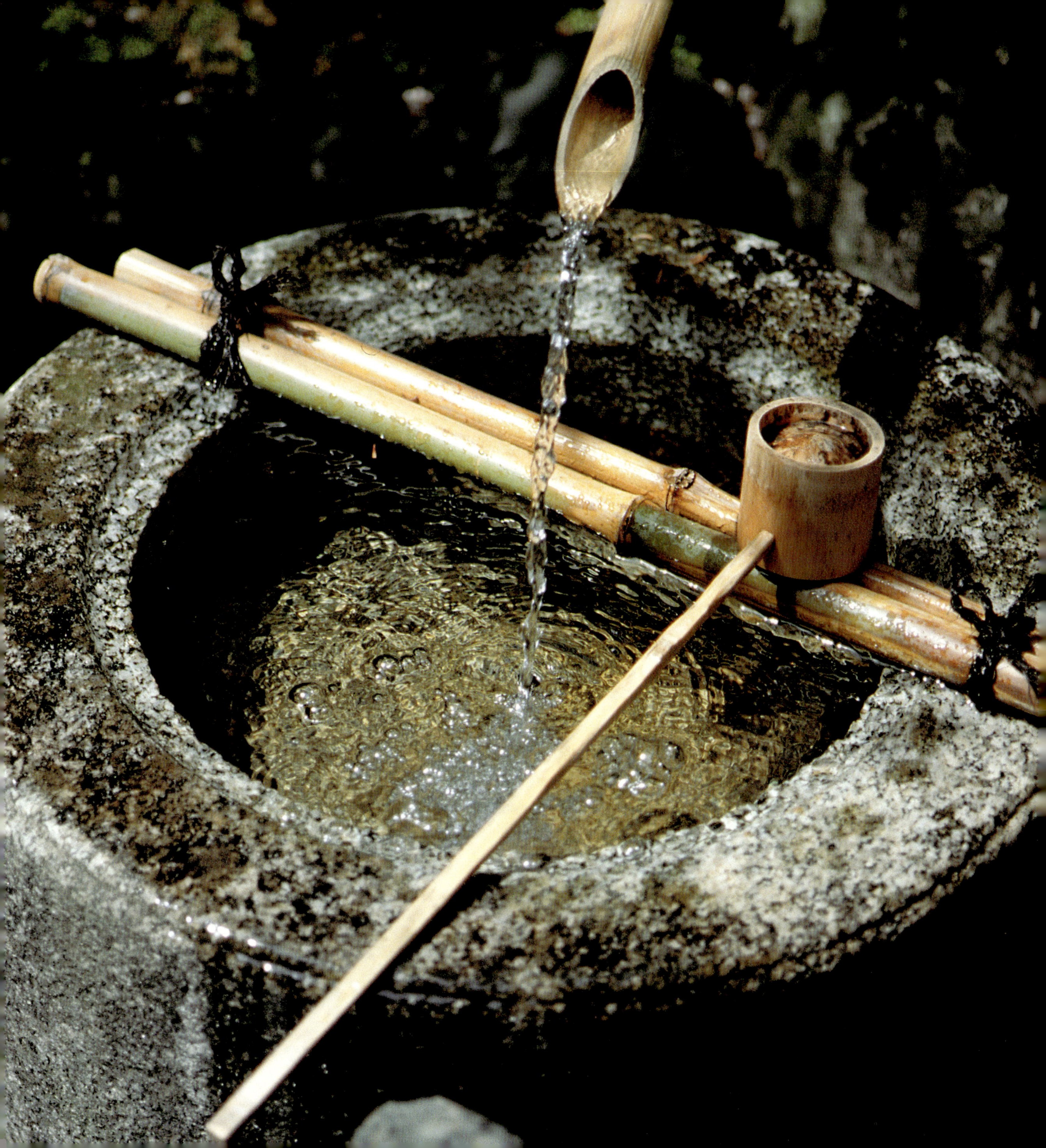

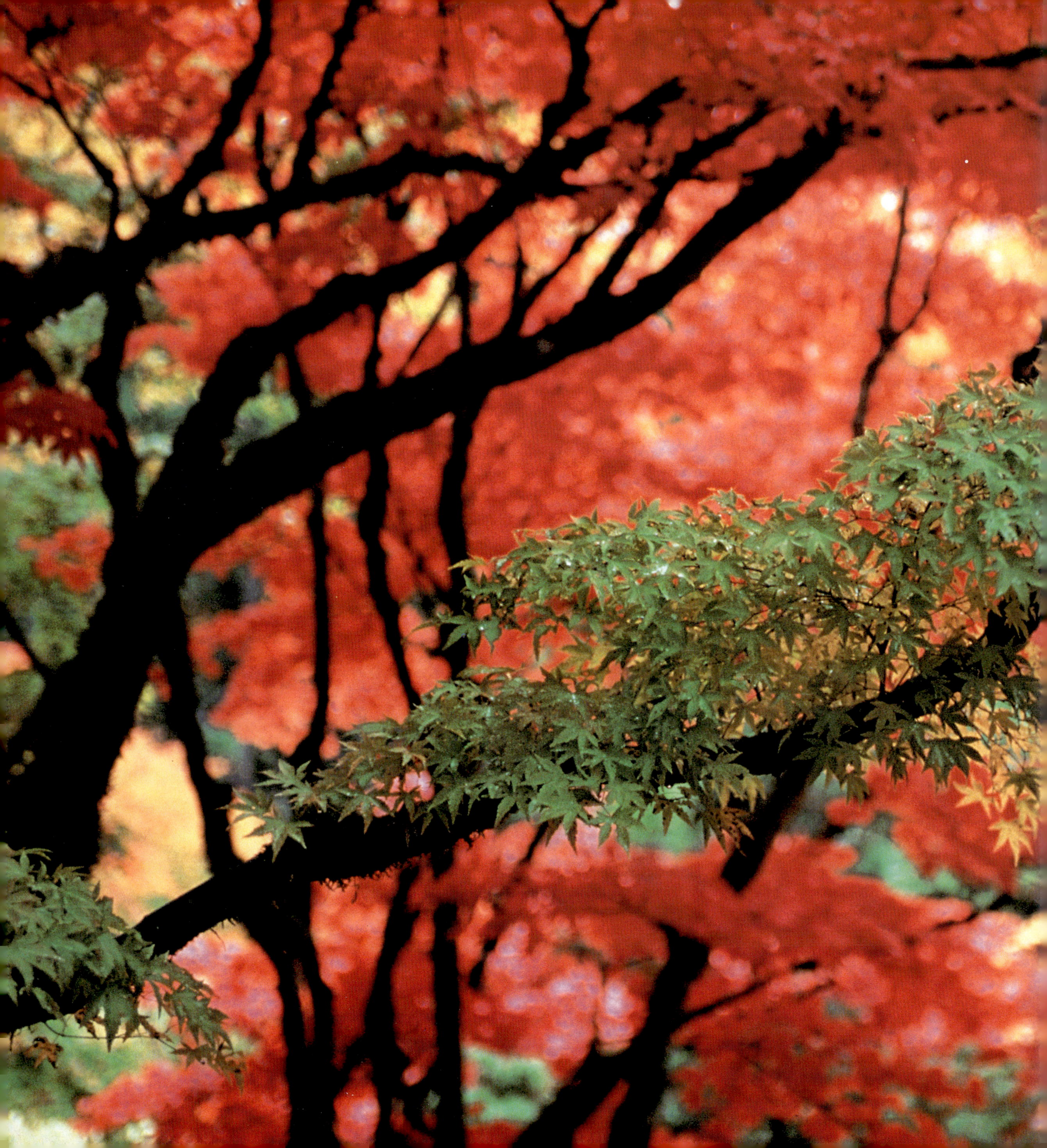

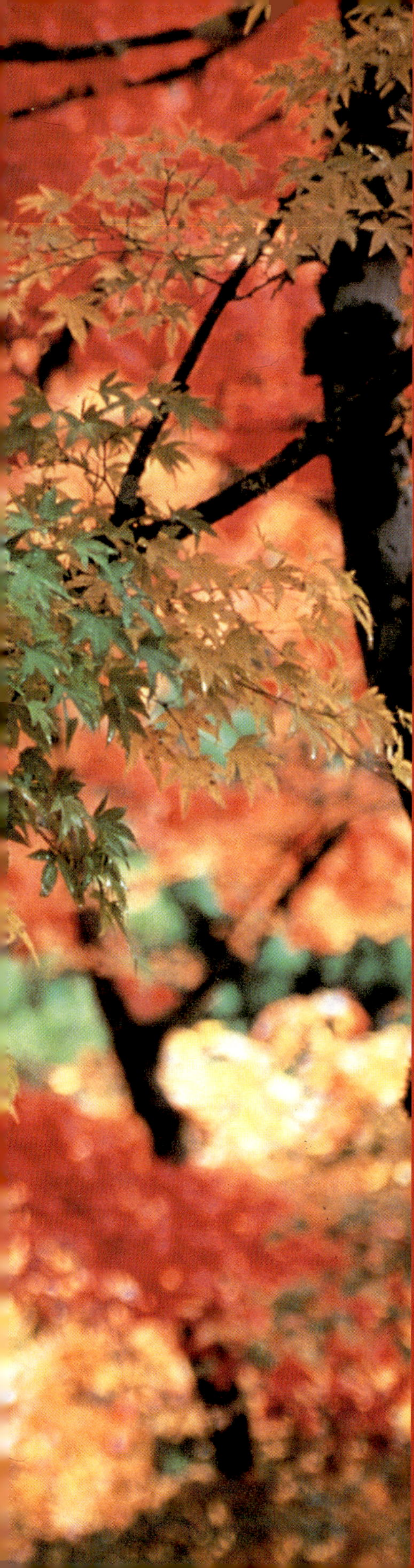

color

The East Asian palette is rich in symbolic meanings, sometimes in harmony with our own understanding of color, sometimes at variance with it. Although we in the West share the associations of red with life, green with nature, and gold with opulence, the purity and innocence of our white have transmuted into the Asian color of dissolution and mourning. In ancient Rome, purple was the color chosen by the Caesars to denote their imperial rank, but in dynastic China, the emperors reserved yellow for their robes and the decoration of their palaces.

To the casual Western observer, the tints of China's recent past are limited to the monochrome drab imposed by ideological conformity, enlivened only by splashes of revolutionary red; while Japan, much praised and imitated by Western designers for the subtlety of its natural hues, is seen primarily as the home of industrial efficiency and of the minimalist Zen aesthetic. Yet both these preconceptions overlook the opulent decorative tradition of the temples, palaces, and castles of pre-modern China and Japan, as well as the rich, sometimes riotous, use of color and pattern in their traditional costume, folk art, and everyday utensils.

The glowing, jewel-like fall colors of Japanese maple trees provide a rich source of inspiration from the world of nature.

naturals

1 Closely woven Chinese bamboo harvest baskets, dating from the nineteenth century, are now sought-after decorative objects in their own right. They would formerly have been used for storing and transporting rice or other staples.

2 This brick-red earthenware model of a house shows us the kind of dwellings the Chinese lived in during the late Eastern Han period in China (early third century A.D.). The house's veranda has decorative ventilation holes, and inside, pillars topped by *dougang* brackets support the eaves.

Natural colors range in tone from hot to cold; shades of beige, cream, brown, and gray echo the colors of the earth and sky. In traditional Japanese homes, the use of color is subtle and muted to create a calming atmosphere. Natural hues and textures create the basic framework of the living space: the rice straw woven into *tatami* mats for flooring, the paper of the *shoji* sliding screens, and the unpainted wood of pillars and roof timbers. These understated colors and varied, sensuous textures have been a great influence on the development of tranquil, minimal interiors in contemporary Western design.

The use of natural materials to create objects that combine form and function is typified by the ancient art of weaving bamboo, cane, and reed into baskets, boxes, and chests. As well as being appreciated for their aesthetic qualities, these objects serve the very practical purposes of storage, transport, and display.

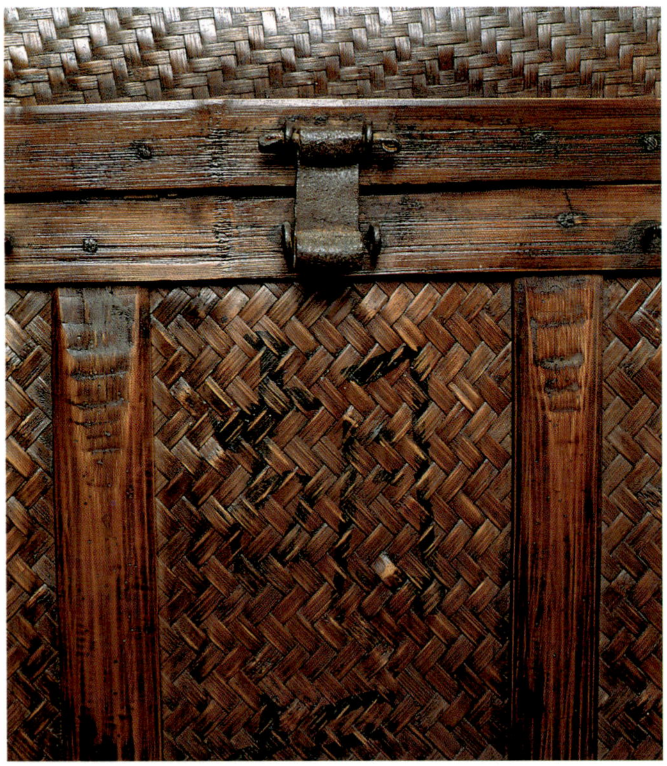

1 2

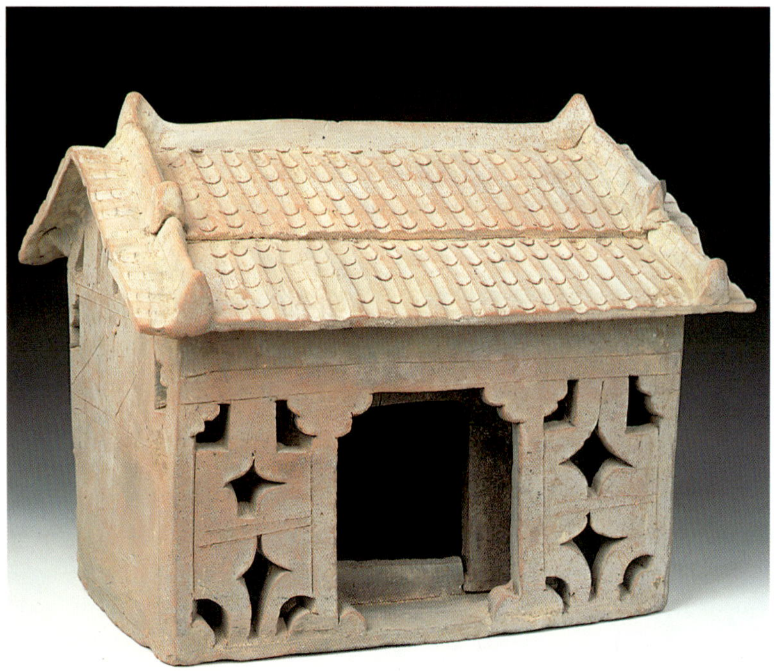

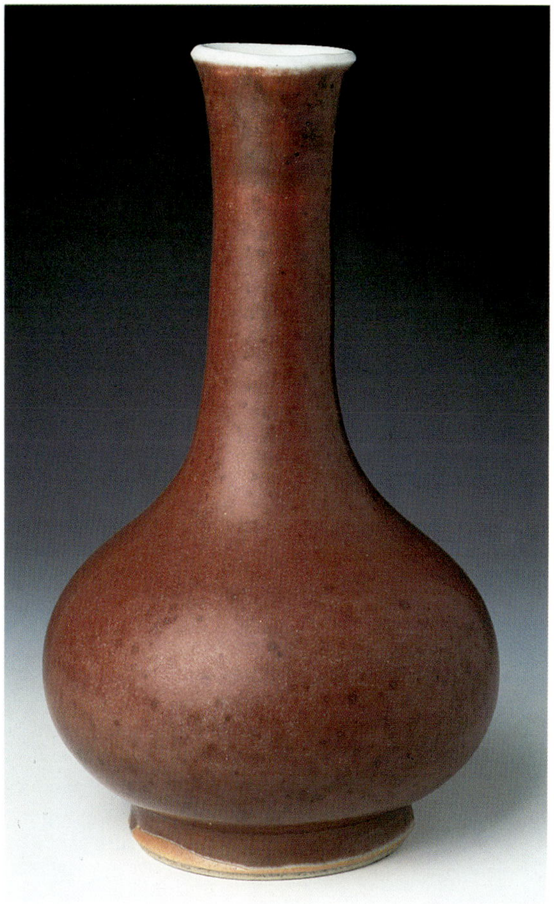

3 4

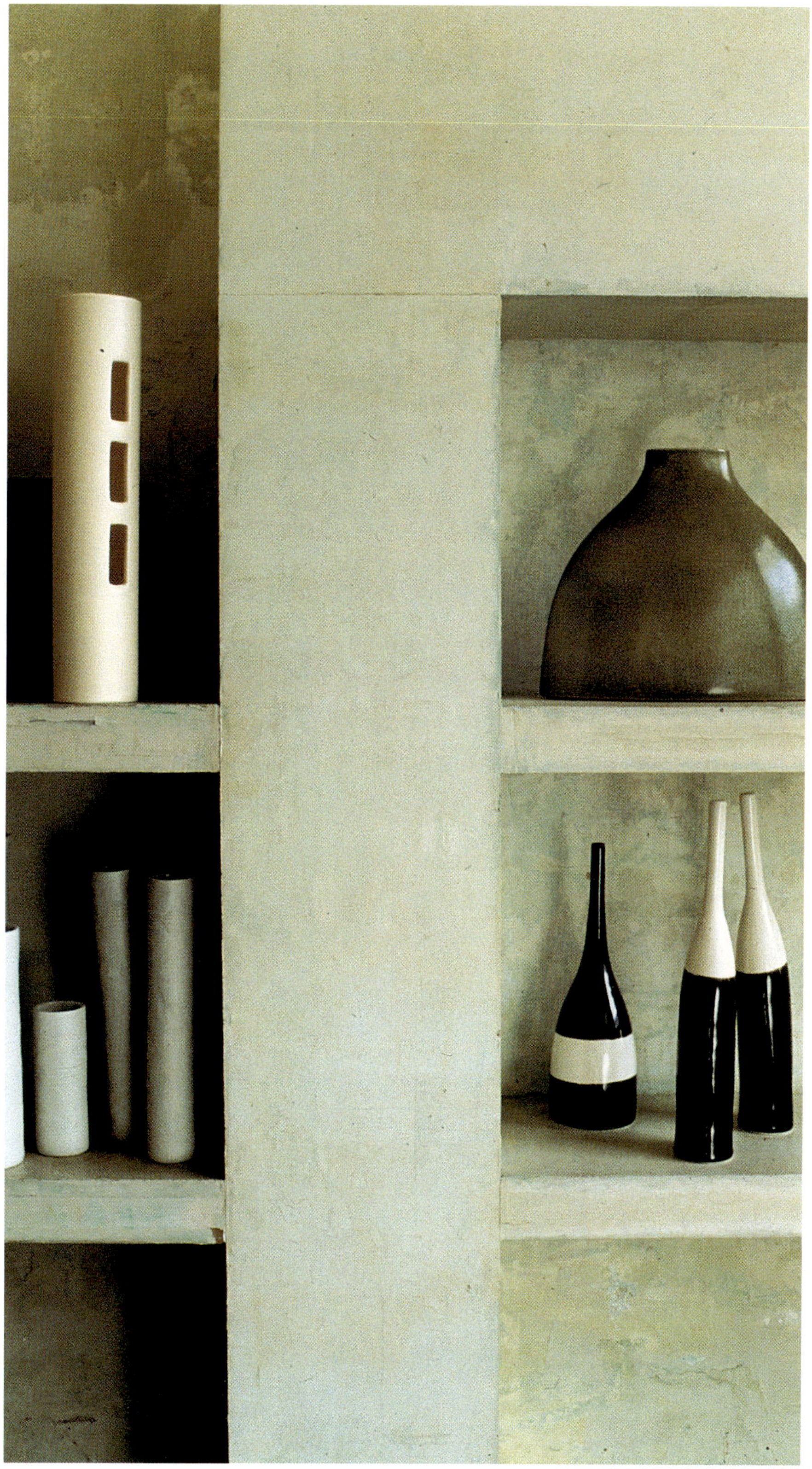

3 A long-necked Chinese *langyao* vase, dating from the early Qing dynasty (1644–1911), covered in a copper-red glaze with areas of dark crushed-strawberry mottling. The mouth rim, base, and interior are decorated in a white glaze. This classic style looks modern and is much copied by ceramic artists over two and a half centuries later.

4 Neutral walls are an ideal backdrop to display a collection of modern Japanese-influenced pottery, sleek and streamlined in its uncluttered design.

black

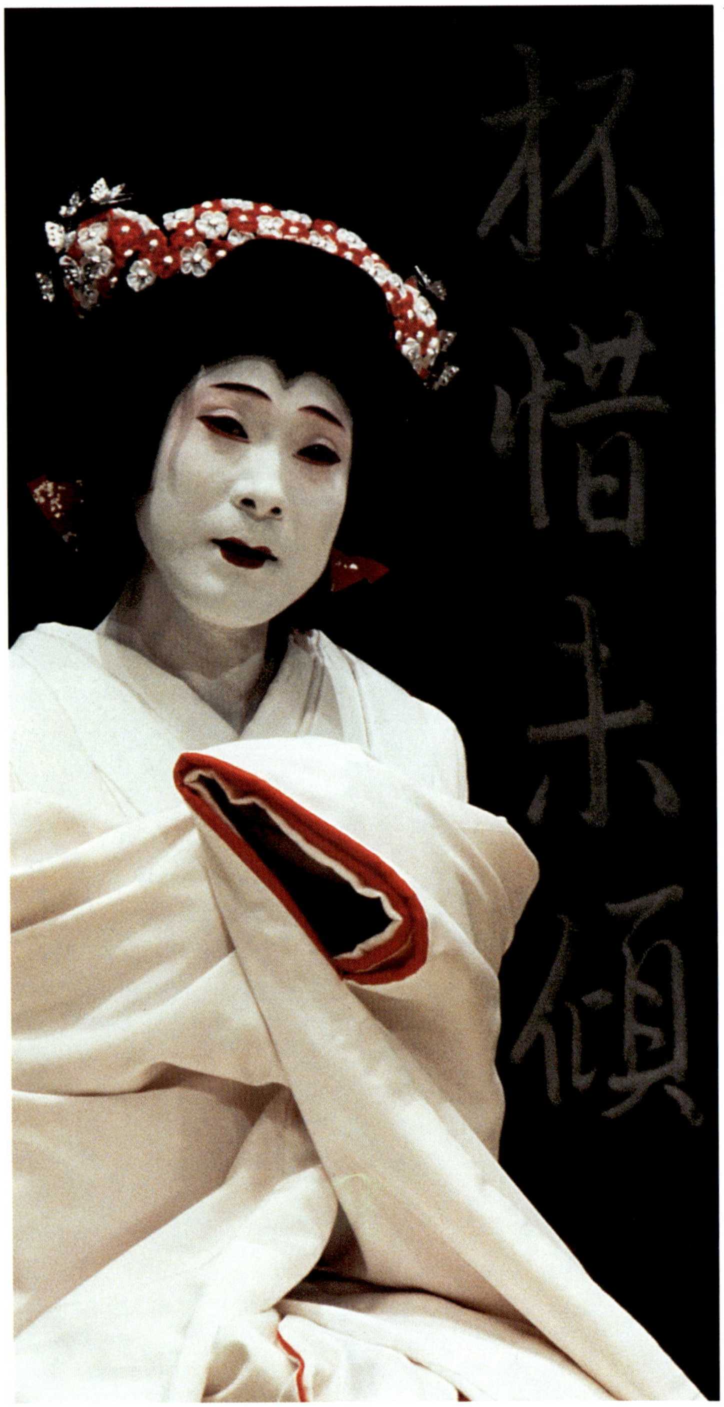

1

Made from charcoal, black was the first pigment used by man across the world. In East Asia, its associations are literary, formal, and martial.

In lacquerwork, black provides the sleek, smooth base coat for the gold, silver, and mother-of-pearl inlays that adorn the most costly eating utensils and furniture, as well as ceremonial weapons and armor. This tradition is echoed in modern Japan in its use of black to encase its electronic goods.

Both Japanese and Chinese calligraphers dramatically pair black in the form of Chinese ink with the white ground to create dramatic effects on banners, posters, lanterns, scrolls, and textiles.

1 A Japanese *kabuki* performer with a white-painted face stands against a background of black and white banners. The dramatic effect of the deliberately artificial makeup is heightened by the use of bright red around the eyes and lips. In contrast to the restraint of the older, more stylized *noh* theater, *kabuki*, which had its heyday in the seventeenth century, is fast-paced and popular. It delights in visually elaborate costumes and make-up and spectacularly fast costume changes.

2 The deadly swords worn by *samurai* warriors had elaborate decorative fittings that make them objects of beauty in their own right. These *tsuba,* or sword guards, protected the wearer's hand from an adversary's blade. The wedge-shaped opening in the center is designed to take the tang of the sword. Made by armorers and swordsmiths as a sideline, *tsuba* were often decorated with symbolic motifs. The ones shown here date from the sixteenth to the eighteenth centuries.

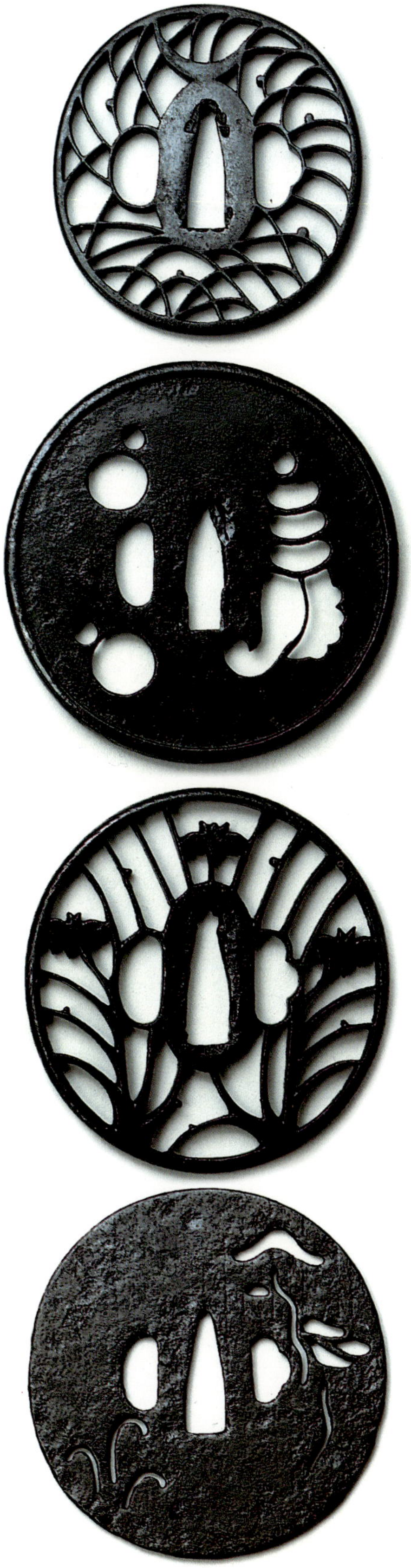

2 3

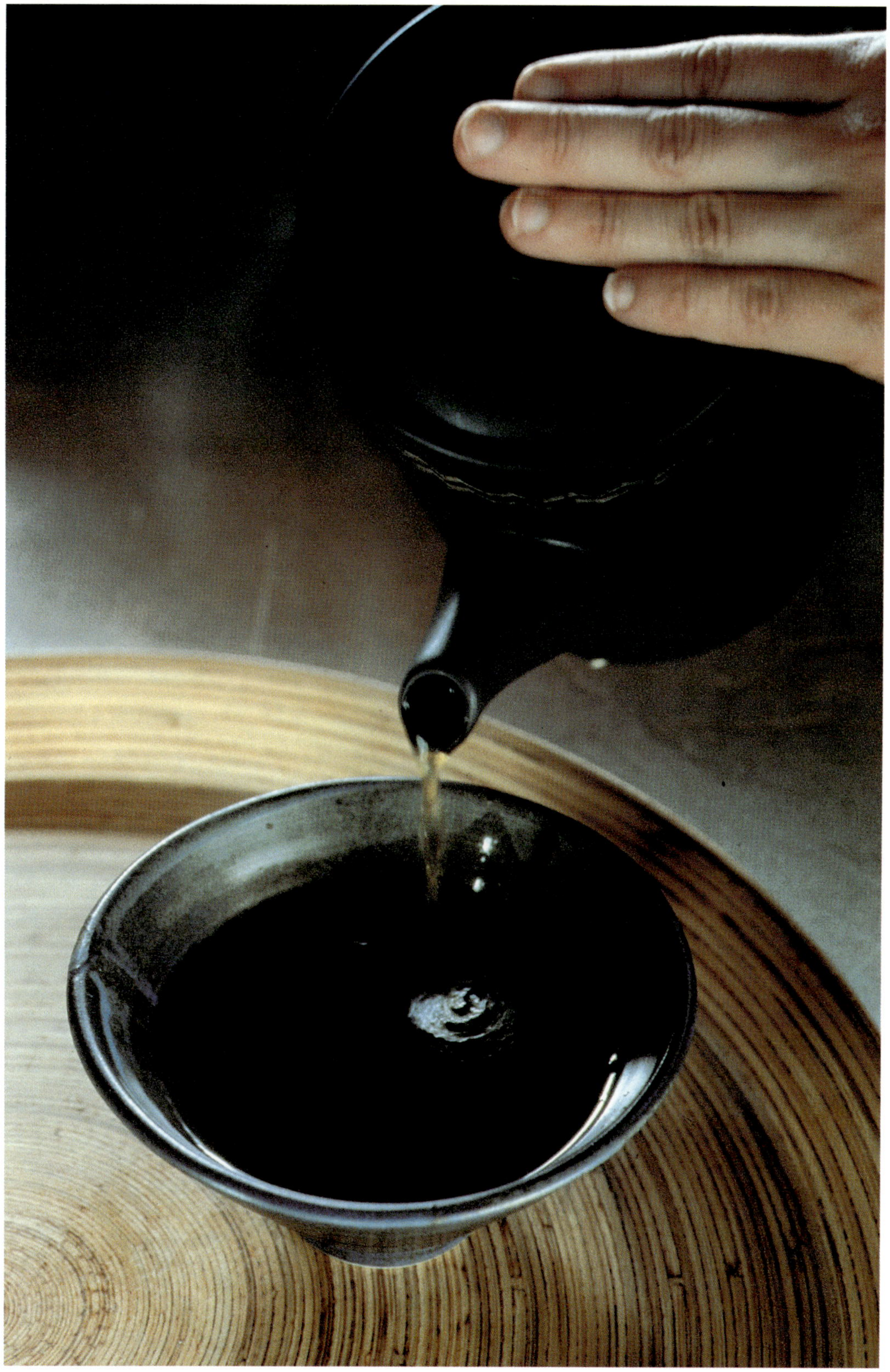

3 Modern pottery, although in this instance mass-produced, reflects the traditional design of handmade wares. The shape and the rough texture of the teabowl are two of the most instantly recognizable symbols of simple Eastern style.

red

Since prehistoric times the Chinese have seen red as a "life-giving" color. In the art of *feng shui*, red is associated with the element of fire and the most propitious of the cardinal directions, south. The Chinese bride does not wear virginal white, which is the color of mourning, but a crimson robe as she sets out to meet her husband. The Taoists have three gods of good fortune, each with his own color. The one dressed in red confers riches, so the color is associated with wealth. In Shinto, the traditional religion of Japan, shrine gates, or *torii*, are painted red, and festival decorations, lanterns, and offerings often form rich red visual displays.

1

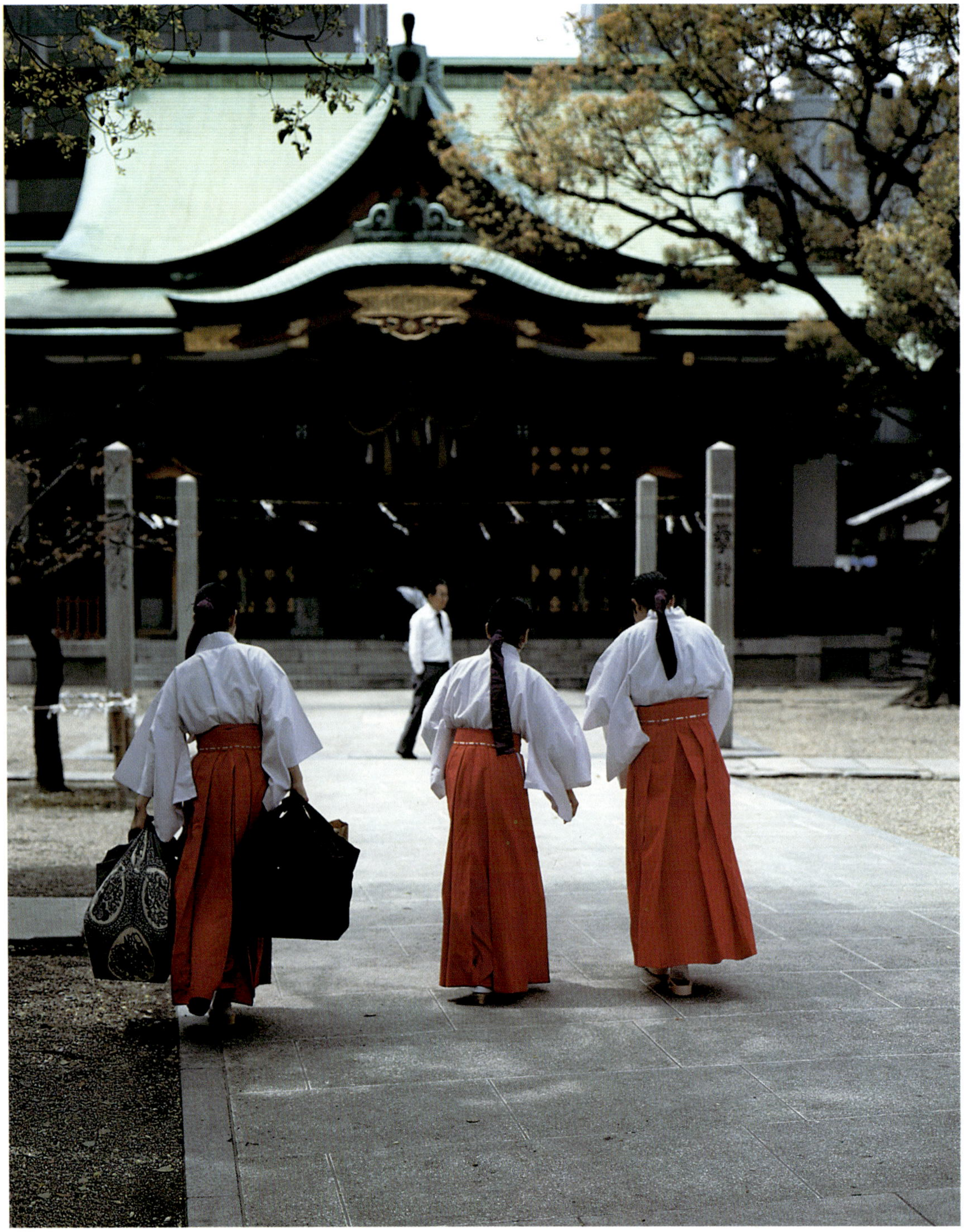

1 Shinto priestesses on their way to Sumiyosi Grand Shrine in the port city of Osaka wear crisp red *hakama*, formal baggy trousers. The shrine is home of the gods of the sea.

2 Six red wooden fire buckets, ringed in green, are stacked in a shelter outside a wooden house in Kyoto. As traditional buildings are built of wood, precautions against fire are essential, but, as in this stunning and rare example, they can also be appreciated as a decorative feature.

3 Chinese characters are hand-painted onto this traditional lantern, outlined in gold, echoing the red, white, and gold decorations of the Asakusa Kannon temple in Tokyo.

4 These banners, edged in red, are strong, graphic examples of the Japanese calligrapher's art.

2

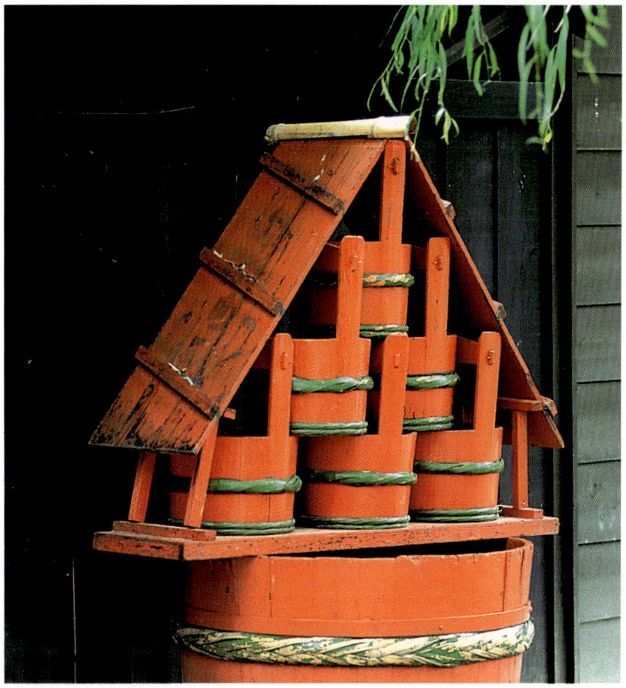

3

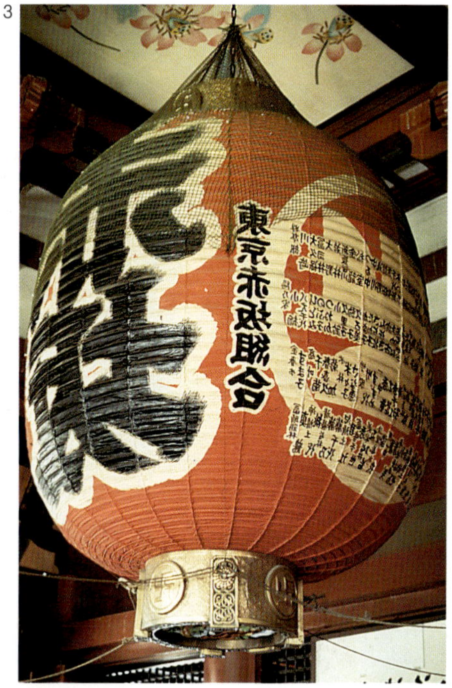

4

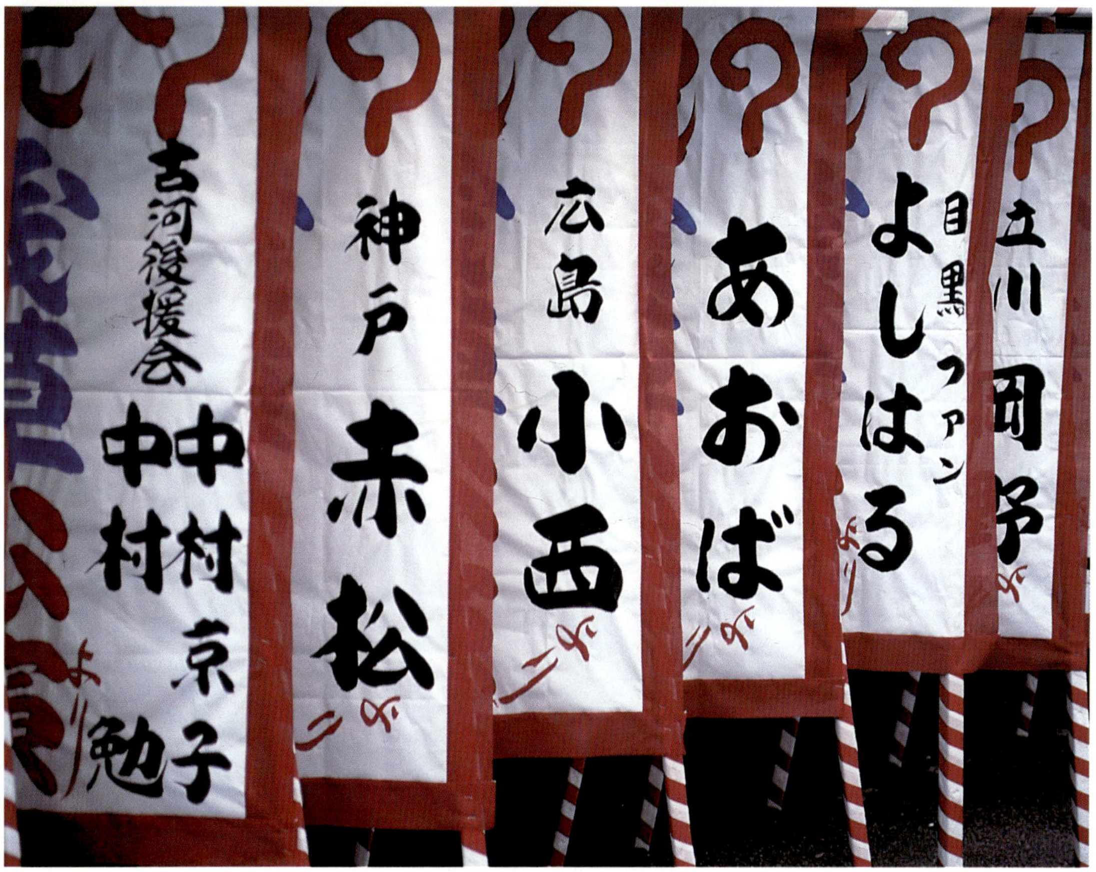

1

1 The *torii* or entrance gate of Itsukushima shrine at Miyajima in Hiroshima Bay, Japan. In the evening light, the *torii,* painted vermilion red and 52½ ft (16 m) high, silhouetted against a dramatic sky of the same hue, is one of the most beautiful sights in Japan. The gateway, with the pronounced upward-slanting curves of its roof, dates from 1875. It is the seventeenth version since the original was erected by the warlord Taira-no-Kiyomori in the twelfth century. It stands in front of a shrine built in the *shinden* style. The sea laps beneath low halls and red-colonnaded corridors, where a sea deity has been worshiped since the sixth century A.D.

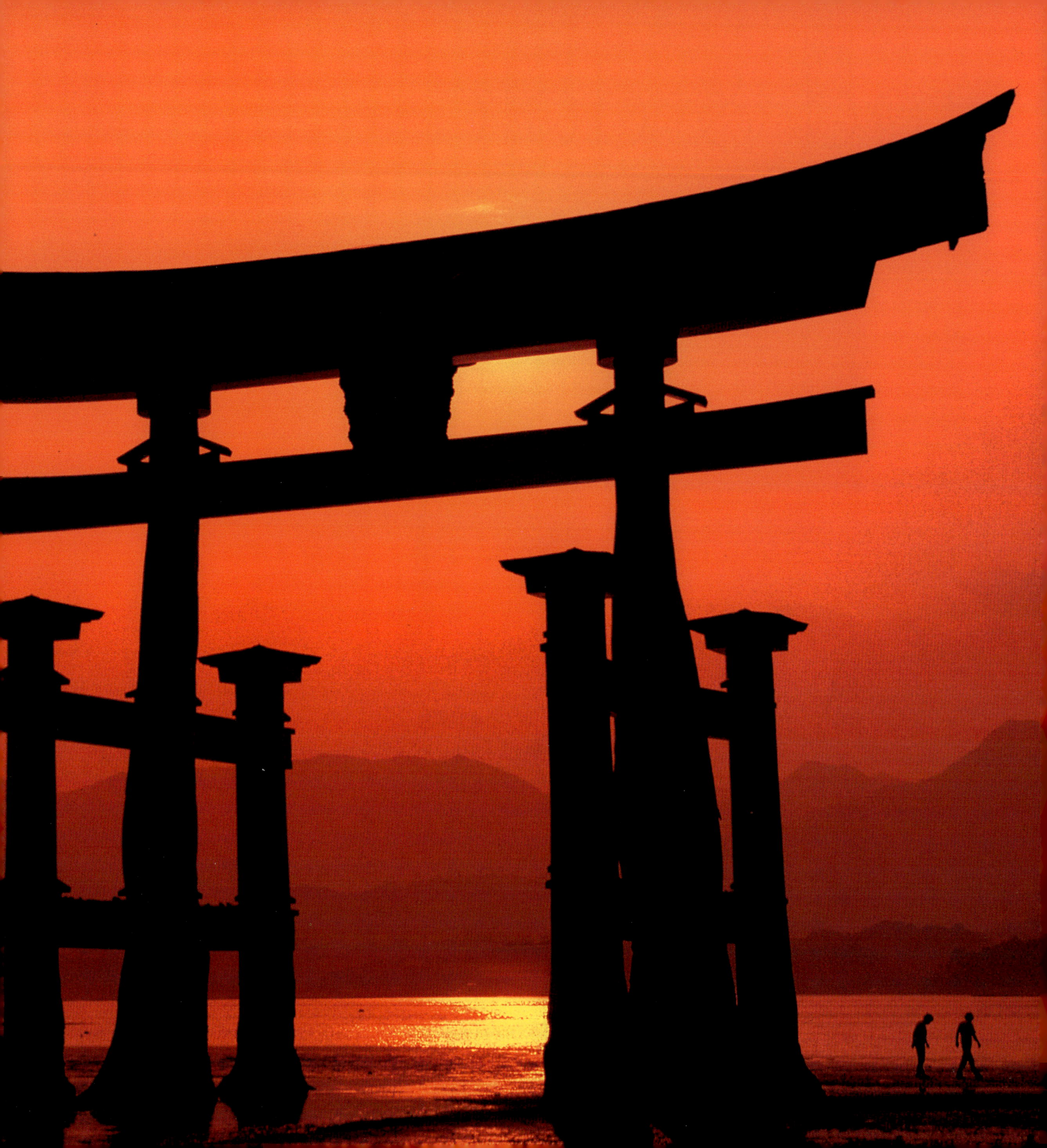

red & gold

The pairing of these two propitious colors is common in Chinese interiors and in its art, and is found in Chinese restaurants worldwide. The scheme, however, has its roots in far grander buildings dating back to medieval China. Red, symbolic of the element fire, was the color of the Ming dynasty (1368–1644). Courtiers dressed in red, the walls of palaces were lacquered in red, and their ceilings burnished with gold leaf. Chinese characters executed in gold are still used as decorative devices, though today the messages they convey are much more likely to be commercial than poetic.

1

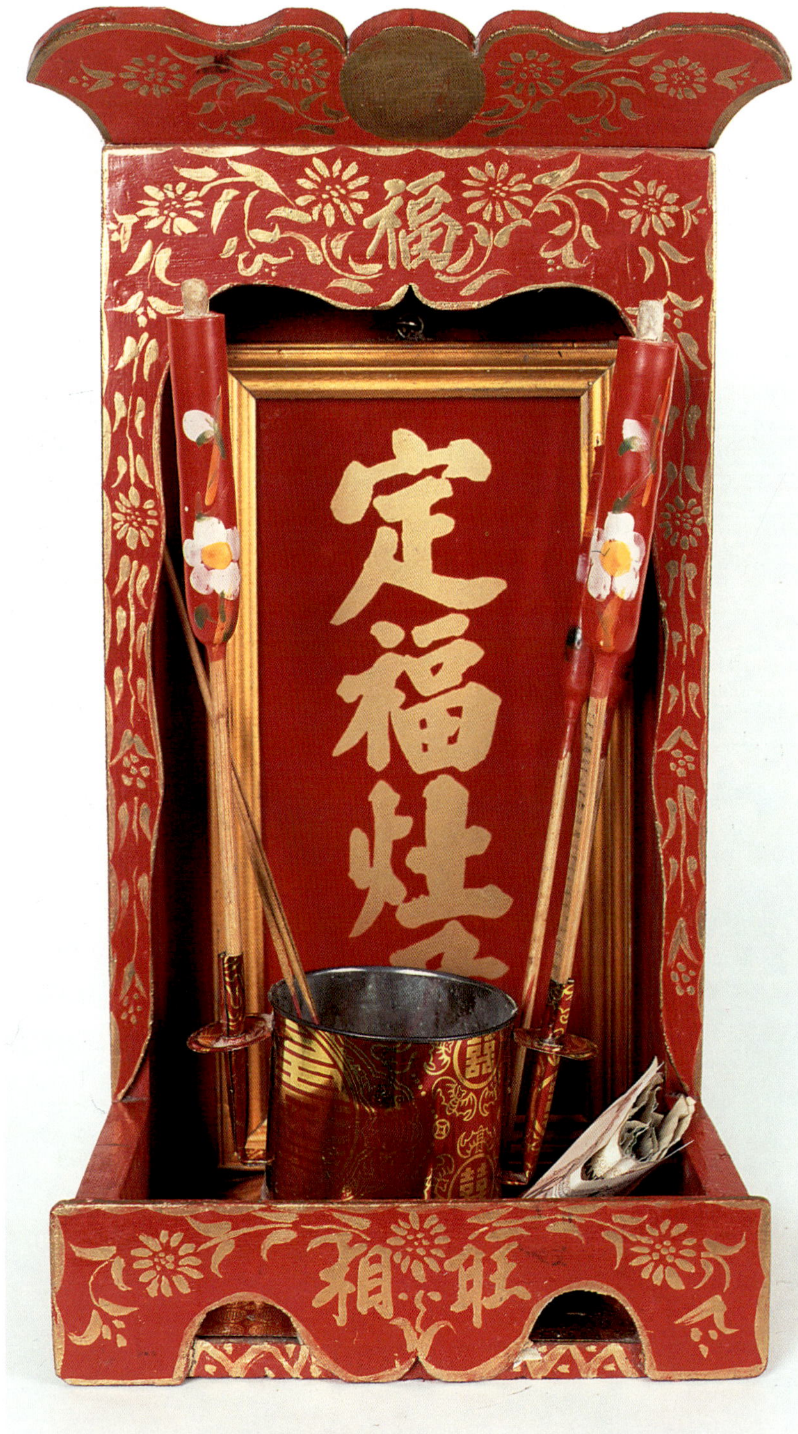

1 A personal Taoist shrine for use in the home highlights the use of red and gold—the red symbolizing good fortune. Offerings of money and personal trinkets are made to the gods at the shrine.

2 The largest of all the imperial halls within the Forbidden City in Beijing is the Taihe Dian, measuring some 210 x 120 ft (64 x 36.5 m). Completed in 1417, it was burnt and rebuilt several times and was used for celebrations such as the imperial birthday, the lunar new year, the winter solstice, and for coronations and audiences with the emperor. The screen walls and columns are red, and the beams and brackets are gold and green; the roof tiles are yellow, as was required of an imperial building.

3 The richness of red and glints of gold accentuate delicate patterns of light on a spiral incense burner in Man Mo Temple, Hong Kong.

4 As any school child knows, the Chinese invented gunpowder. Fireworks, however, existed even before the invention of gunpowder—pieces of bamboo were thrown into fires to cause explosions—so their advent was merely a natural progression of the desire to celebrate by making loud noises. Firecrackers, used symbolically to dispel evil influences following processions for ceremonial feasts or other celebrations, are irresistible to a nation passionate about fireworks.

2

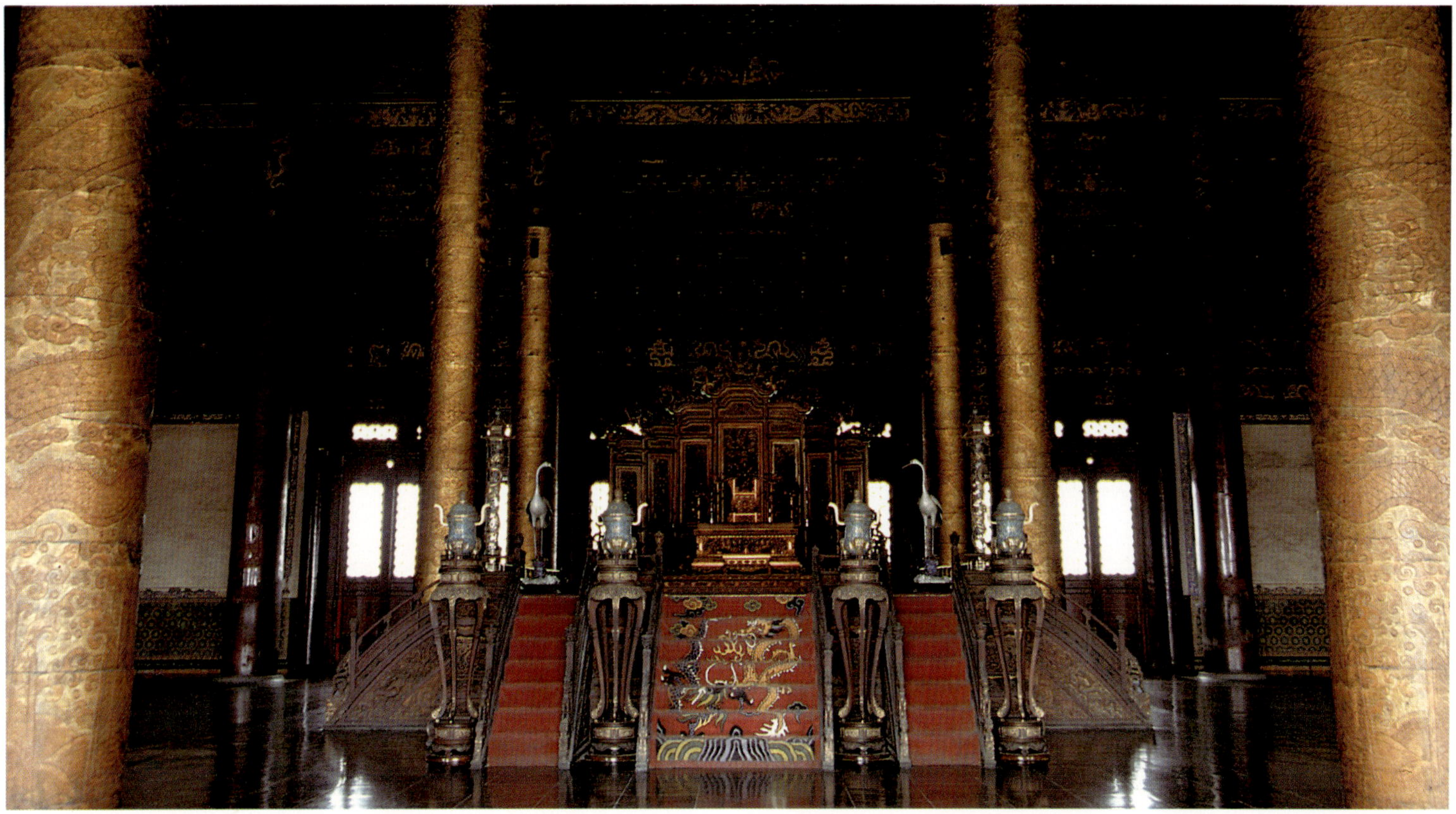

3

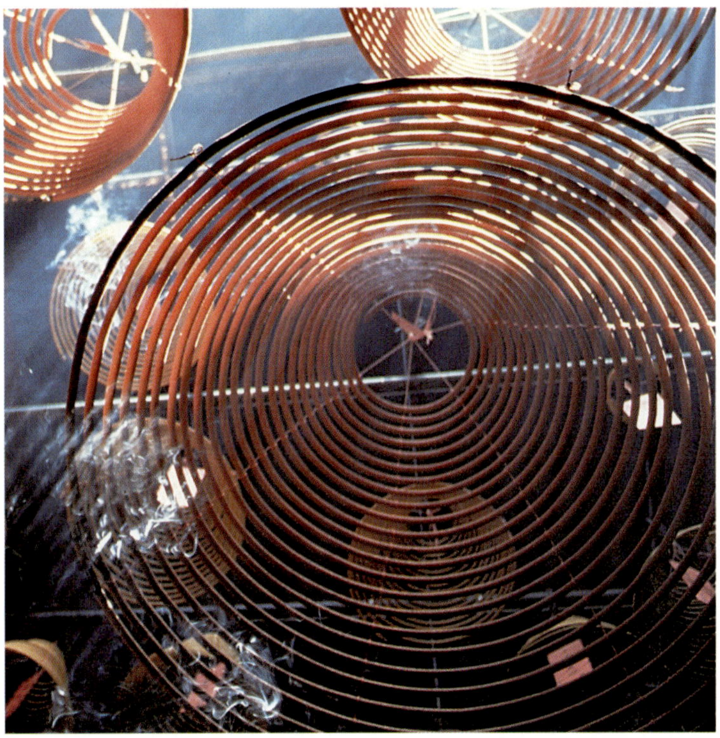

4

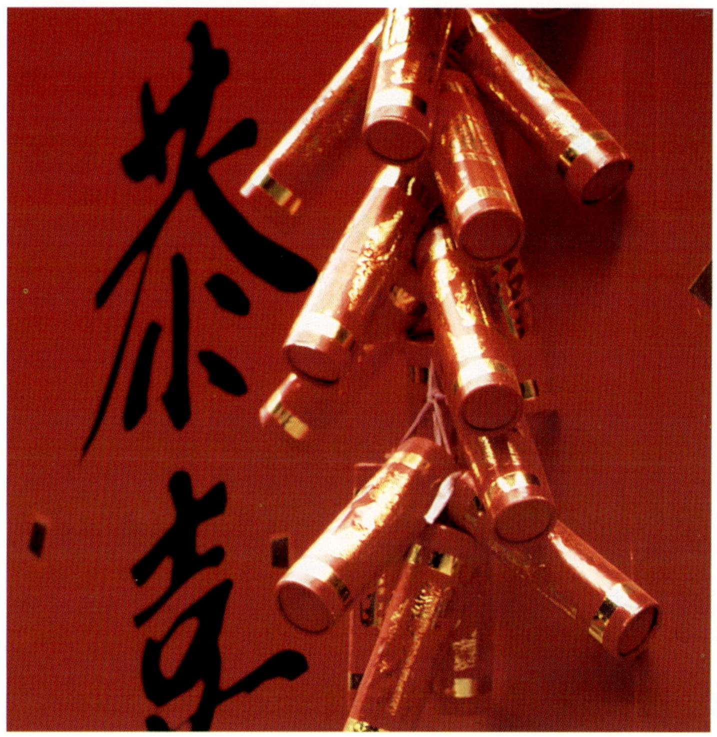

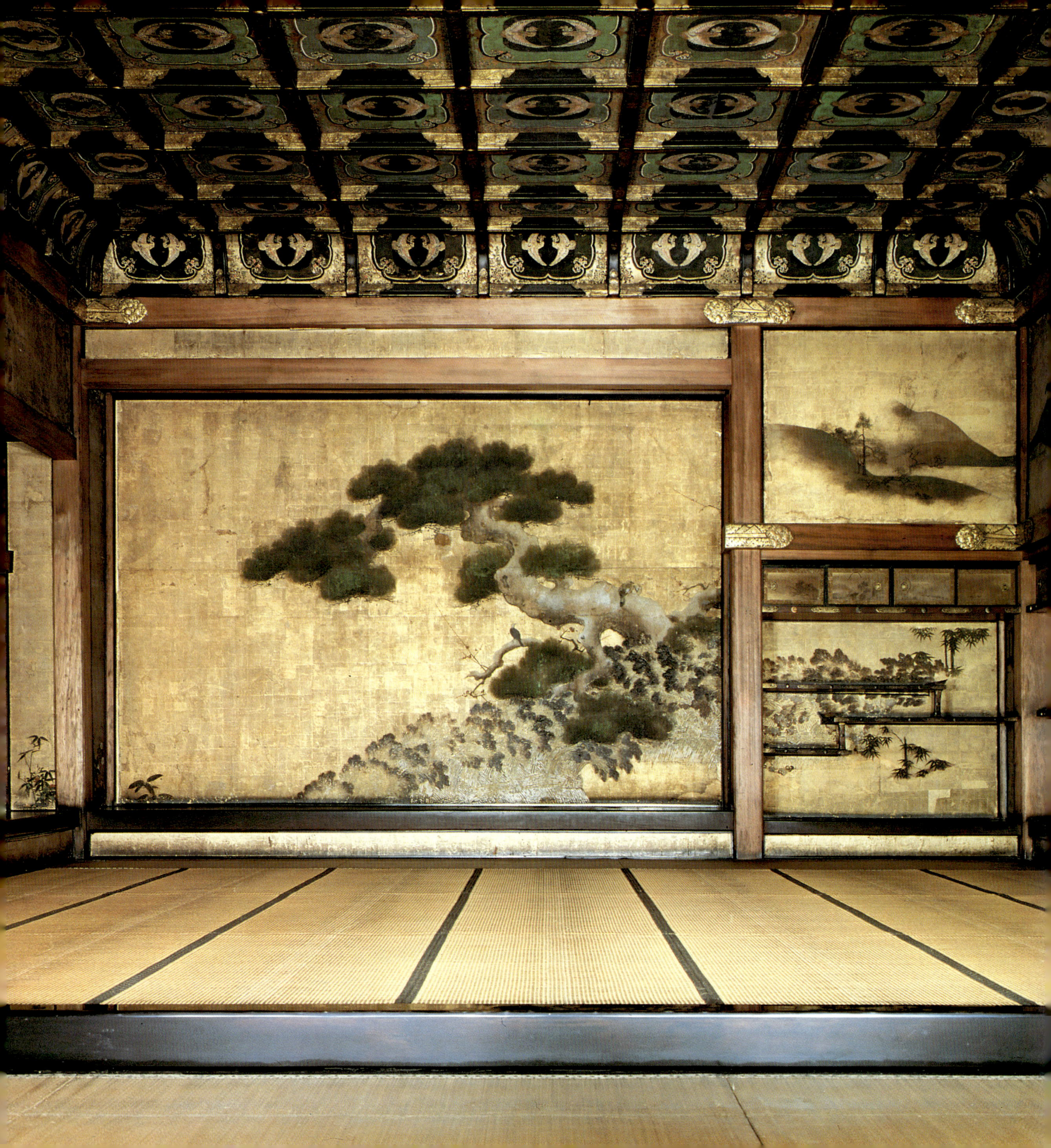

gold

1 The first room of the Kuroshoin in Nijo Castle built by the shogun Tokugawa Ieyasu in 1603 as his residence in Kyoto. *Shoin* were originally conceived as temple reading rooms, which doubled as reception rooms. During the Momoyama (1568–1600) and Edo (1600–1853) periods, they became the formal reception rooms in the mansions of the *samurai* elite. Elaborately decorated by masters of the *Kano* school, this room shows how painted panels were used to create the overall decorative effect. Few examples of complete rooms survive from this period.

2 & 3 Intended to be "read" from right to left, a pair of six-fold screens depicts spring and fall. The symbolism is one of marital fidelity, longevity, and the fulfillment of parental duties, and contains the essence of "auspicious imagery." Dating from the *Meiji* period (1868–1912), and painted in colored pigment and black ink on a gold ground, the first screen shows a white-naped crane and egret in a spring landscape of bamboo, plum, iris, and peony (below). The river runs to join the second screen (above), where a red-capped crane and its young are in a fall landscape of maple, pine, *kiku,* and other flora and exotic birds.

Unlike China, Japan is rich in silver, but has few gold deposits. For centuries this most precious of metals was reserved for the gilding of Buddhist images and temple fittings. During the Momoyama period (1568–1600), artists working for rival warlords who fought a protracted civil war to unify Japan created a style of interior decoration and architecture unprecedented in Japan for its lavish use of color and gold. Determined to outshine his rivals by the magnificence of his principal residence, the warlord Oda Nobunaga built Azuchi Castle on the shores of Lake Biwa near Kyoto. The outer walls of the castle were painted blue, and the painter Kano Eitoku was commissioned to decorate the rooms of the lofty inner keep. Each floor depicted a different theme painted on gold leaf. Sadly, Azuchi, along with many other palaces and castles of the period, was destroyed during the civil war.

2

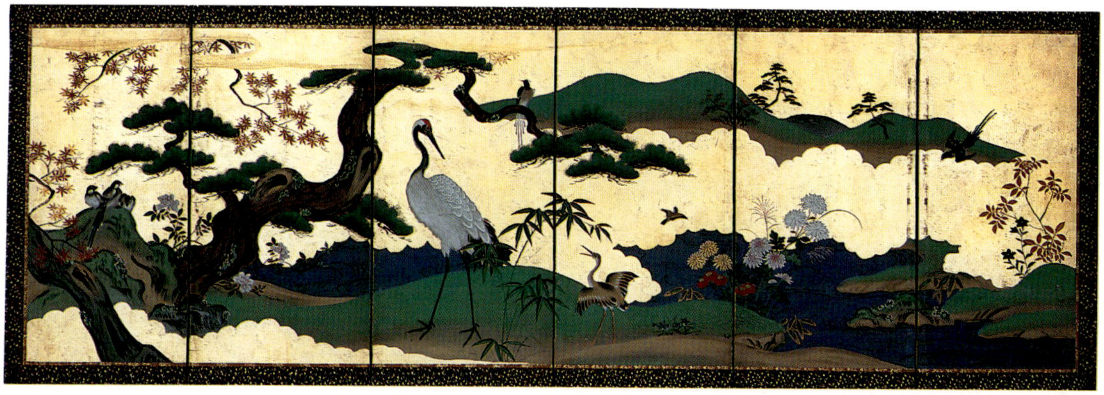

3

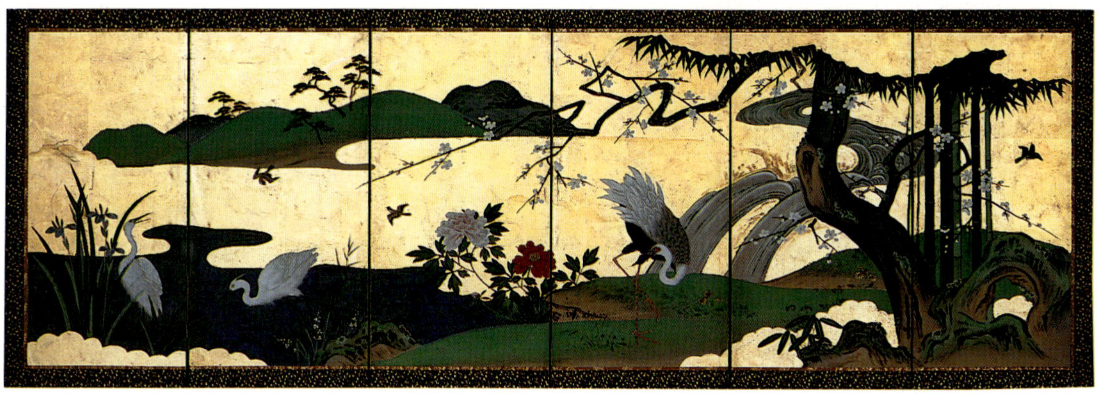

blue & white

1
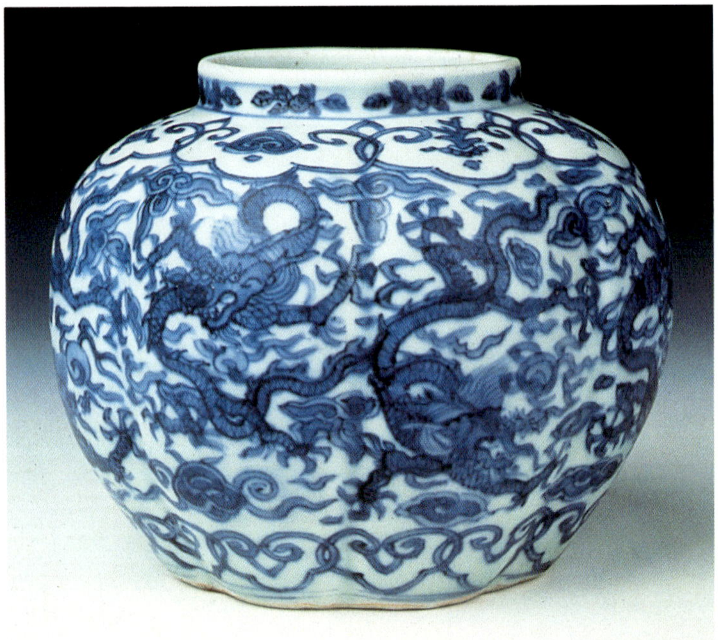

Porcelain was perfected in China during the Tang dynasty (618–906). Along with silk, it was one of the most sought-after items traded on the Silk Route between East and West until the secret of its manufacture was discovered in Europe. Blue and white porcelain reached perfection during the Ming dynasty (1368–1644). Such was the demand from collectors in Europe that it was soon imitated in inferior export wares made for the European market. Its trademark blue pigment, cobalt, was originally imported from Persia. During the Yuan period (1260–1368), however, when China was ruled by a foreign Mongol dynasty, blue and white wares were decorated with domestically mined cobalt. 3

2
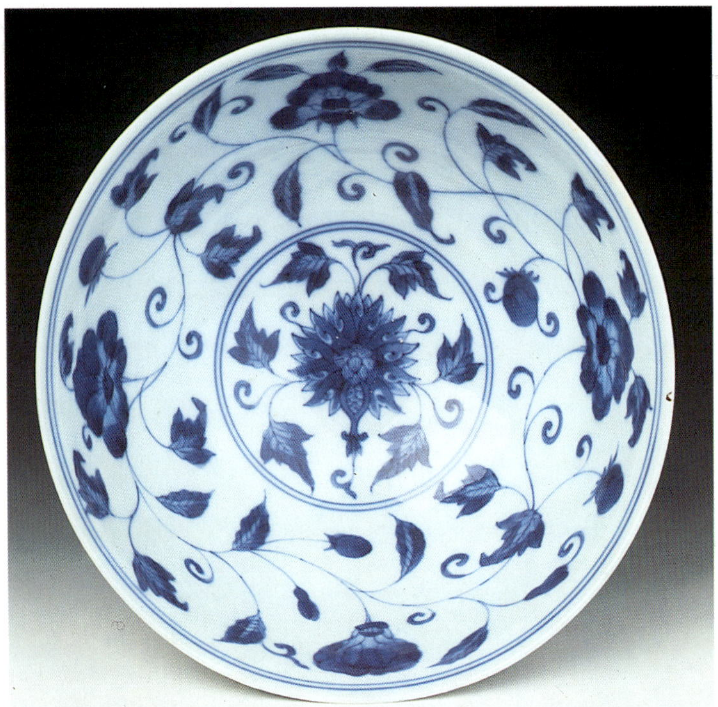

1 A Ming dynasty (1368–1644) eight-lobed blue and white jar, decorated with eight dragons in pursuit of flaming pearls through clouds. Dragons were seen as the embodiment of the masculine principle, *yang*, and clouds, too, are a *yang* element. The eight precious emblems of Buddhism are depicted around the shoulder of the jar; the wheel, conch, umbrella, standard, lotus, vase, two fish, and endless knot are all auspicious symbols. The jar's shape is classical and timeless, and the perfection of the glaze and coloring distinguishes it from many later copies.

2 From a hundred years after the Ming dynasty, a *Chenghua* blue-and-white palace bowl is decorated on the outside in underglaze blue with a continuous scroll of five-pointed camellia flowers. Inside there is a continuous peony scroll with a central peony medallion. The peony symbolizes spring and was known in Chinese legend as the Queen of Flowers.

3 The collar of a nineteenth-century blue silk mandarin's robe is embroidered with scenes of Chinese landscapes and pleasure gardens. It is less stylized and symbolic than the court robes of earlier periods.

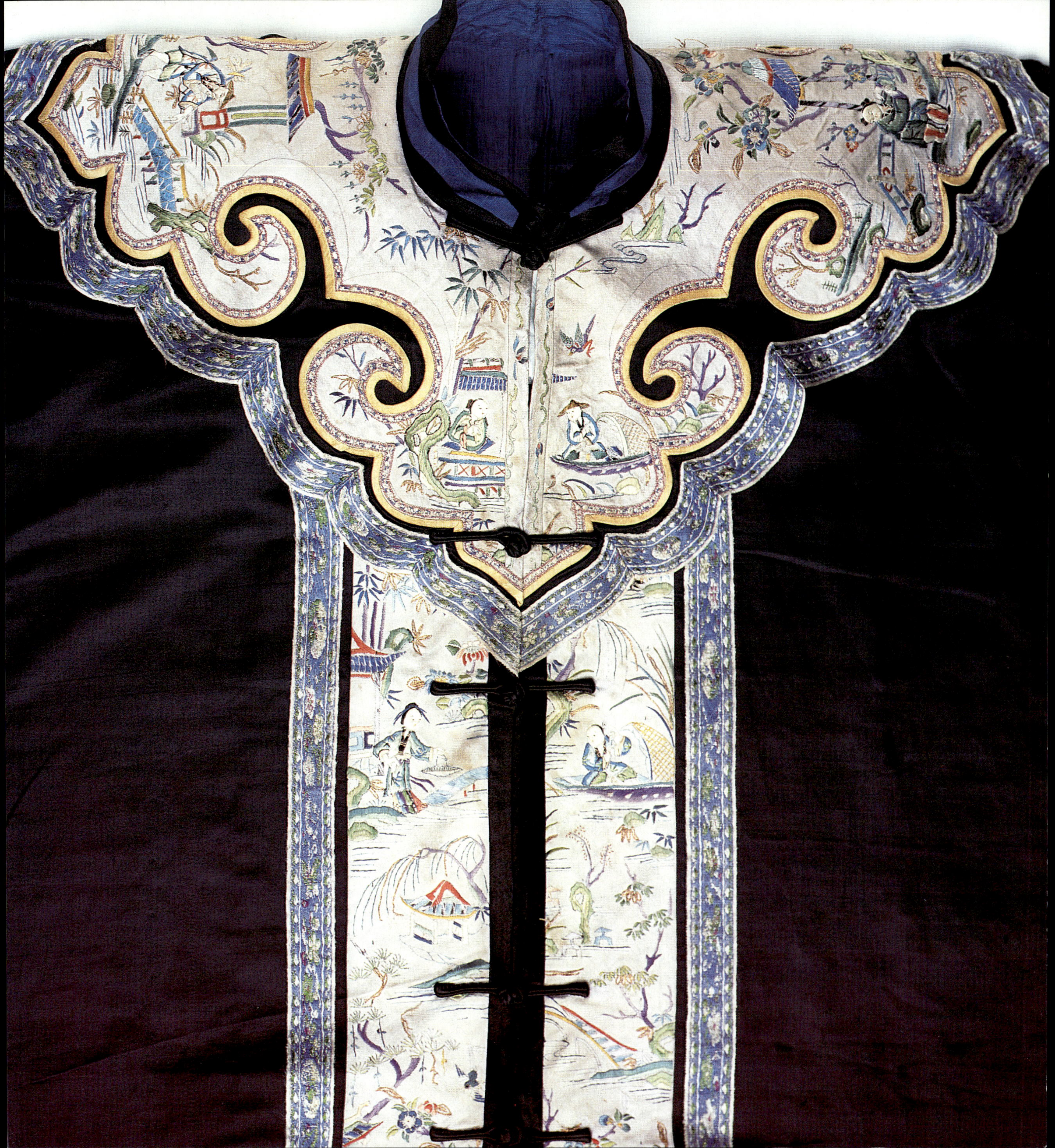

yellow

In China, the emperor Wudi of the Western Han dynasty (206 B.C.–A.D. 12) chose to rule under the aegis of the element earth, whose color is yellow. The color became a symbol of imperial power during the Han period, a tradition which continued during the later Yuan, Ming, and Qing dynasties. All the roofs of the imperial palace in Beijing, The Forbidden City, are covered in yellow glazed tiles.

The reigning emperor was the only person allowed to wear the sumptuous yellow dragon robes of state (see picture at right), although his near relatives could wear shades of the color, such as apricot, worn by the heir apparent, or golden yellow, worn by the emperor's other sons.

1 The yellow walls of this Buddhist temple at Baocheng, Wuxian, China, provide a striking contrast with the dramatic ornamental roof structure.

1

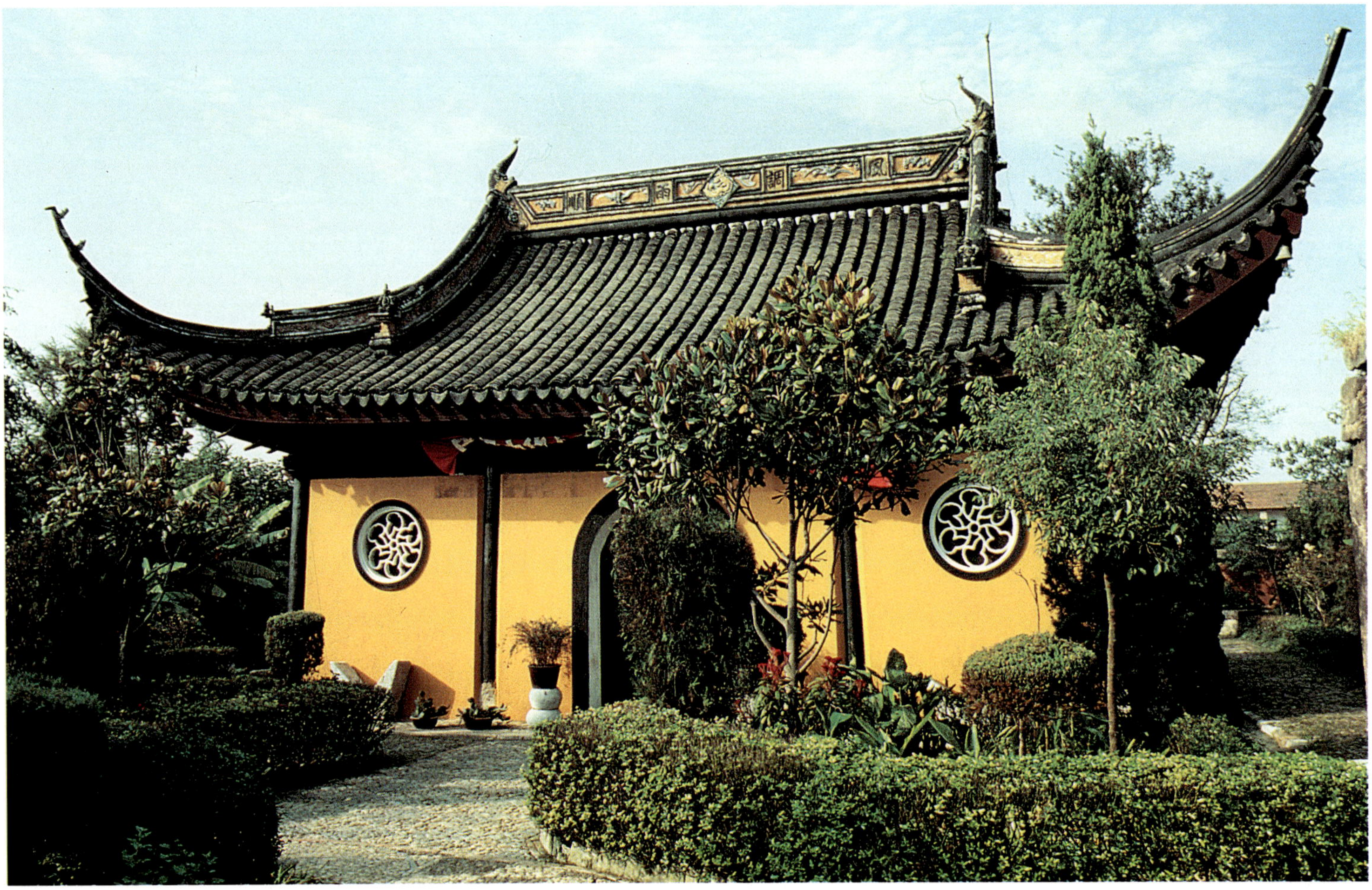

2

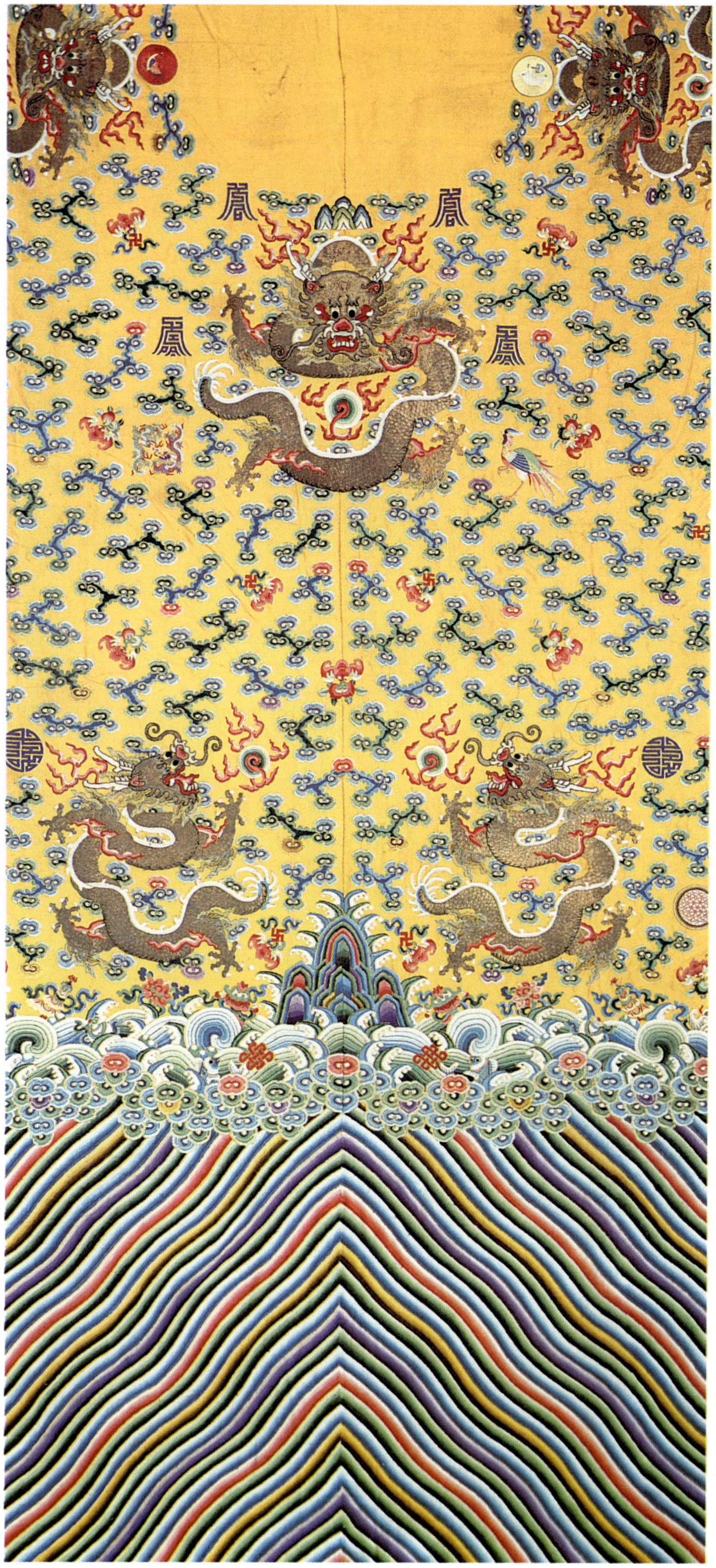

3

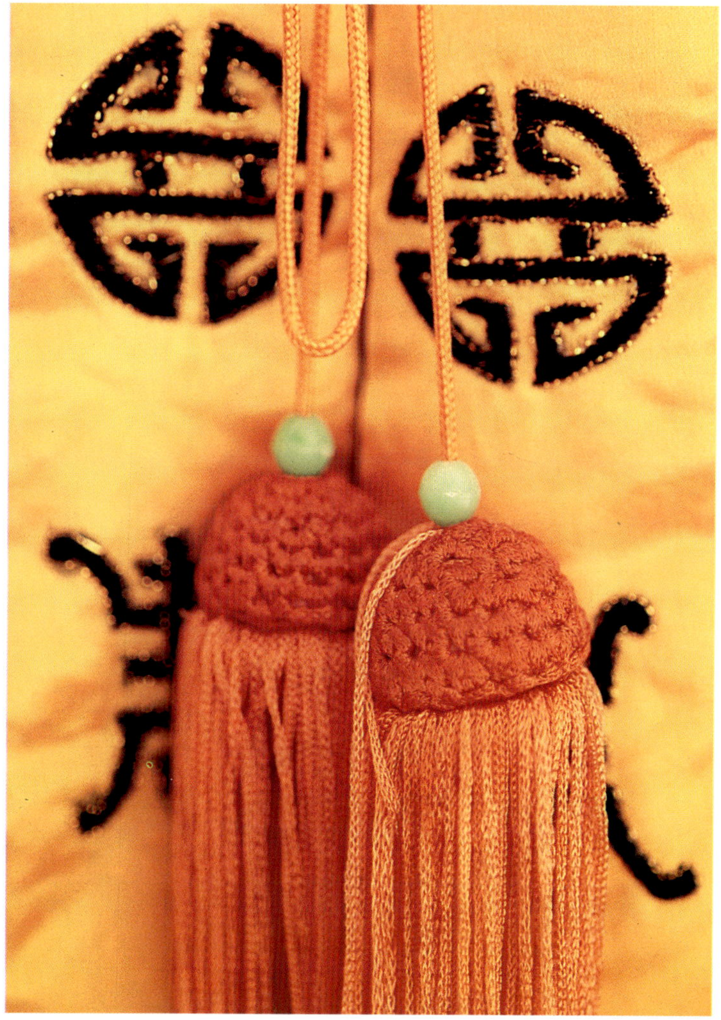

2 Detail of the uncut silk yardage for a Chinese emperor's Dragon robe from the late nineteenth century, made shortly before the fall of Imperial China. The fine golden-yellow silk is brightly embroidered in silk and gilt threads, with nine dragons chasing flaming pearls among cloud scrolls, and bats carrying peaches and swastika, with auspicious symbols and the twelve imperial symbols of authority, over a deep sea-wave border. The dragon symbolizes the emperor's search for divine truth.

3 Embroidered Chinese characters for longevity and good fortune. The graphical quality of Chinese characters makes them striking decorative motifs that have been used on textiles, ceramics, and furniture.

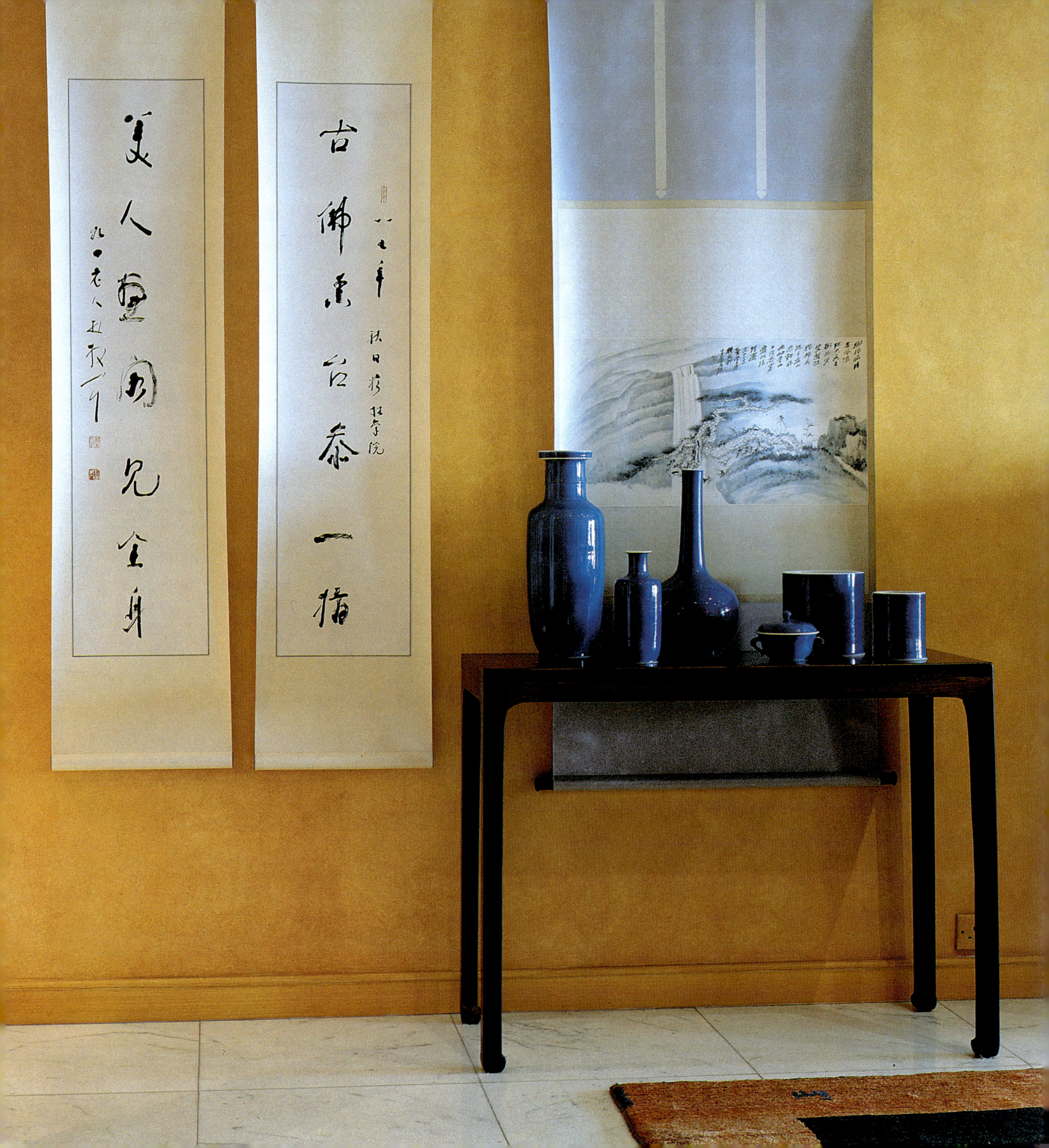

1

1 In this elegant contemporary Hong Kong apartment, old meets new as the traditional color of the walls forms a perfect backdrop to display decorative scrolls and a collection of pottery, set on a classic Ming-style table.

2 A classic modern Japanese apartment shows Western influence on Eastern style: the giveaways are the scroll painting, the table lamps, and the profusion of silk cushions. The yellow of the walls creates an illusion of light, warmth, and space.

2

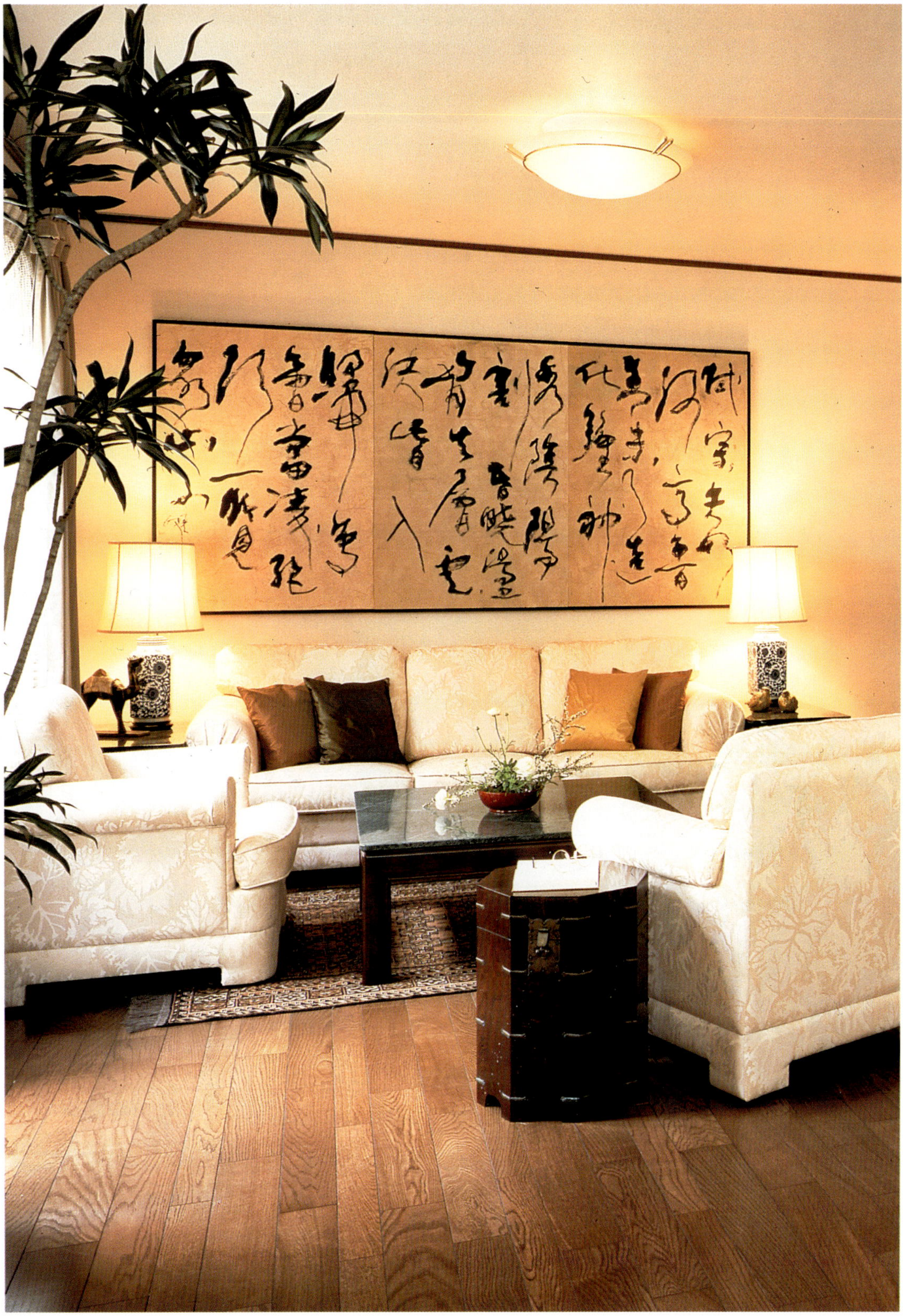

green

The natural world is the main source of inspiration for East Asian art and decoration. Since ancient times, Chinese and Japanese artists in all media have striven to reproduce the subtle hues found in nature. Centuries before the West, the Chinese discovered that iron, lead, and copper could be added to glazes to produce a range of colors, including green and brown.

In China, as in the West, green is emblematic of spring and renewal. For that reason, the Chinese attach great importance to the propitious combination of green and its complementary color, red, which are often paired on *pa kua* mirrors, placed inside and outside the home to deflect negative influences.

1 The soothing combination of trees overhanging water in the garden of the Hamarikyu Detached Palace in Tokyo. Now open to the public, this traditional stroll garden was created in the seventeenth century as a private retreat by the shogun Tokugawa Tsunashige. It suffered damage during the great Kanto earthquake of 1923 and also during the firebombing of Tokyo during World War II.

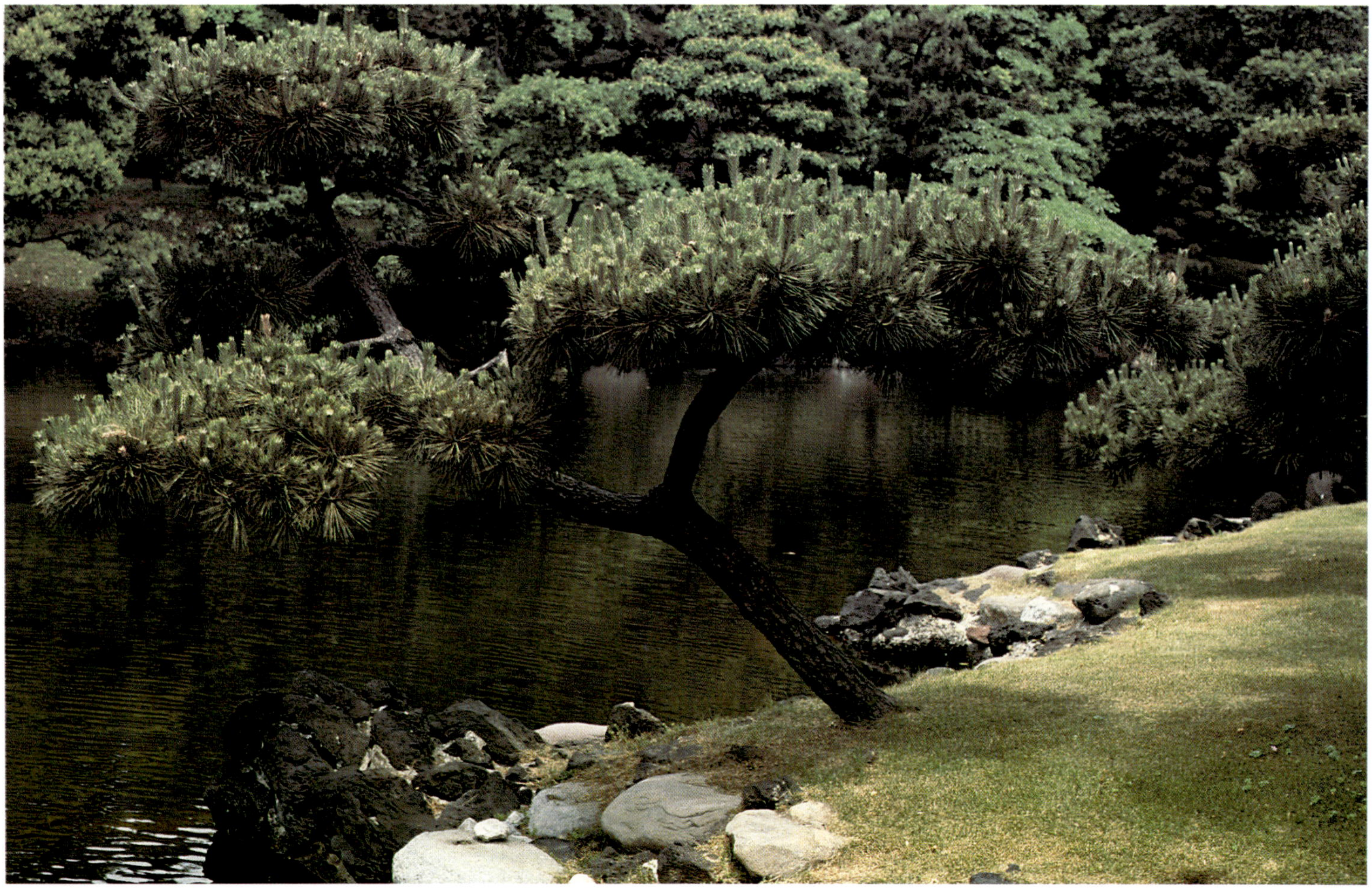

2

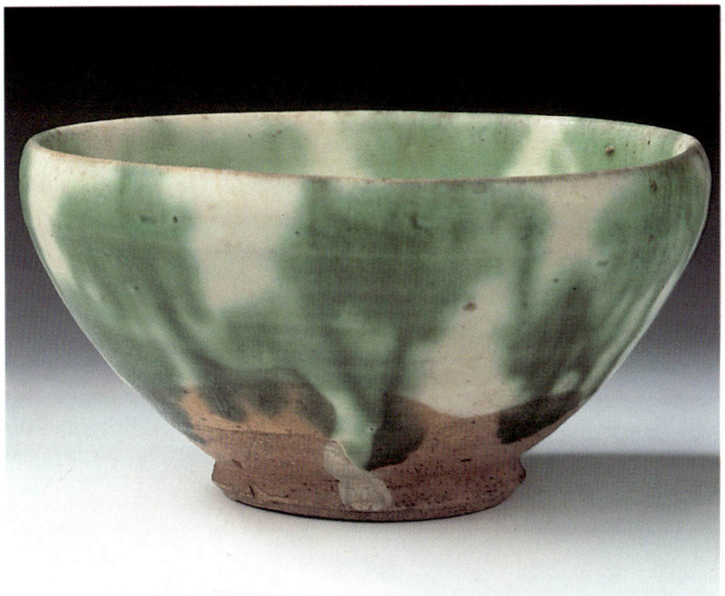

3

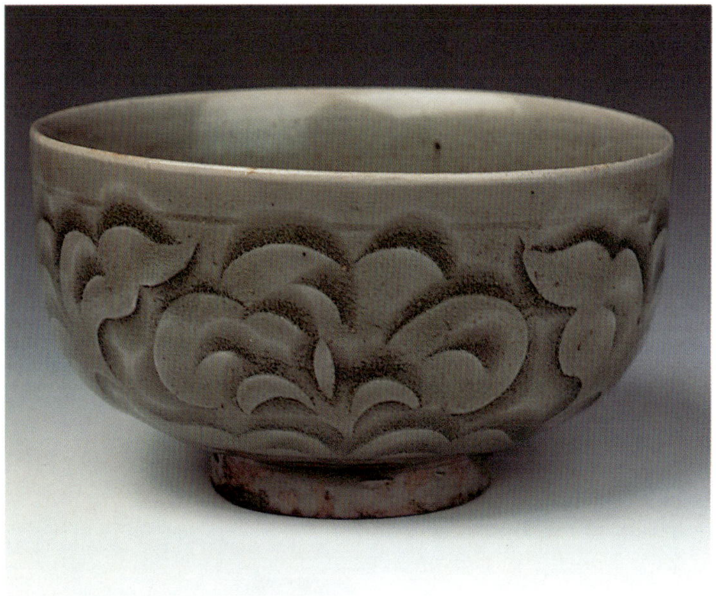

4

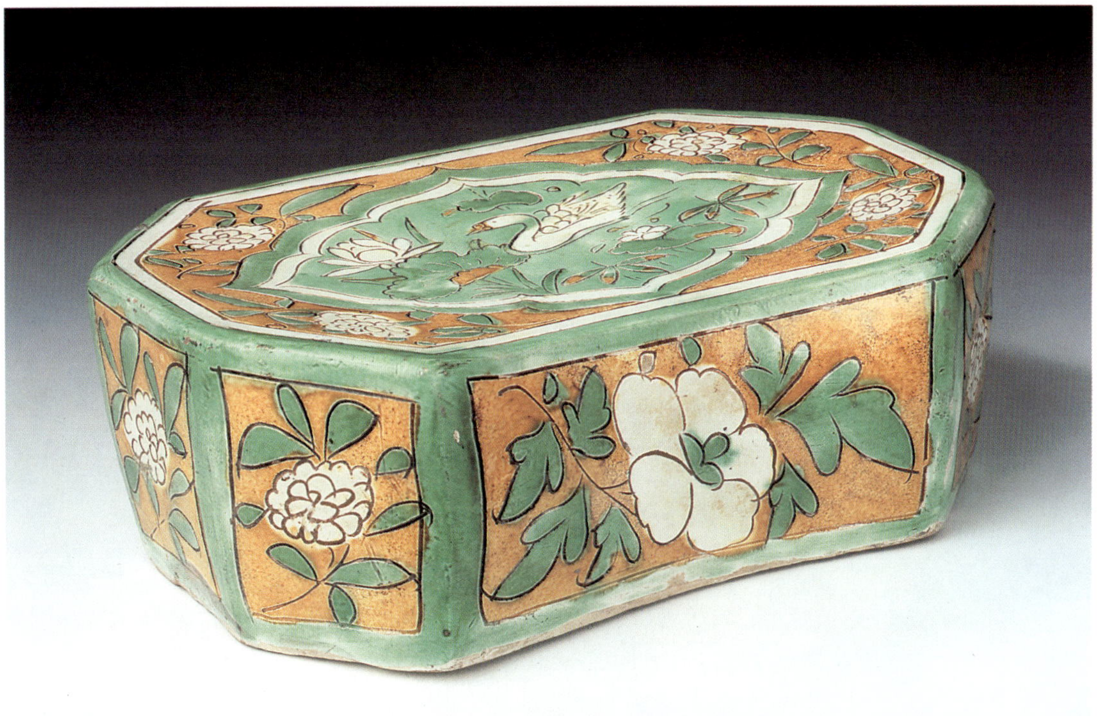

2 Not an example of Mediterranean rustic earthenware pottery, but an eleventh-century bowl. The modern, yet timeless feel of the glaze and design defies the passage of nearly a thousand years, and the bowl looks fresh and contemporary.

3 This is a northern Song dynasty shallow circular celadon bowl from the eleventh century. The celadon glaze is a rich gray-green, with fine bubbles throughout. Celadon is a high-fired green or bluish glaze, gaining its distinctive color from the addition of iron.

4 An octagonal twelfth-century pillow decorated with a scene of a white goose in a green lotus pond, with peony sprays. The combination of green and yellow was popular during the Tang dynasty.

multi-colored

In the past decades China has overtaken Japan as the world's leading manufacturer of textiles for clothing, carpets, and furnishing fabrics. The country owes its success not only to the introduction of mass-production methods and cheaper labor costs, but also to the boldness and freshness of designs that are inspired by traditional Chinese models. However, the garish purples, lime greens, shocking pinks, and bright turquoises that we think of as "typically Chinese" are, in fact, relatively recent additions to the Chinese dye master's palette. These rich, dense colors are only made possible by artificial chemical dyes that were introduced to China from the West in the late nineteenth century.

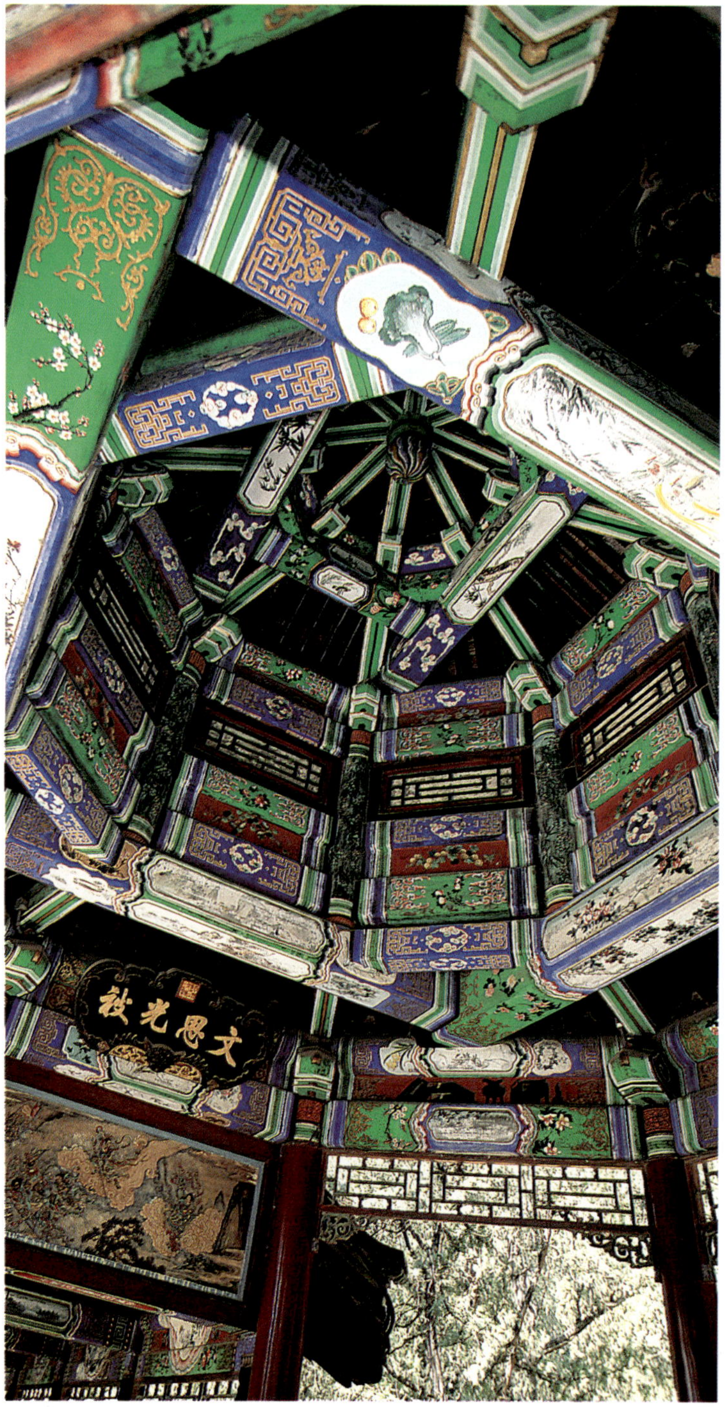

1

1 The Summer Palace built for the formidable Empress Dowager Ci Xi in the late nineteenth century. An escape from the oppressive summer heat of Beijing, it stands on the shore of Kunming Lake twelve miles outside the city. The complex consists of pavilions, halls, temples, and an ornamental covered walkway, painted in luminous greens, reds, pinks, and blues, with white and gold highlights, and embellished with landscape and floral vignettes.

2 The opening of the new airport in 1990 at Jinghong in Yunnan province, China, was the reason for this colorful celebration. The dancers wear traditional dress in the colors of the rainbow and hold matching festive balloons.

2

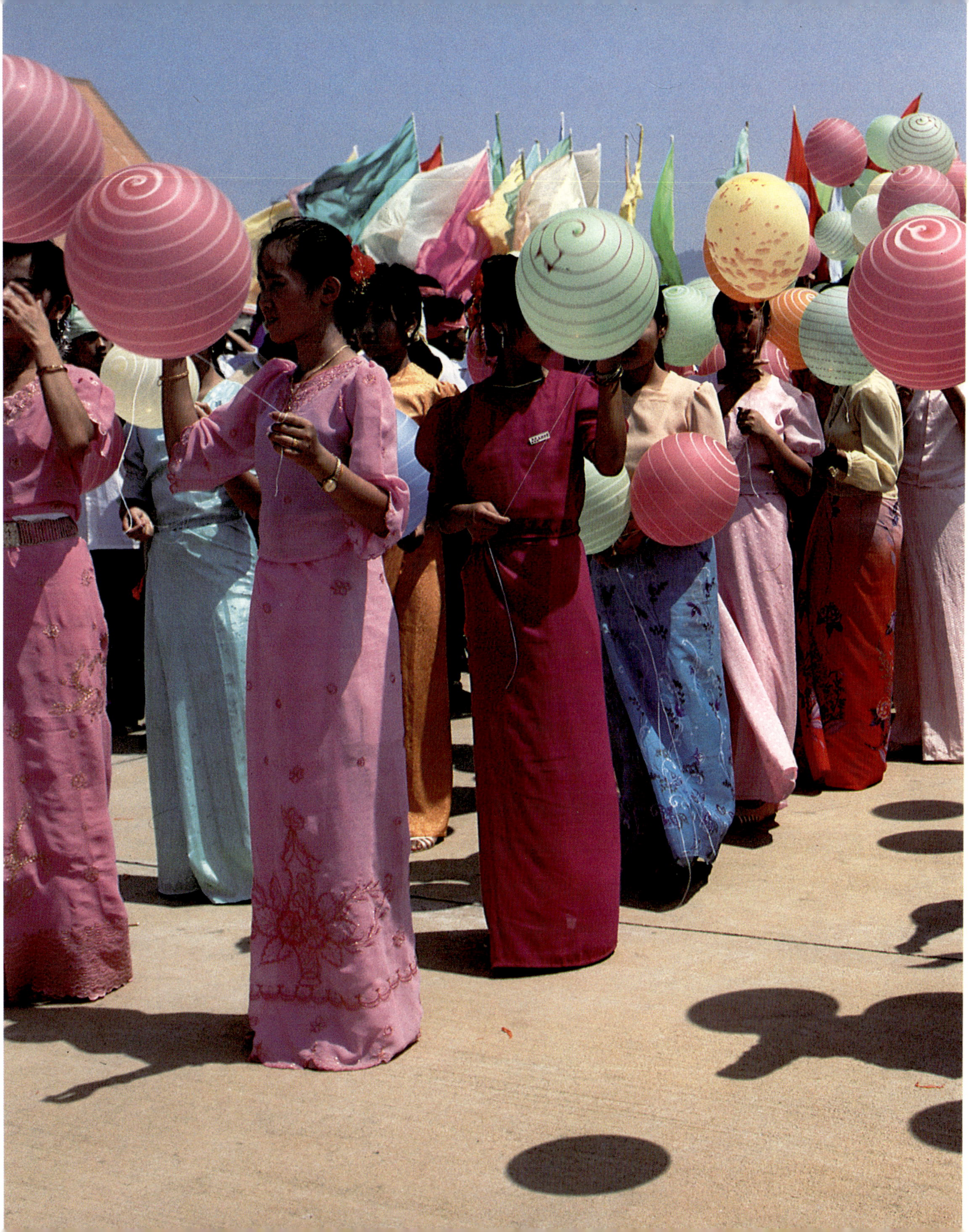

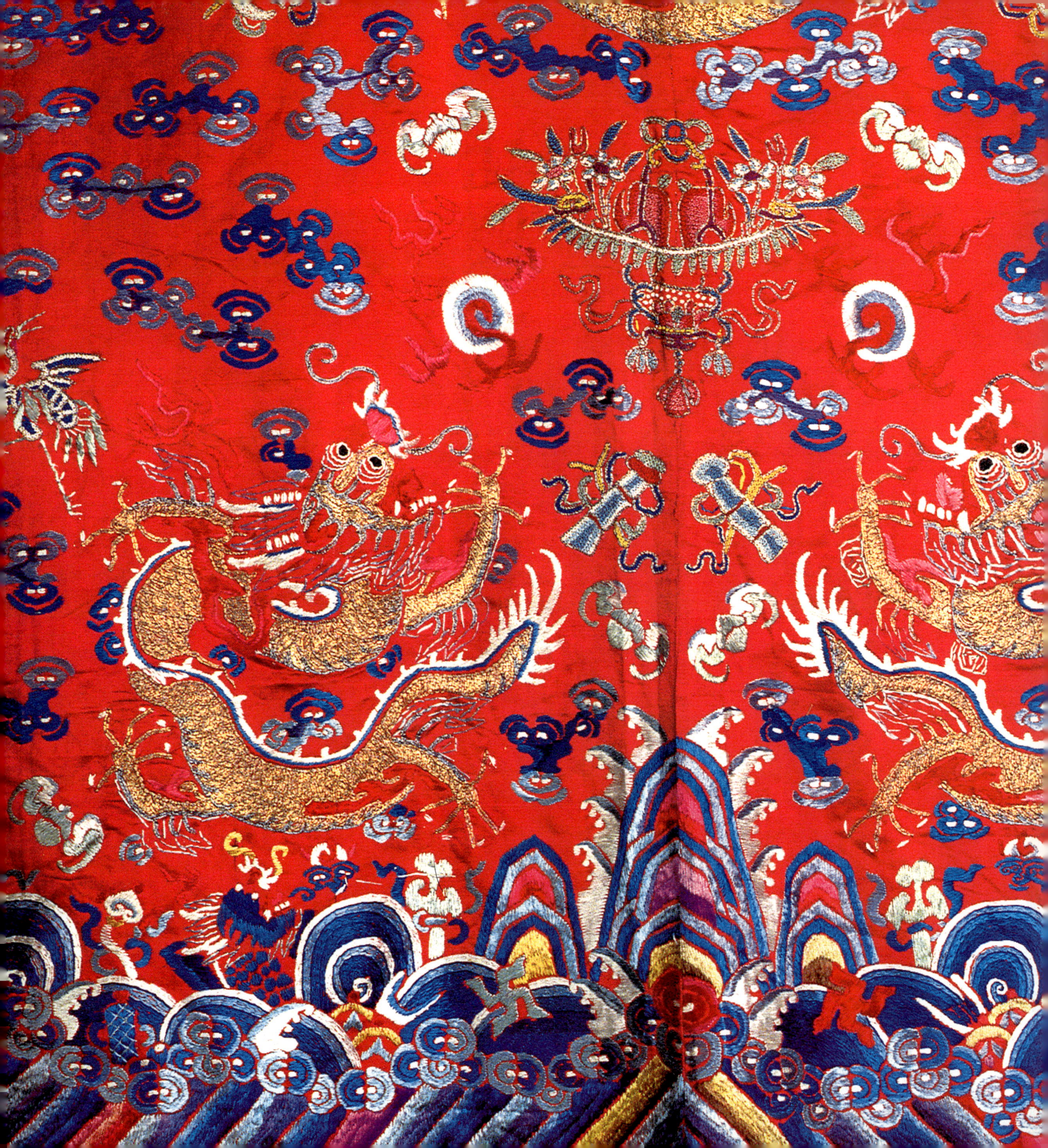

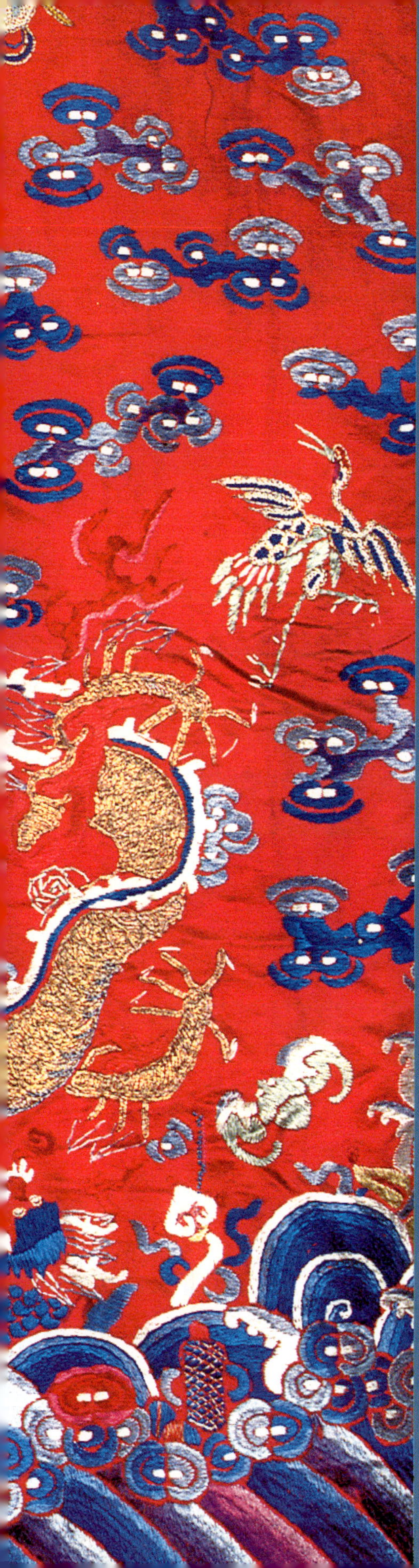

pattern

We in the West can appreciate an embroidered Chinese robe, a porcelain vase, or a Japanese screen on an aesthetic level, but the artist's choice of material, color, and ornament was dictated by a symbolic alphabet deeply rooted in religious and folk beliefs. Where we see only the random juxtaposition of flowers, animals, and geometric designs, the Chinese and Japanese will "read" a story written in a visual language rich in linguistic and literary allusions.

The Chinese language has many homonyms—words with the same pronunciation but very different meanings—providing the Chinese artist with a much richer vocabulary of visual puns than his Western counterpart. Chinese characters are themselves often used as decorative elements, and they also serve as talismans to dispel evil influences and attract good fortune.

In more recent times, the political upheavals of the twentieth century have swept away the beliefs and social hierarchies that underpinned traditional decoration. Communist China adopted the heroic Socialist Realism of the Soviet Union in the visual arts, and the stark lines of modernism for its official architecture.

A detail from a nineteenth-century embroidered Chinese robe depicts the dragon, the bringer of water, who chases thunderbolts among the clouds. He pursues the flaming pearl, the essence of life. The colorful wavy lines on the hem of the robe depict the ocean, the boundary of the universe.

flora

1 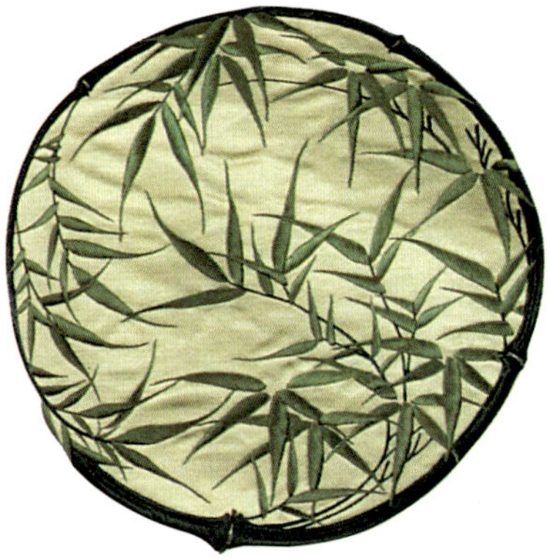

2 

When man first wanted to beautify his surroundings, it was to the world of plants that he turned for inspiration. Throughout the centuries, the meaning of each flower became codified. The lotus is an emblem of purity, because it grows in mud yet its blossom is pure and undefiled, while the peony, the flower of spring, represents love and affection. The East has many floral symbols of longevity, including the pine tree, the plum blossom, and the chrysanthemum, which is often used to represent a contented middle age. Conversely, when the plum blossom is shown on leafless, wintry branches, it symbolizes the transience and fragility of beauty.

3 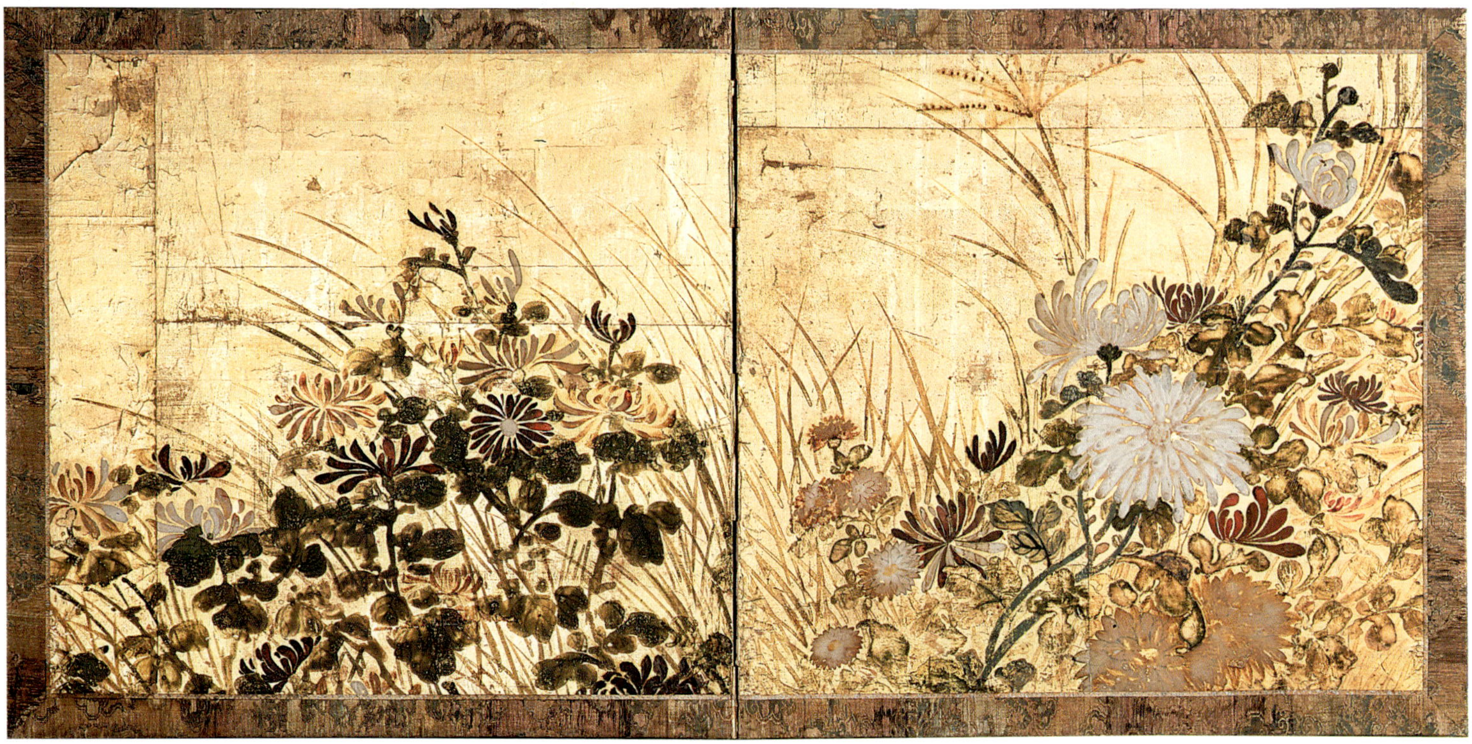

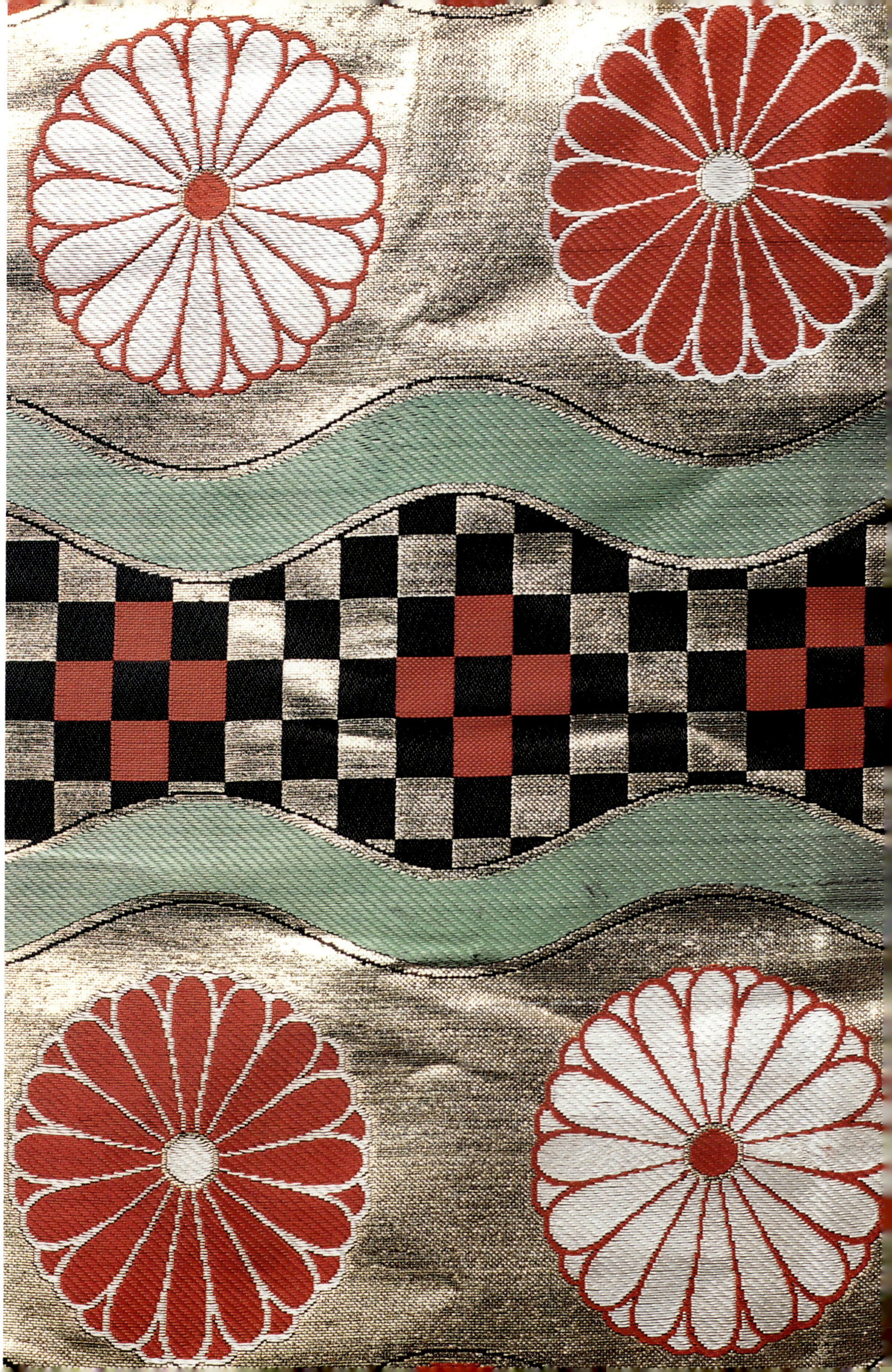

4

1 and 2 Details from a nineteenth-century woman's over-kimono. On a green satin-weave silk ground, floral and foliage roundels are exquisitely embroidered in satin stitch, creating a delicate pattern of blossoms and leaves.

3 A two-fold screen painted in colored pigment and black ink on a gold ground with *kiku* (chrysanthemums) and fall grasses. An early example of Japan's Rimpa School of painting, dating from the Edo period (1600–1867), this gentle depiction contrasts with more graphic modern interpretations of flowers, such as those on the picture at right.

4 The *obi* or kimono sash has been described as "an expression of beauty fastened to a woman's back." Only in the act of tying it and giving it its true form does its real significance become apparent, as it was believed possible to transfer one's love or spirit through the highly symbolic tied knot. Subtle differences in the ways of wearing *obi* differentiate between married and unmarried women. This 1920s *obi* is almost abstract with its stylized chrysanthemum and checkered patterns.

1 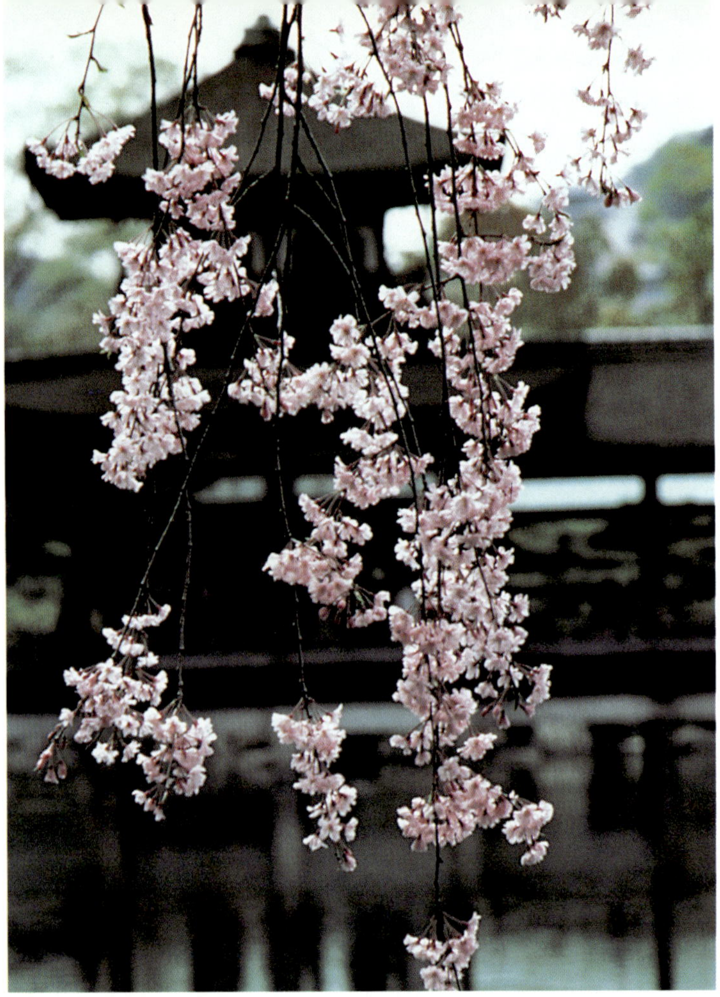

1 Cherry blossoms trail evocatively over water in the gardens of the Heian shrine in Kyoto, Japan. Flowering cherry trees are the embodiment of spring and are celebrated in *hanami,* cherry-blossom viewing parties in March and April. Once literary and poetic outings, *hanami* are now drunken revels held in the country or city parks.

2 Part of a large hanging, this fragment is an exquisite example of early fifteenth-century Ming dynasty textiles. Embroidered in polychrome silks, it depicts a lotus flower and peony blossom within encircling tendrils and leaves. Wall hangings also served practical purposes within a house to keep out drafts.

2 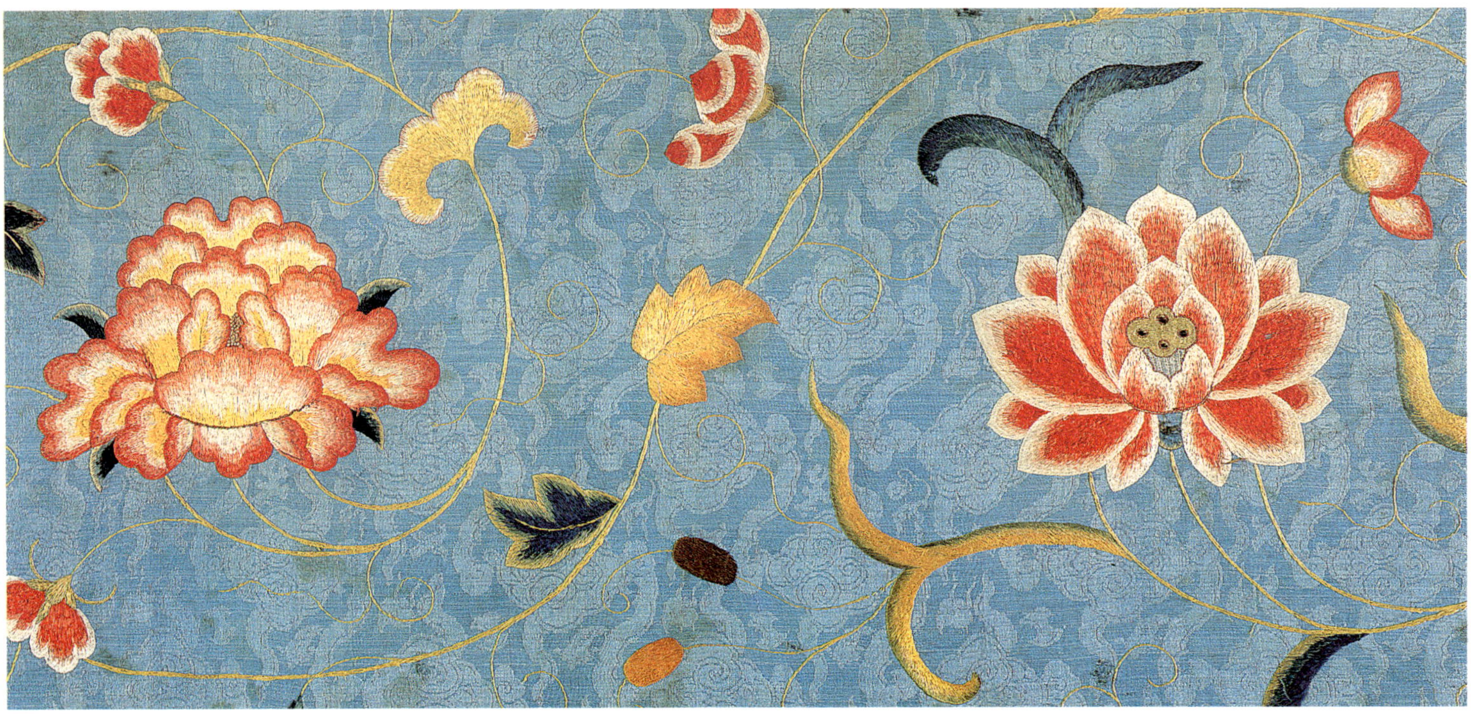

3

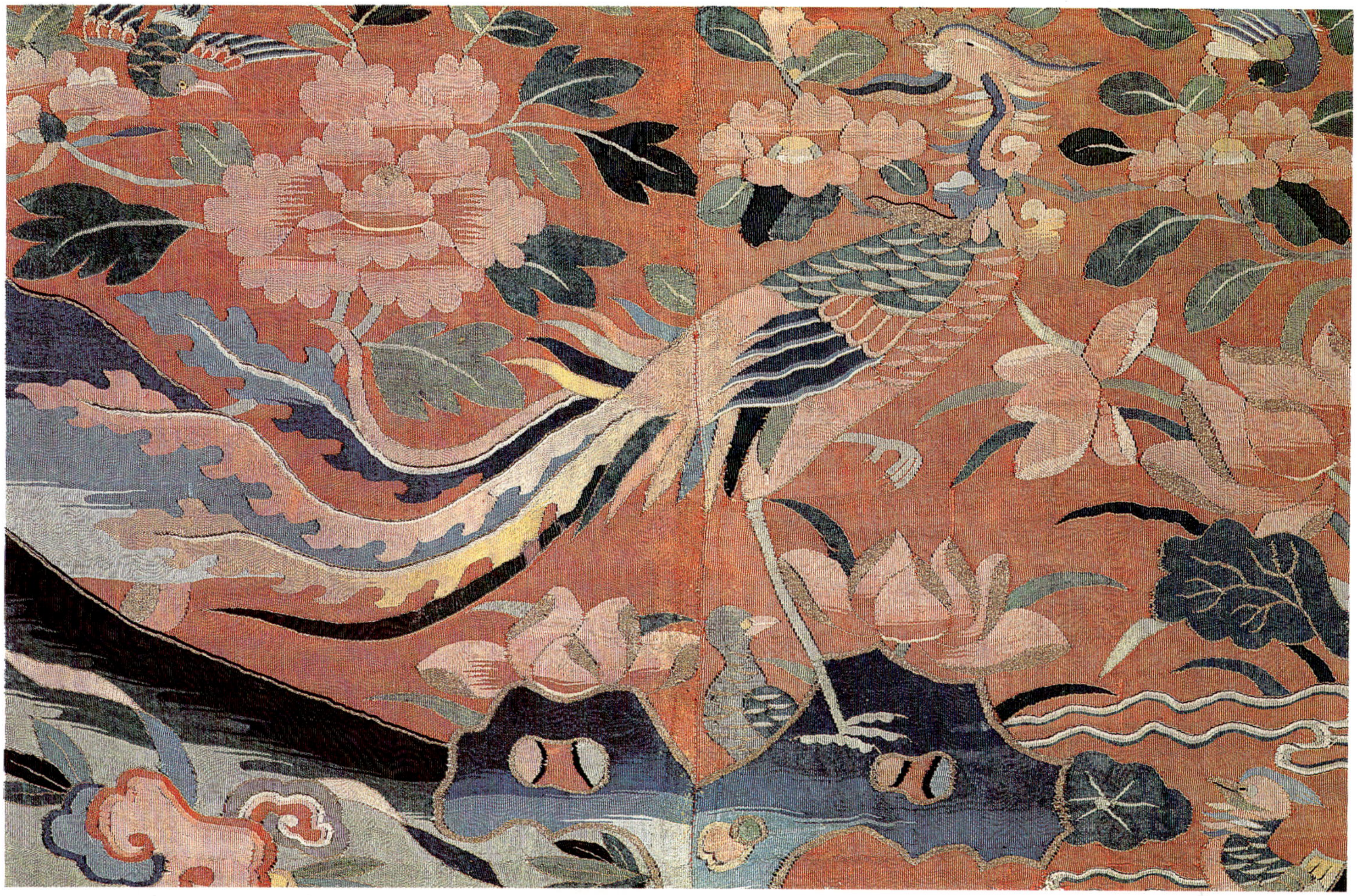

4

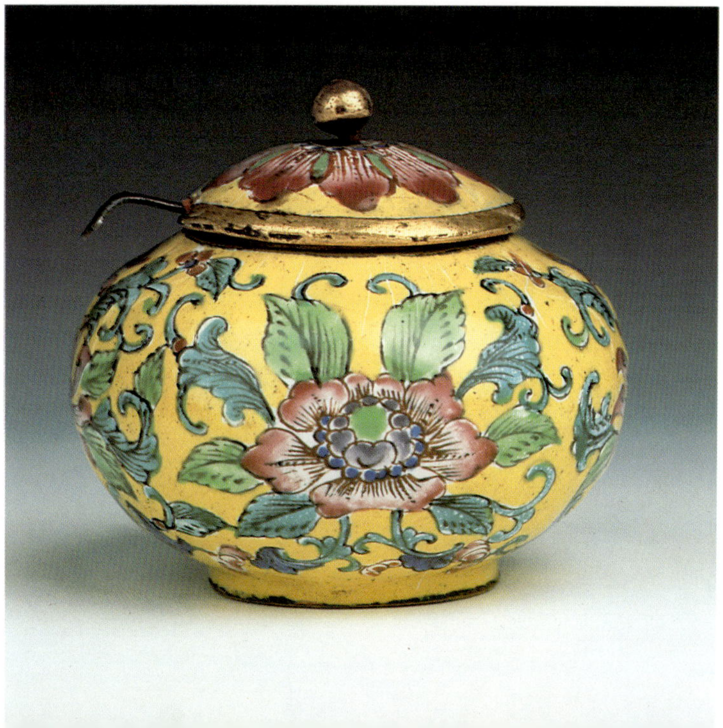

3 The phoenix, or *feng,* representing prosperity, is the most important bird in Chinese decorative symbolism. It is one of the celestial animals central to *feng shui*. It was the symbol for the empress and it adorned her apartments. This seventeenth-century Ming dynasty silk *kesi* (tapestry) panel shows a phoenix perched on a blue rock, with a lotus-filled pond to one side, with peony and lotus flowers, and a branch of *lingzhi* fungus, symbolizing immortality, to the left.

4 A yellow-ground Canton enamel condiment jar and spoon made for the Annamese court. The jar was made between 1820 and 1840, the spoon in 1830.

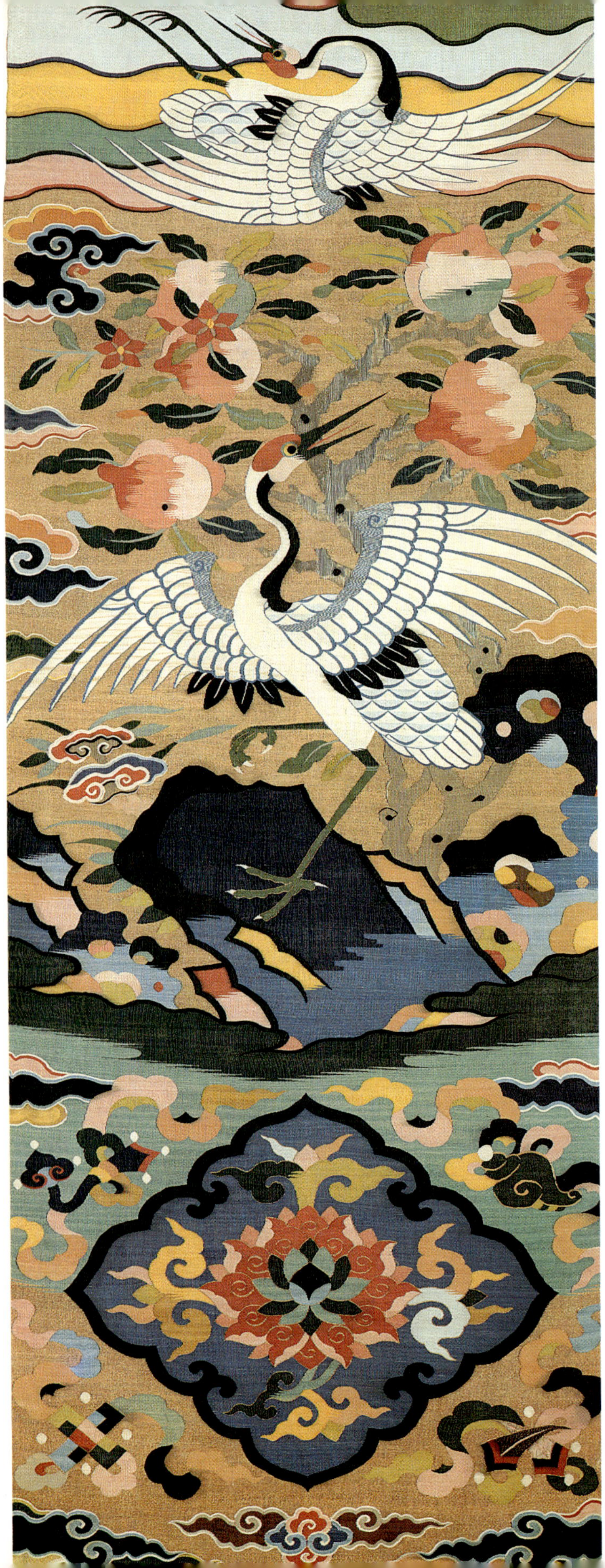

fauna

Animal representation in East Asian art dates back to prehistoric times. In the earliest religions, animals were the sacred totems of tribes, but as religions became more abstract, animals were demoted to symbolic components, representing qualities such as longevity, wisdom, and fertility, or used as talismans to ward off evil. Chinese lends itself to visual puns. The word for bat, *fu*, also means "happiness," hence the representation of bats is not sinister, as in the West, but signifies good fortune.

1 Detail of an extremely fine and rare silk Ming dynasty *kesi* (tapestry) chair cover, woven in polychrome silks with a design of a large Manchurian crane perched on a rock, with a branch of fruiting peaches (both emblems of longevity) with *lingzhi* fungus above and below. The medallion is decorated with a large formalized lotus flower, flanked with four symbols of wealth: a pair of rhinoceros horns, a pair of books (also a symbol of wisdom), a *ruyi* scepter (also for granting wishes), and a conch shell (also a Buddhist symbol of victory). This particular cover has an intriguing history; it was thought to have been given to the Russian Tsar Peter the Great by the Kangxi Emperor.

2

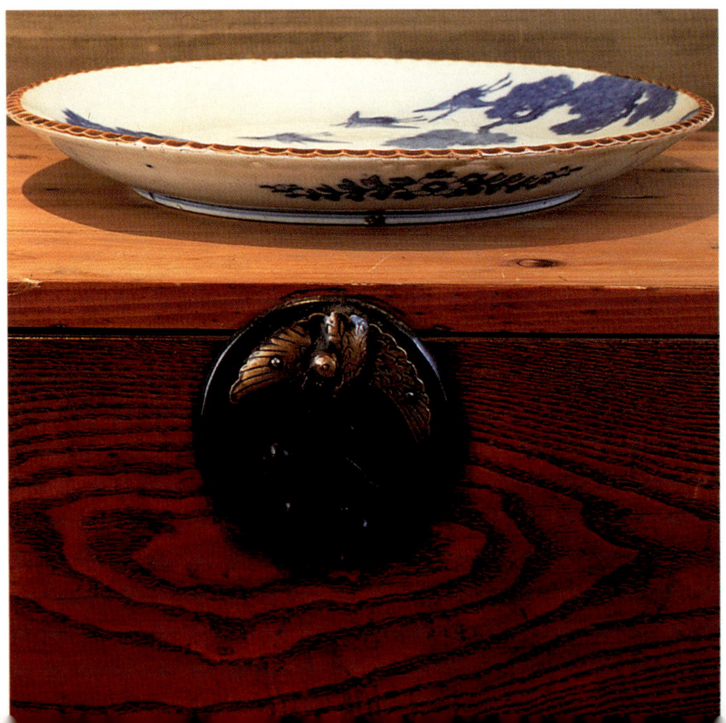

2 Detail of a decorative lock on a Japanese *tansu* chest, showing a crane and tortoise. The crane is one of the most popular symbols of longevity in Japanese art, and is depicted in all media for its grace and beauty. It is often shown with a tortoise; together they stand for good fortune and a long life. The blue-and-white plate also shows cranes in flight, representing many good wishes.

3 A cotton kimono from the eighteenth or nineteenth century. Patterned by resist stenciling, the naturalistic design shows water plants beside a stream with pairs of ducks, which are symbolic in both China and Japan of marital affection, love, and faithfulness.

4 The portrayal of five bats signifies the Five Blessings of health, wealth, virtue, longevity, and a natural death. This detail from a silk *kesi* robe has a design of bats among rows of *shou* symbols (for long life) woven in threads of gold leaf on paper wrapped around a silk core.

3

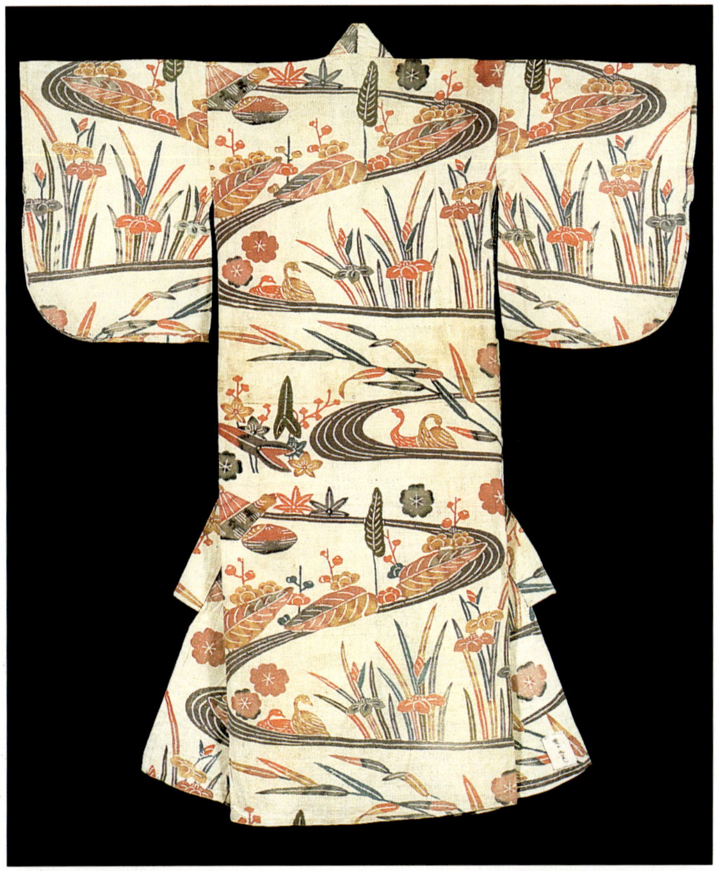

4

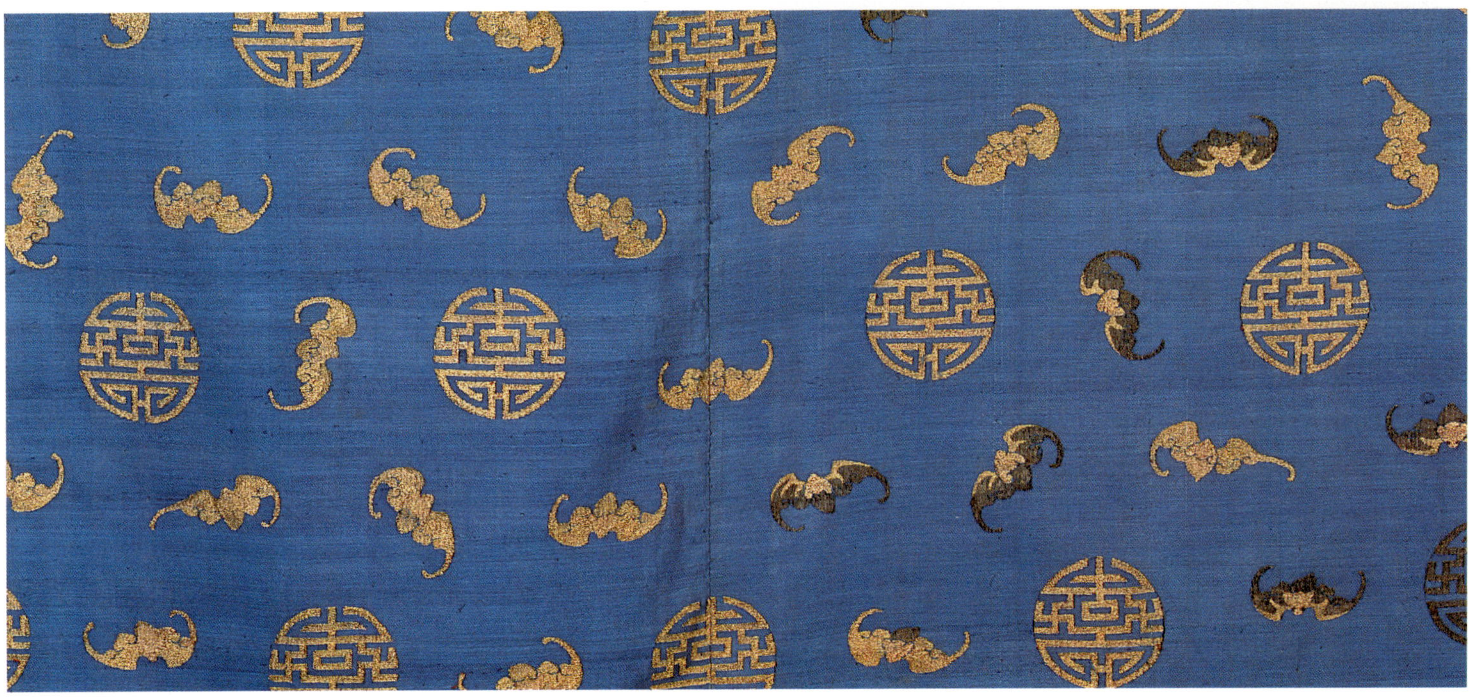

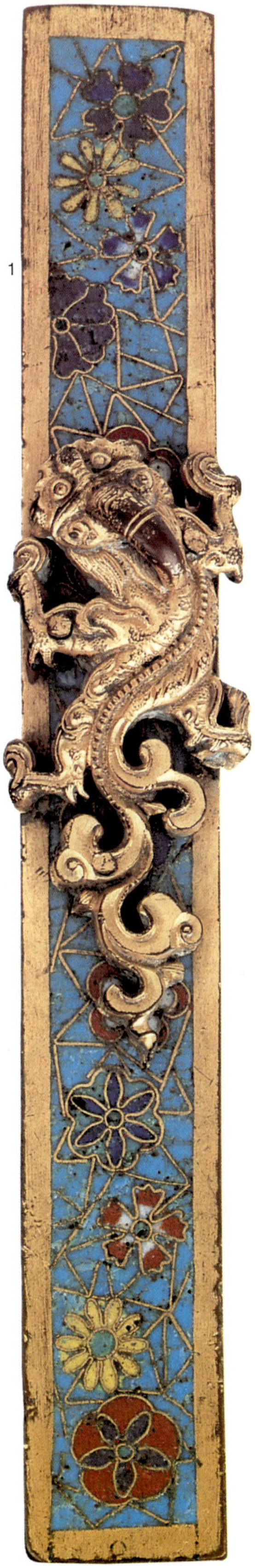

1

dragons

The fifth animal of the Chinese zodiac, the dragon, is the mythical beast most closely associated with East Asia. In contrast to our own tradition of rapacious, evil monsters, hoarding gold, which were slayed by knights in armor, the Chinese dragon is a benign creature, which symbolizes fertility and vigor. Until the end of imperial rule in 1911, the dragon was the symbol of the Chinese emperor, who wore sumptuously embroidered "dragon robes" on state occasions.

One of the most frequently seen dragons in Chinese art and decoration is the five-clawed *long*; these were reproduced on textiles, cast in bronze, gold, and silver, and painted onto porcelain and roof tiles. There are three principal orders of dragon: of sky, earth, and water. The dragon-kings, who are believed to rule the four seas encompassing earth, are celebrated in yearly dragon-boat races held on the fifth day of the fifth lunar month.

1 A cloisonné enamel paperweight decorated with flower blossoms on a turquoise ground, decorated with a gilt bronze *kui* dragon dating from the late Ming dynasty (*c.* 1600). The stylized and decorative dragon has a foliated tail, pronounced claws, and a snarling mouth.

2 A ferocious dragon head detail from a bronze replica of the world's first seismograph, or earthquake detector, built in A.D. 132.

3 Datong, the largest town in northern Shanxi province, has two important stone dragon screens. The Nine Dragon Screen (*Jiu Long Bi*) was built early in the Ming dynasty, and portrays nine dragons rising out of the sea. A smaller three-dragon screen from the same period is at the nearby temple of Guan Yin Tang.

4 A yellow silk panel from a sixteenth-century court robe. The complete robe would have had a lobed-collar design around the chest, back, and shoulders, decorated with dragons.

2

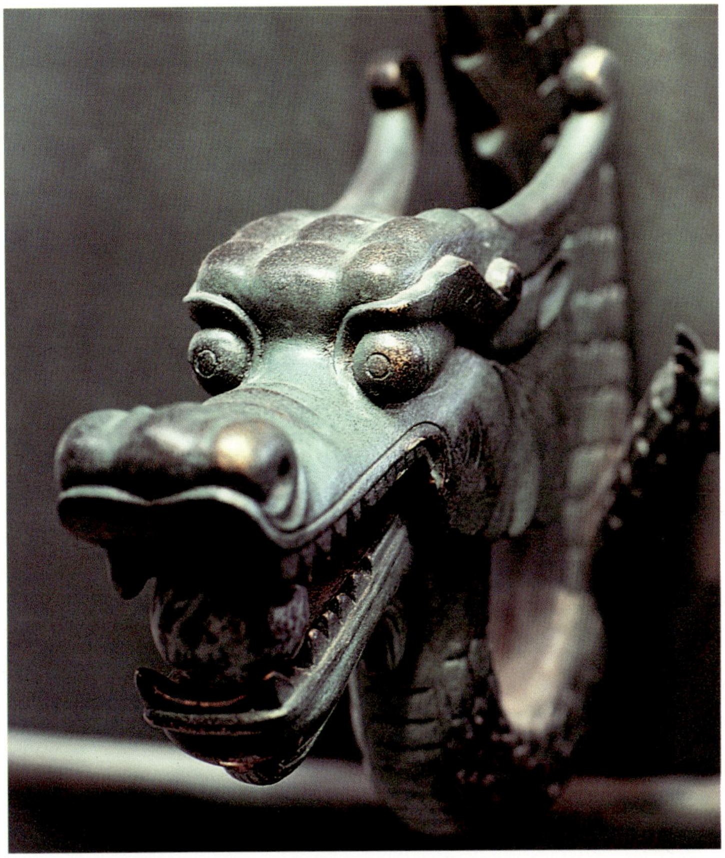

3

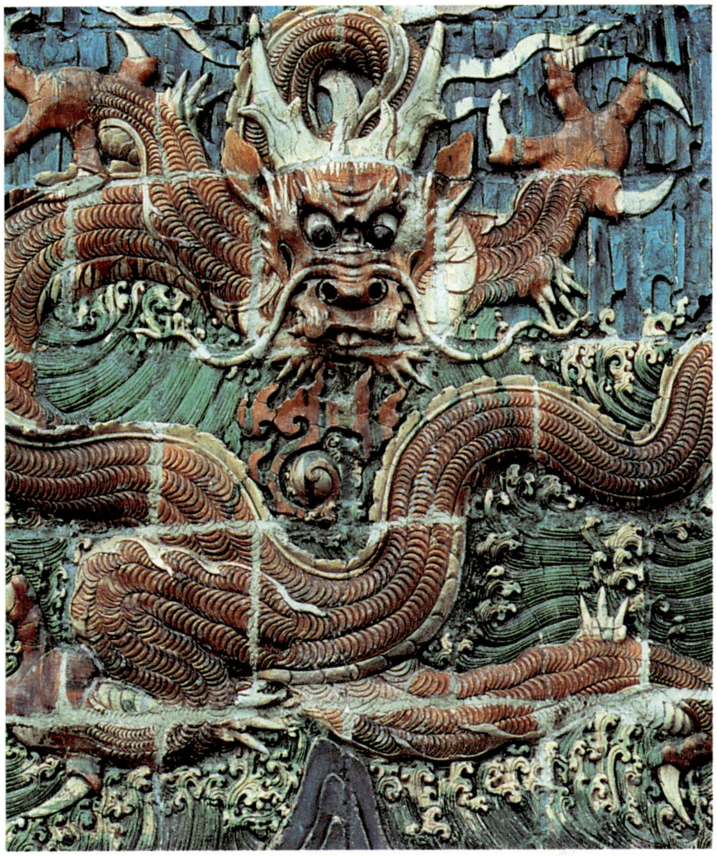

4

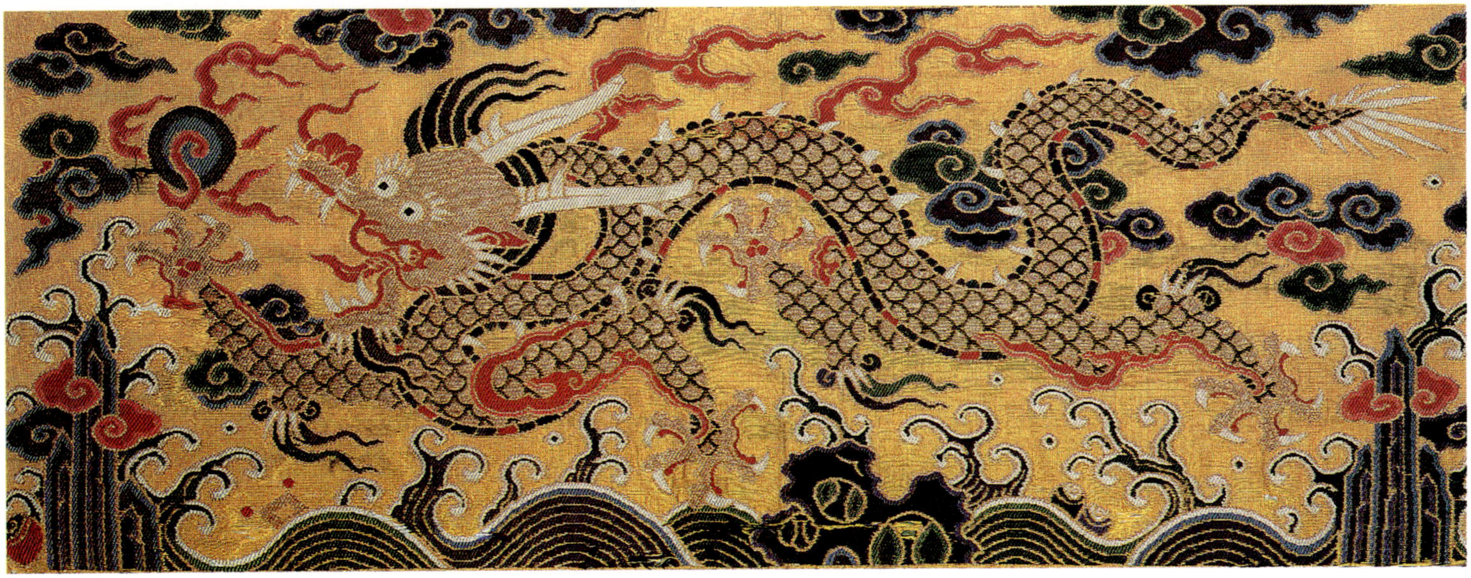

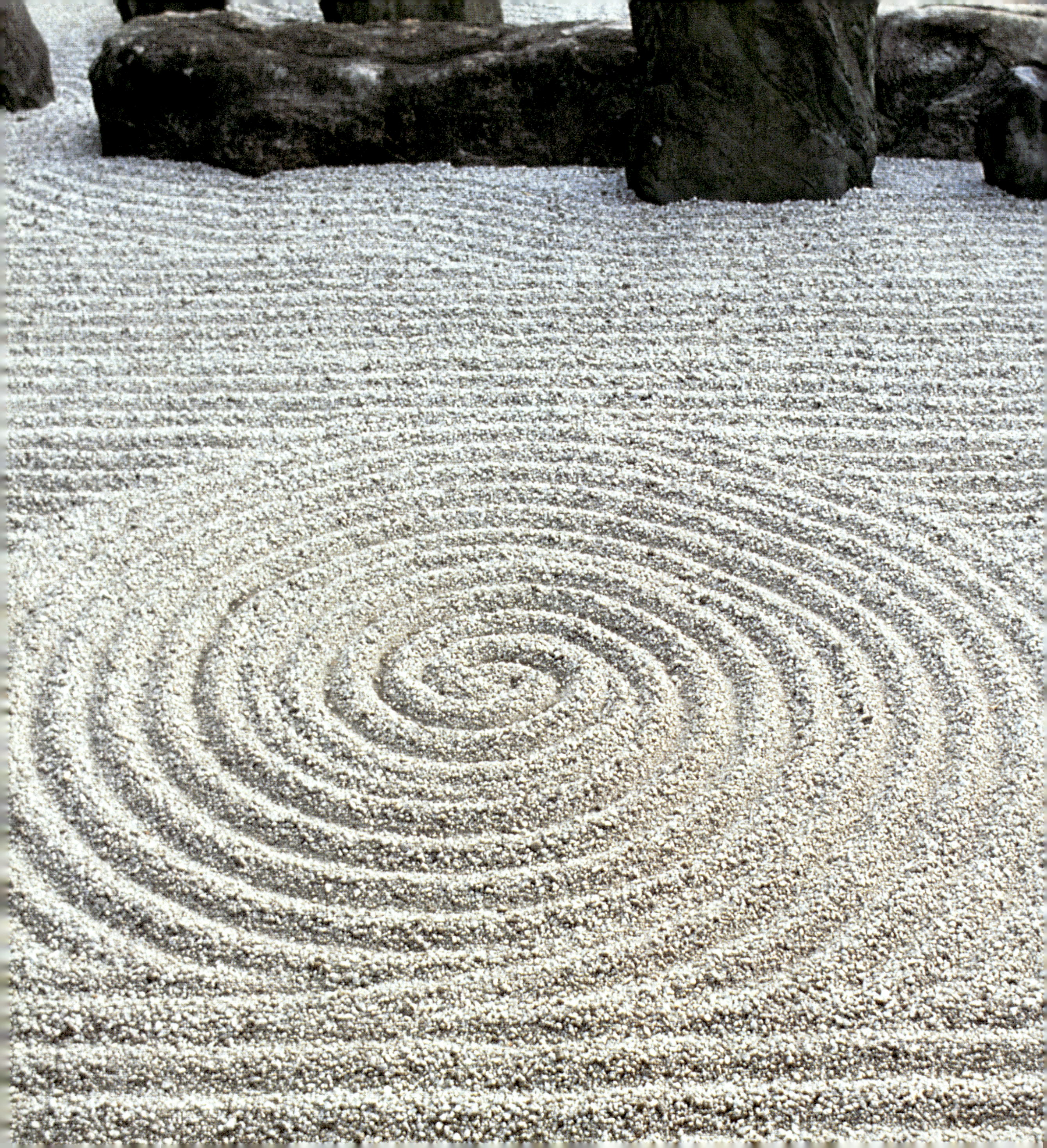

abstract

1 Detail of the south garden of Tofuku-ji temple in Kyoto, created in 1939. The temple has four gardens: north, south, east, and west. The South Garden is the largest and most important. Three oblong rocks form the islands of paradise, and four other sacred islands are surrounded by whirlpool-patterned gravel, representing a body of water, raked to create ripple and wave effects.

2 A collection of decorative jade pieces displayed on a bamboo table in Hong Kong. The endless knot design, shown here, symbolizes the Buddhist path and the "thread" that guides us to happiness. The knot is one of the eight Buddhist symbols of auspiciousness.

The genius of Eastern art is perhaps best seen in the abstraction of natural elements into symbolic and decorative patterns. With a few deft strokes of the brush or the masterly combination of form and color, the essence of an object is extracted, simplified, and reproduced.

We often forget that many of the decorative designs we see around us were originally imported from the East. In the nineteenth century, the intricate floral scrollwork, animals, and abstract symbols that adorned Western chinaware and furnishing fabrics were directly inspired by Chinese models. In the twentieth century, interior and commercial designers have looked for their models in Japan's centuries-old tradition of abstract representation.

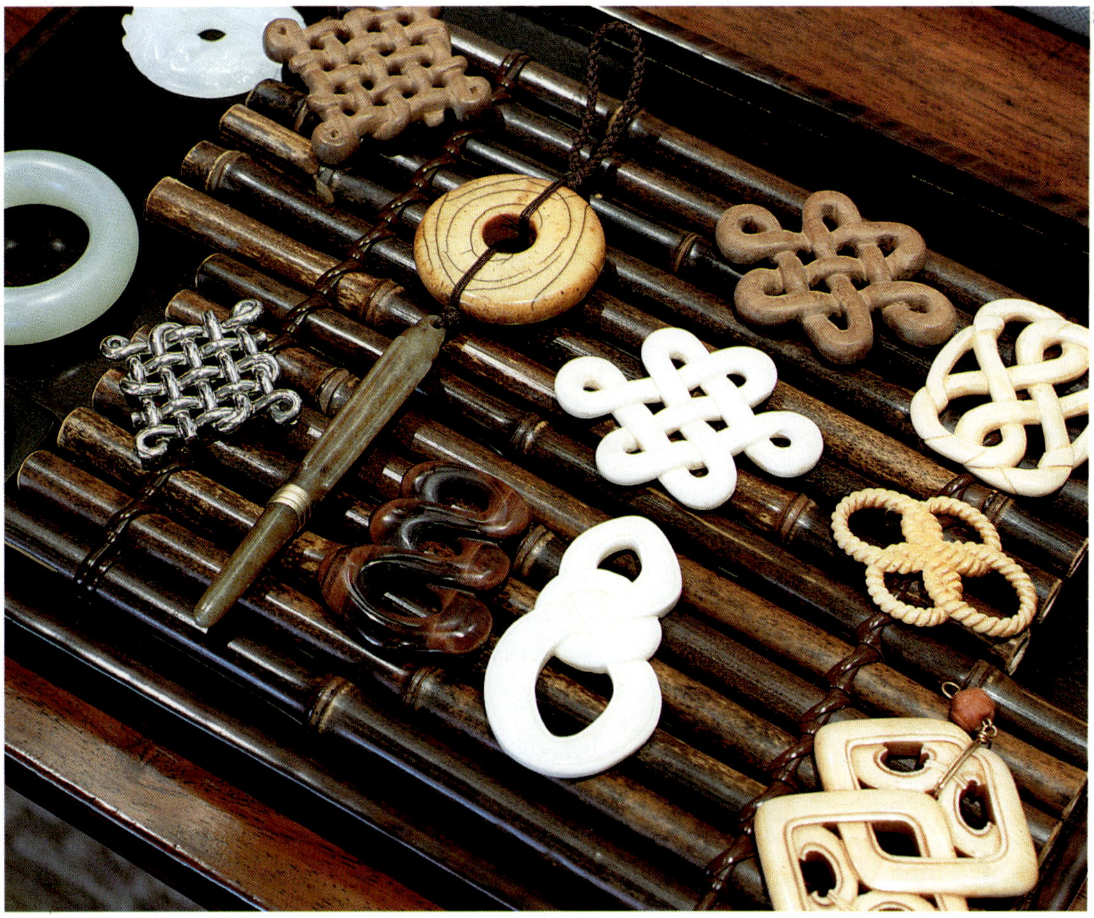
2

1

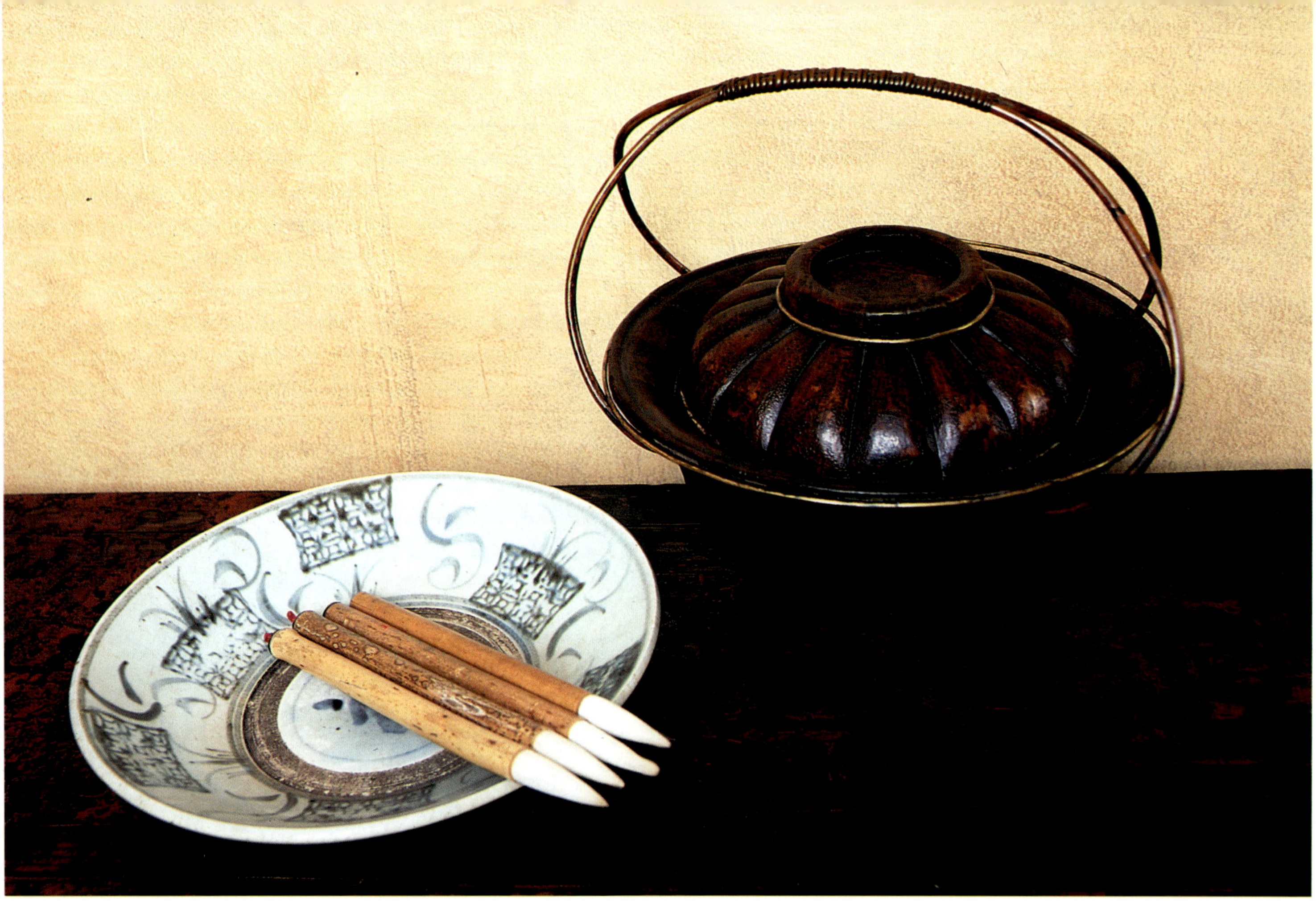

2

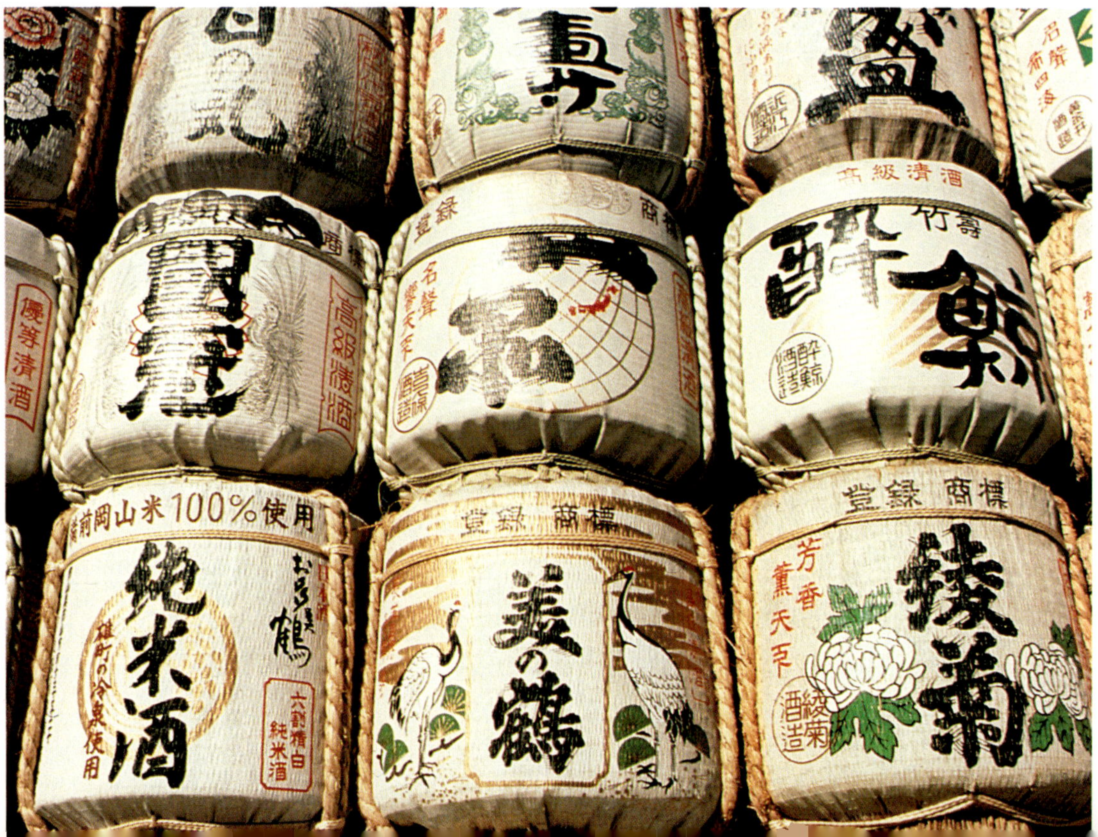

3

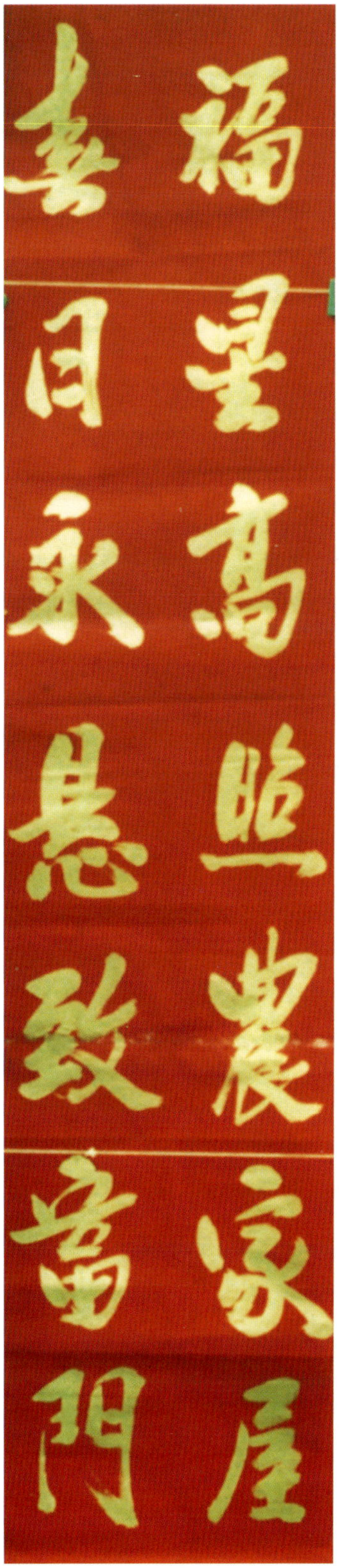

calligraphy

In the West, writing is seen primarily as a functional activity, used as a means to convey information, but in the East, calligraphy is an art form in its own right. To the Chinese or Japanese poet, it would seem absurd that his words be buried in the lifeless and graceless straitjacket of printed letters. Equipped with the "Four Treasures" of the calligrapher—brush, ink, inkstone, and paper—he can express his work in a visual style that best suits its content.

The Chinese language has more than 20,000 ideograms, ranging from the simple upturned "v" made by two brushstrokes that means "man," to elaborate characters made up of twenty or more strokes. The Japanese, who adopted Chinese characters in the seventh century, have supplemented them with two syllabic alphabets or *kana*, to allow them to write their own, different language.

1 Displayed here on a nineteeenth-century red lacquer document chest, with a *piyou*-covered lunch box, calligraphy brushes are decorative items in their own right.

2 Ceremonial *sake* casks at a Japanese shrine. The labels are decorated with birds and flowers, but the most striking element of the design is the calligraphy and the balance of the brush strokes.

3 Before Chinese New Year celebrations, stalls are set up in the streets, selling couplets on slips of paper, known as *duilians*, written to order by street calligraphers.

4 Graphic design using a repeating pattern for a black and white contemporary Japanese kimono. Here, a series of Chinese characters are used as the pattern.

4

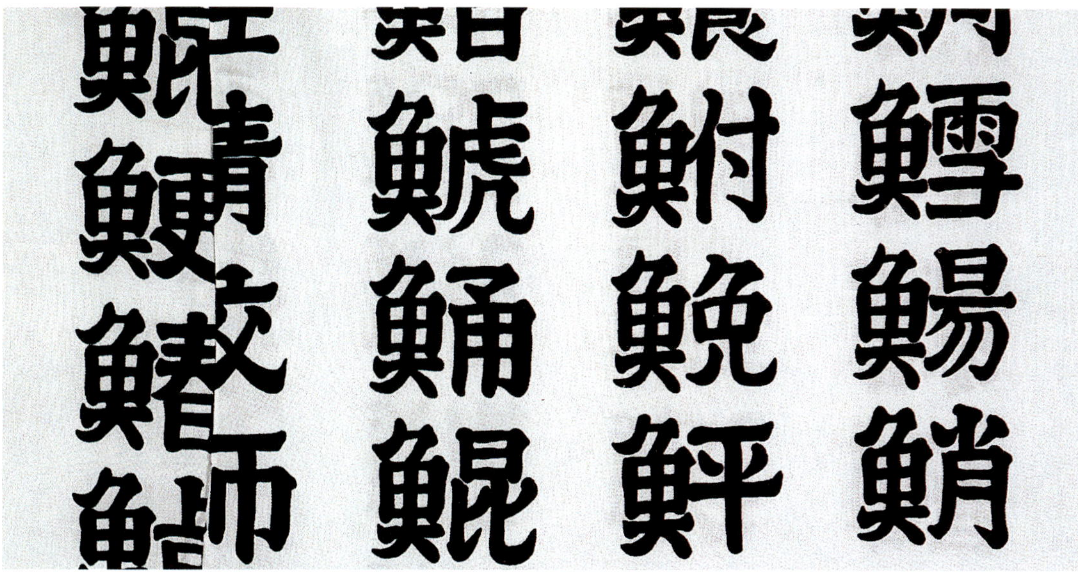

narrative

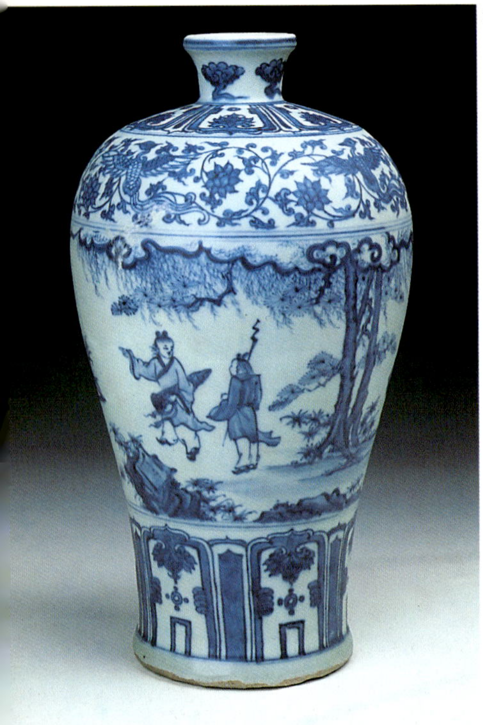

1

The tradition of decorative schemes based on literary, religious, and folk narratives is an ancient one in both China and Japan. China's pictorial art is inseparable from its poetic tradition, as both were thought to be the supreme accomplishments of the poet and scholar.

The world's first novel, *The Tale of Genji*, was written in eleventh-century Japan by the Lady Murasaki. Strikingly modern in its attitudes toward love and sex, it gives us a glimpse of the sumptuous world of court life in the Heian period (794–1185). *The Tale of Genji*, first illustrated in a twelfth-century picture scroll, is a masterpiece of Japan's ancient tradition of pictorial narrative that lives on today in *manga* (comic books). As one slowly unrolls the scroll scene by scene, one discovers the ceremonies of the imperial year, as well as the most intimate moments of courtship. Courtiers stroll in the gardens of the palace, while their female admirers, shielded from view by screens, make their presence known to their admirers by showing the sleeves of their many-layered court robes.

2

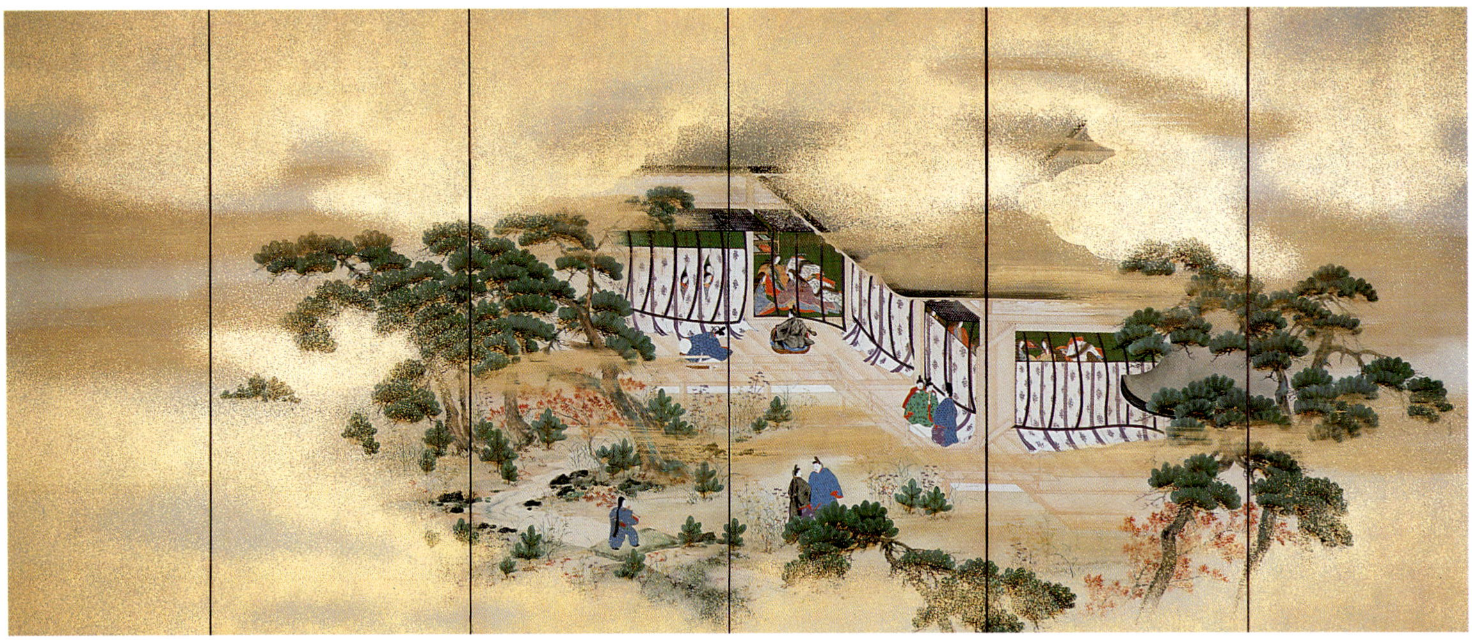

3

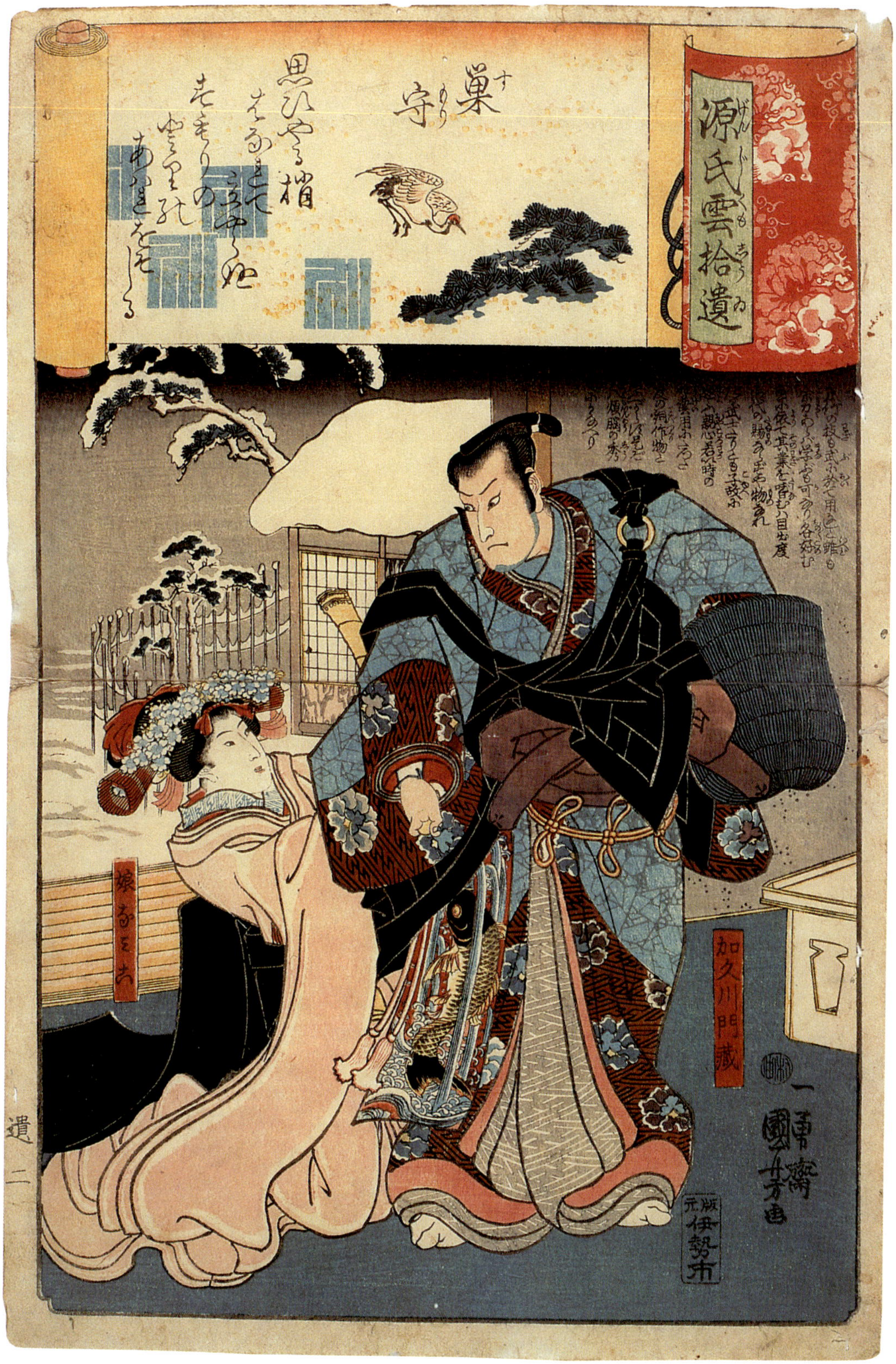

1 A fifteenth-century Ming dynasty vase depicts two scholars meeting in a landscape. One carries a dragon-headed staff and their attendants are on the reverse of the vase, separated by pine and willow trees.

2 One of a pair of nineteenth-century Meiji-period screens depicting the Japanese legend, *The Tale of Genji*. In the first (not shown) it is springtime, as Prince Genji and his courtiers view cherry blossoms while writing poems beside a stream, and in the other (shown here), set in fall, an attendant carries a maple branch toward a terraced pavilion, where ladies-in-waiting peep through blinds at the courtiers in the garden.

3 A nineteenth-century Japanese *ukiyo-e* (floating world) woodblock print by the nineteenth-century artist Kuniyoshi. *Ukiyo-e* prints were used as playbills and advertising posters for the *kabuki* theater from the seventeenth to the nineteenth century. The prints typically show the leading actors of the day in scenes from the play. Bound into lavish albums, *ukiyo-e,* depicting the famous courtesans of the Yoshiwara pleasure district, were collector's items. Collections of woodblock prints were also used to illustrate landscapes and famous places, such as Hiroshige's *Fifty-Three Stations on the Tokaido (Eastern Sea Road)* and Hokusai's *Hundred Views of Fuji.*

display

The reality of modern-day life in metropolitan China and Japan is that of a frenzied drama of industrial and commercial activity, played on a stage overcrowded to bursting point. Amid this visual tumult, the art of display for business and advertising exploits to the fullest the East's traditions of abstract patterning and decorative calligraphy.

Replacing the nineteenth century's woodblock prints, announcing the latest productions at *kabuki* theaters, and the painted banners and flags of temples and shrines, vertical neon signs cascade down from high-rise buildings in multi-colored showers of characters and symbols, denoting department stores, banks, and corporate headquarters. Restaurant windows reveal visual menus for the eyes to feast on, while the cheapest purchase is packaged with the same attention to detail and style as the most extravagant gift.

1

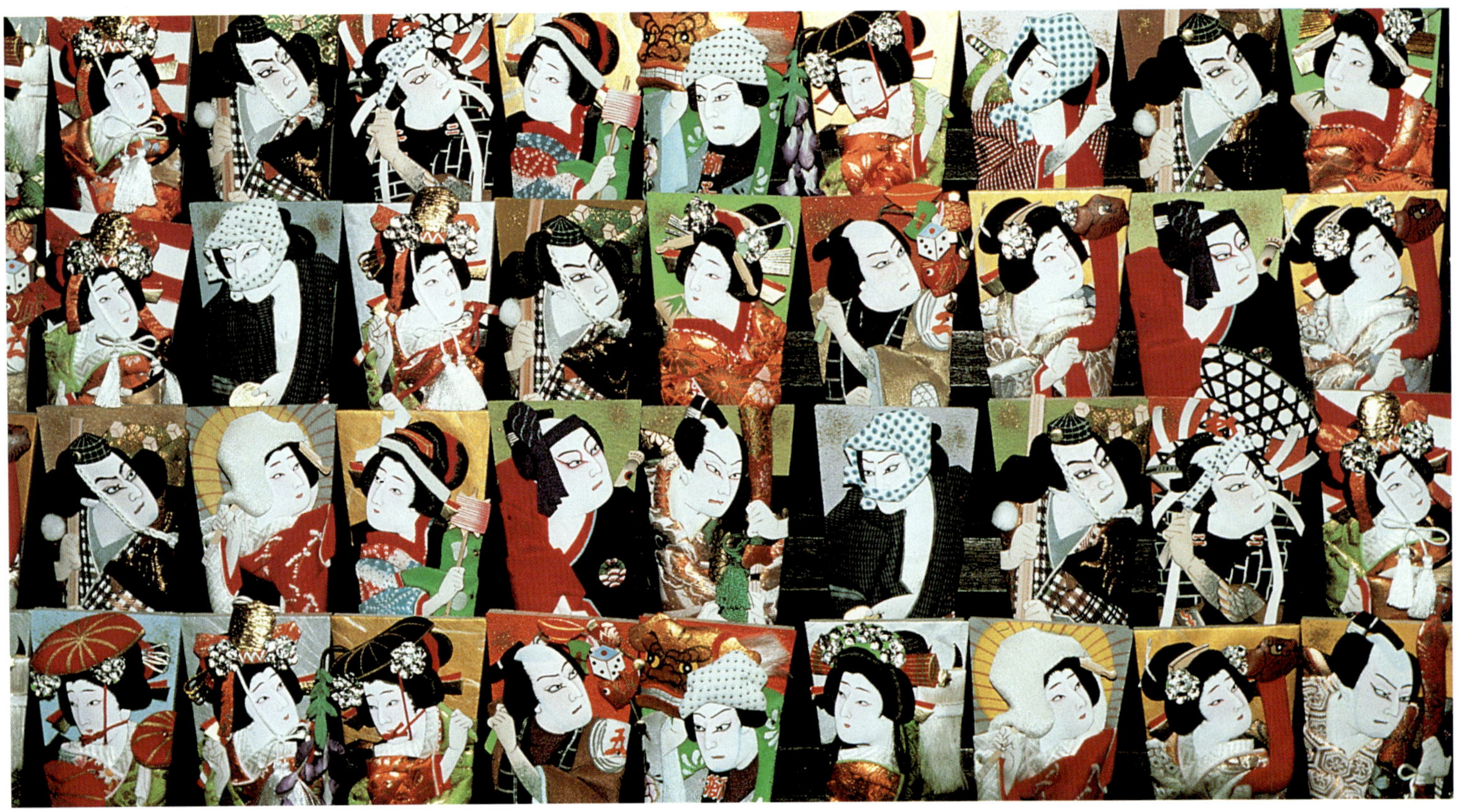

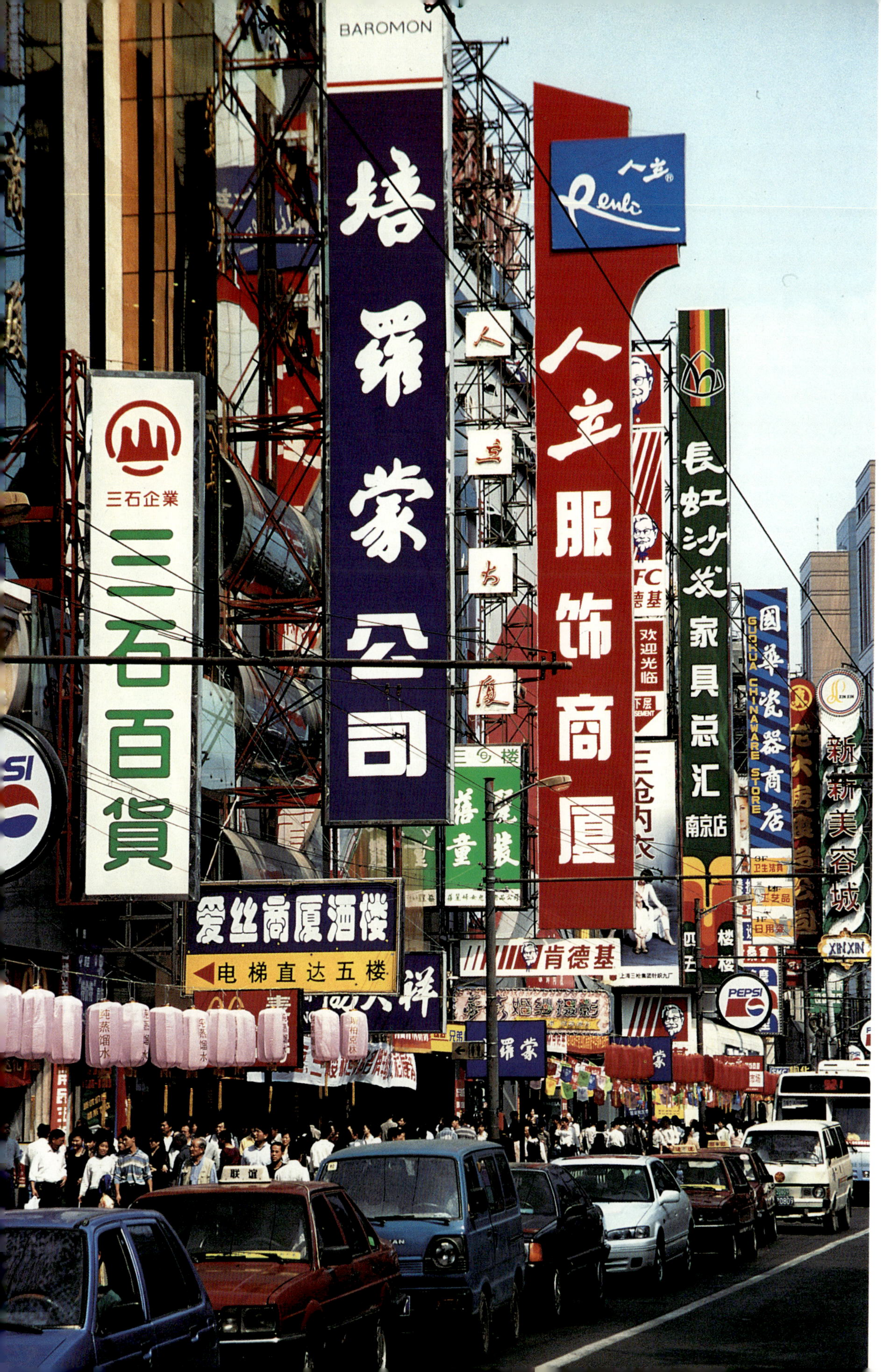

1 *Ukiyo-e* woodblock portraits of actors and courtesans create the repetitive patterns on the bats for a set of battledore, a game played with a bat and ball or shuttlecock during the New Year celebrations in Japan.

2 The hectic confusion of a busy street scene in Shanghai, one of the busiest international ports in the world. The face of the city is constantly changing as it races toward the future, reflecting the contrasts of modern China. The street signs of Shanghai's main commercial street, Nanjing Dong, are the outward signs of the growing commercialization and rapid economic expansion of contemporary China.

2

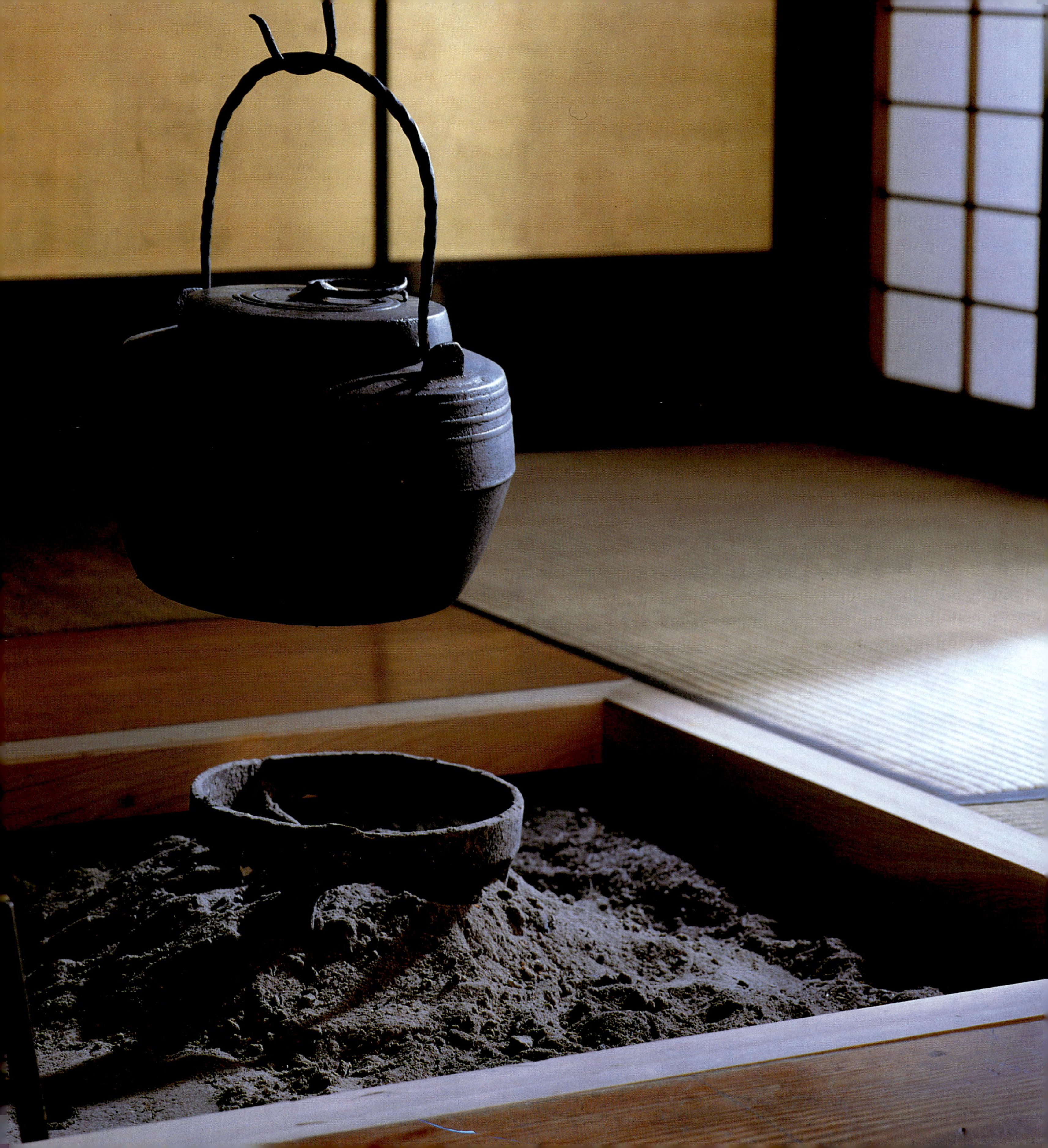

texture
and materials

The complex relationship between man and nature is reflected in his use of materials. The early cultures of China and Japan, finely balanced between survival and extinction, sought to tame the natural world. They transformed its raw materials so as to banish nature from their dwellings: wood was carved, lacquered, and painted; stone was cut and polished; fibers were spun, dyed, and woven; and clay was shaped, decorated, and finally glazed.

In later times, when men lived in comfort and safety in cities, they yearned to recover their lost connection with the natural world. They began to create gardens that imitated natural scenery, and to introduce natural elements into their homes. In sixteenth-century Japan, a new aesthetic of harmony with nature emerged, which extolled the virtues of the simple, rustic, and unadorned. This philosophy is perhaps best expressed in the ceramic wares, architecture, and garden design associated with *Sado*, the Way of Tea.

A metal kettle hangs over an open *irori* hearth in a traditional Japanese interior. The combination of the subtle shades and textures of natural materials creates the calming, restrained atmosphere associated with the Japanese tea ceremony.

stone

As an emblem of the earth, one of the five elements of East Asian cosmography, stone creates a link between the natural and human worlds, and also acts as a physical bridge between internal and external space.

Stone and brick, the most prevalent building materials in China, are not suited to the Japanese climate and lifestyle. The Japanese have traditionally built in wood, which allows their houses to breathe throughout the humid summer, while keeping them warm in winter.

In Shinto, Japan's ancient religion, certain groupings of large natural stones are seen as the abode of the *kami*, or gods. They are often found in the grounds of shrines, and their sacred nature is symbolized by binding them with rice-straw rope hung with folded paper decorations. Stepping stones, too, are important elements in Japanese garden design, guiding the visitor from vista to vista, and allowing him to cross ponds and streams.

1 2

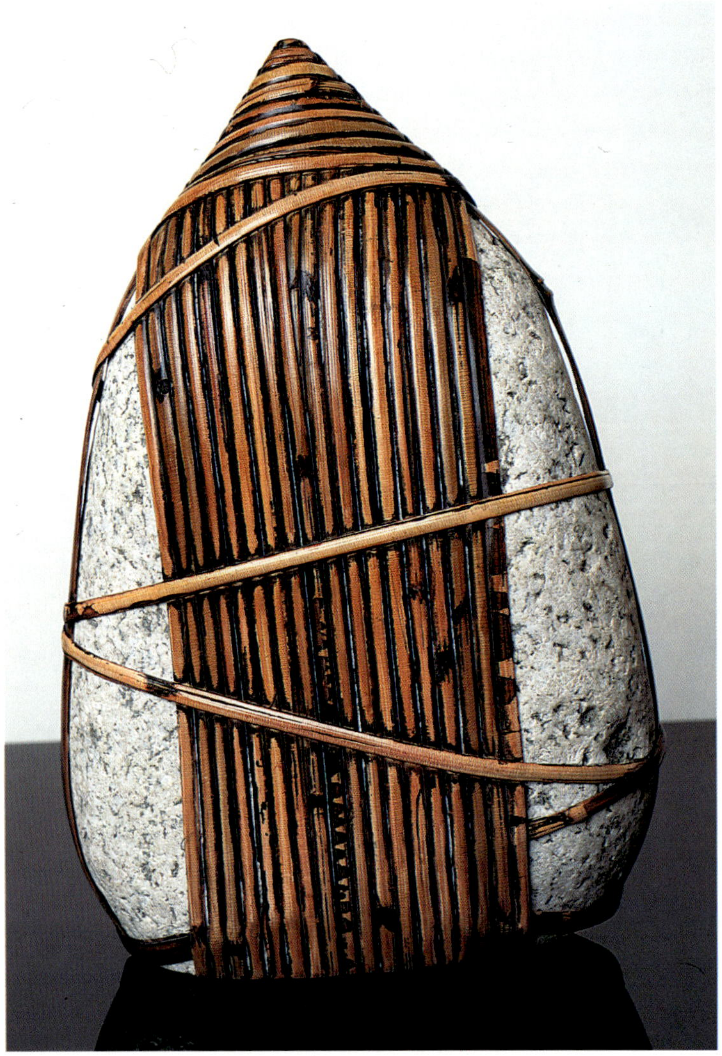

1 Stones can be decorative items in their own right. In East Asian beliefs, they are also imbued with special powers: the bound stone is symbolic of entry into another world. This piece by American artist Del Webber is a contemporary re-interpretation of traditional crafts.

2 The use of natural rocks and stone in this modern bathroom creates the soothing and restorative atmosphere of a Japanese *onsen* or hot spring: these are popular destinations in modern-day Japan.

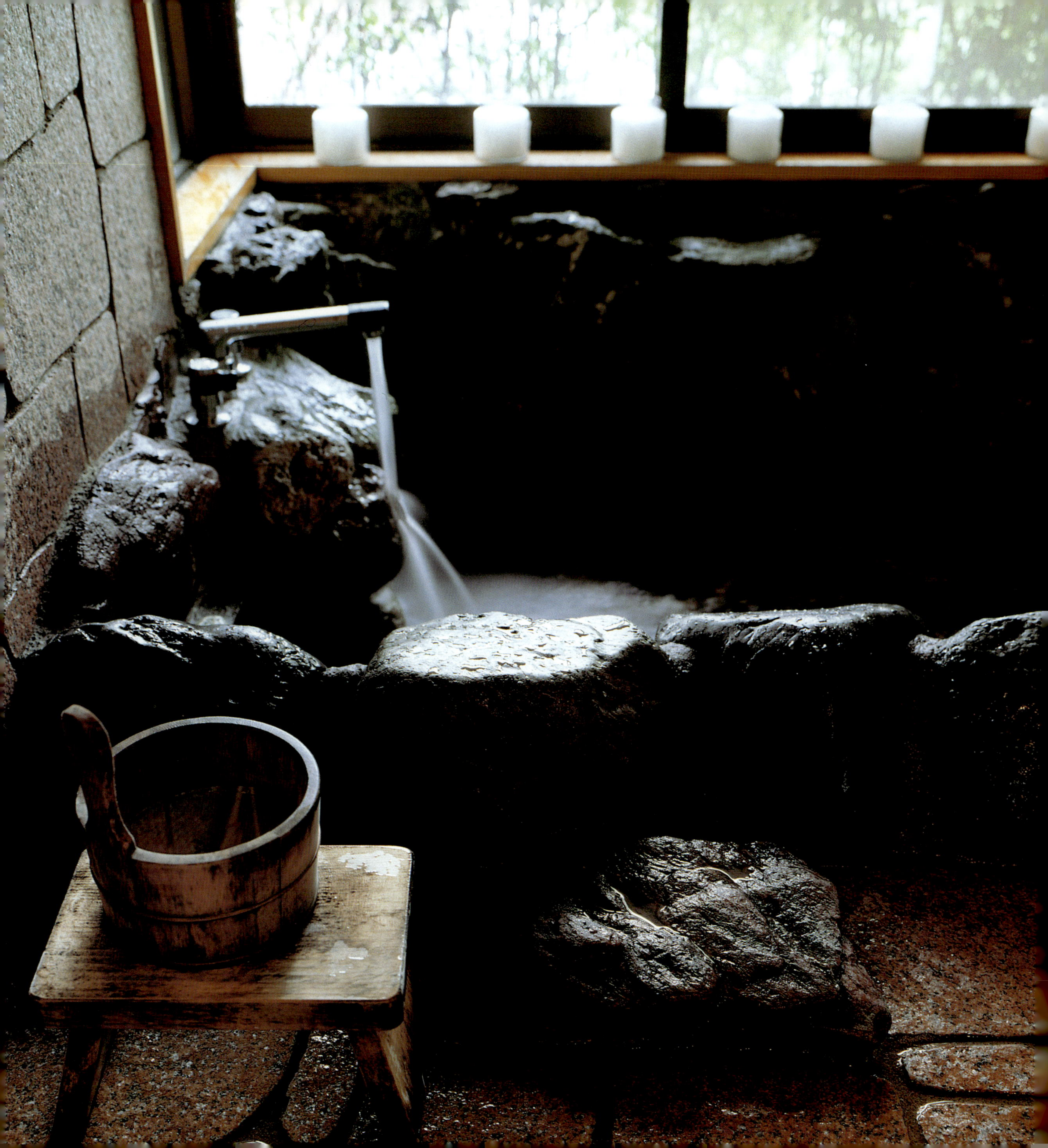

1

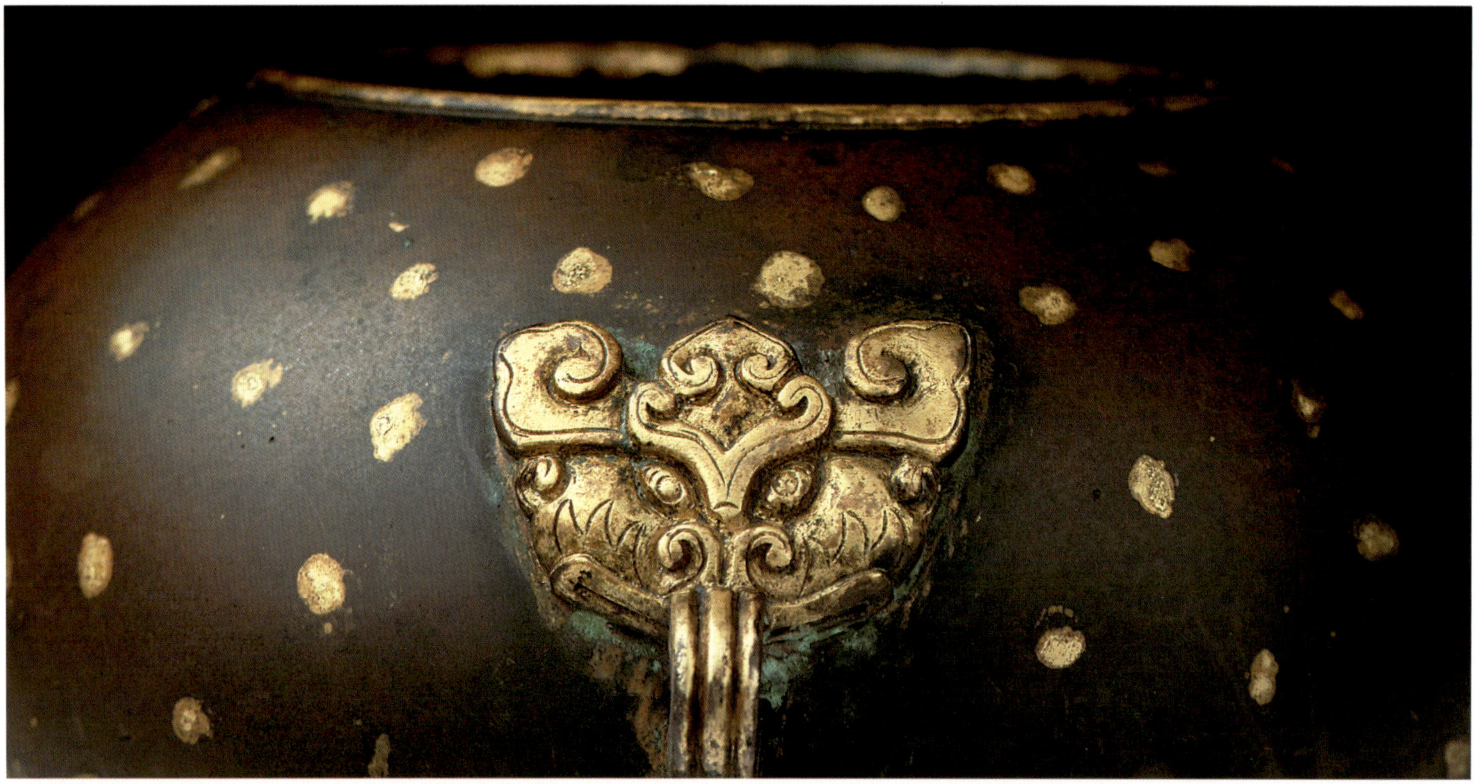

2

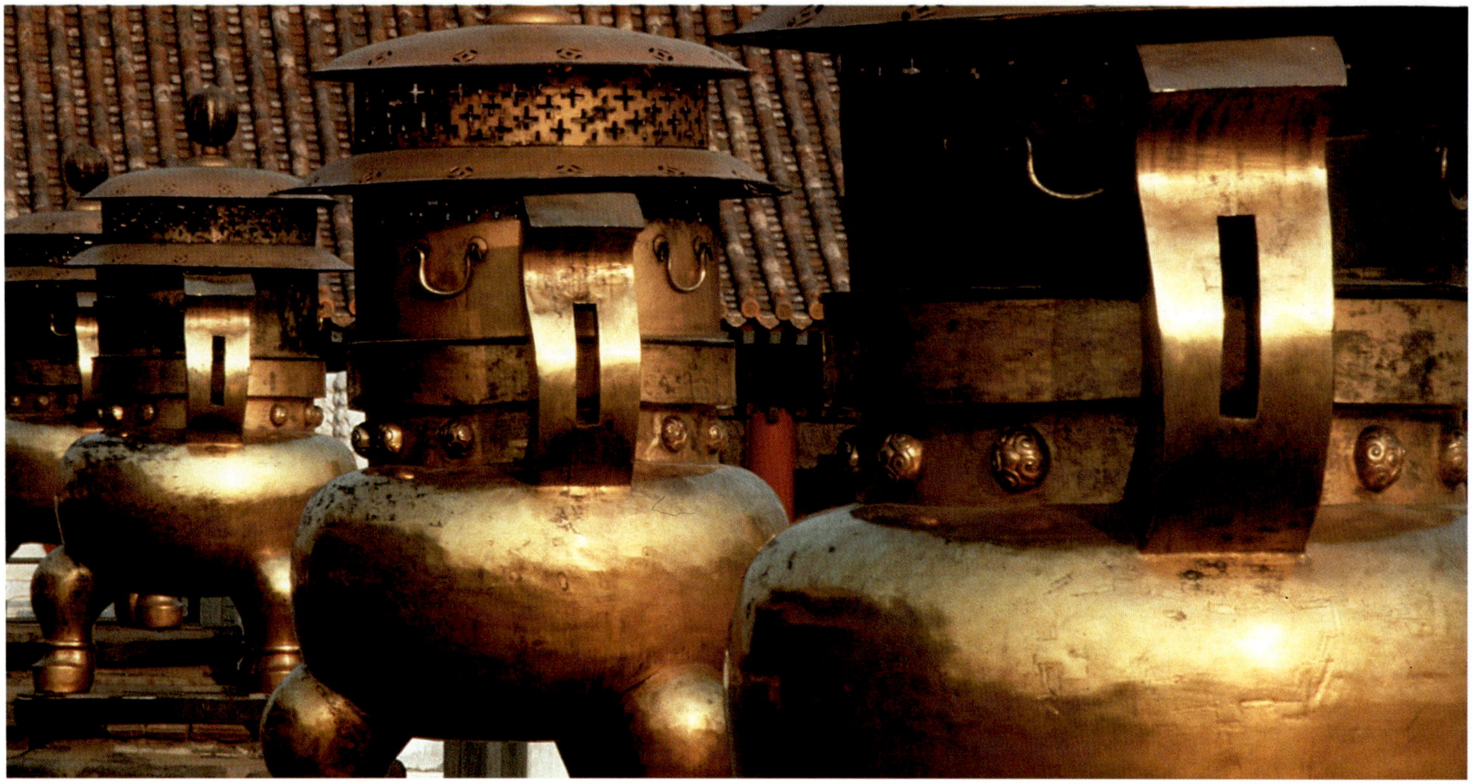

metal

The Chinese were crafting exquisite objects from bronze when our own ancestors were still using stone tools. In ancient China, bronze ritual vessels and musical instruments symbolized wealth and power, and many of these objects have been found in royal and aristocratic burials. The Chinese were the first to smelt iron, and they made steel of such quality that it was not equaled in the West until the eighteenth century.

Gold and silver were as precious in East Asia as in the West, and gold, which does not oxidize, was a symbol of immortality. It was an ingredient of the Taoist Elixir of Life, and was believed to prolong life if consumed.

Unlike its continental neighbors, Japan has poor iron ore and gold deposits, which had to be imported from China and Korea. Such was its scarcity that, for centuries, gold was reserved for the decoration of religious and imperial buildings.

3

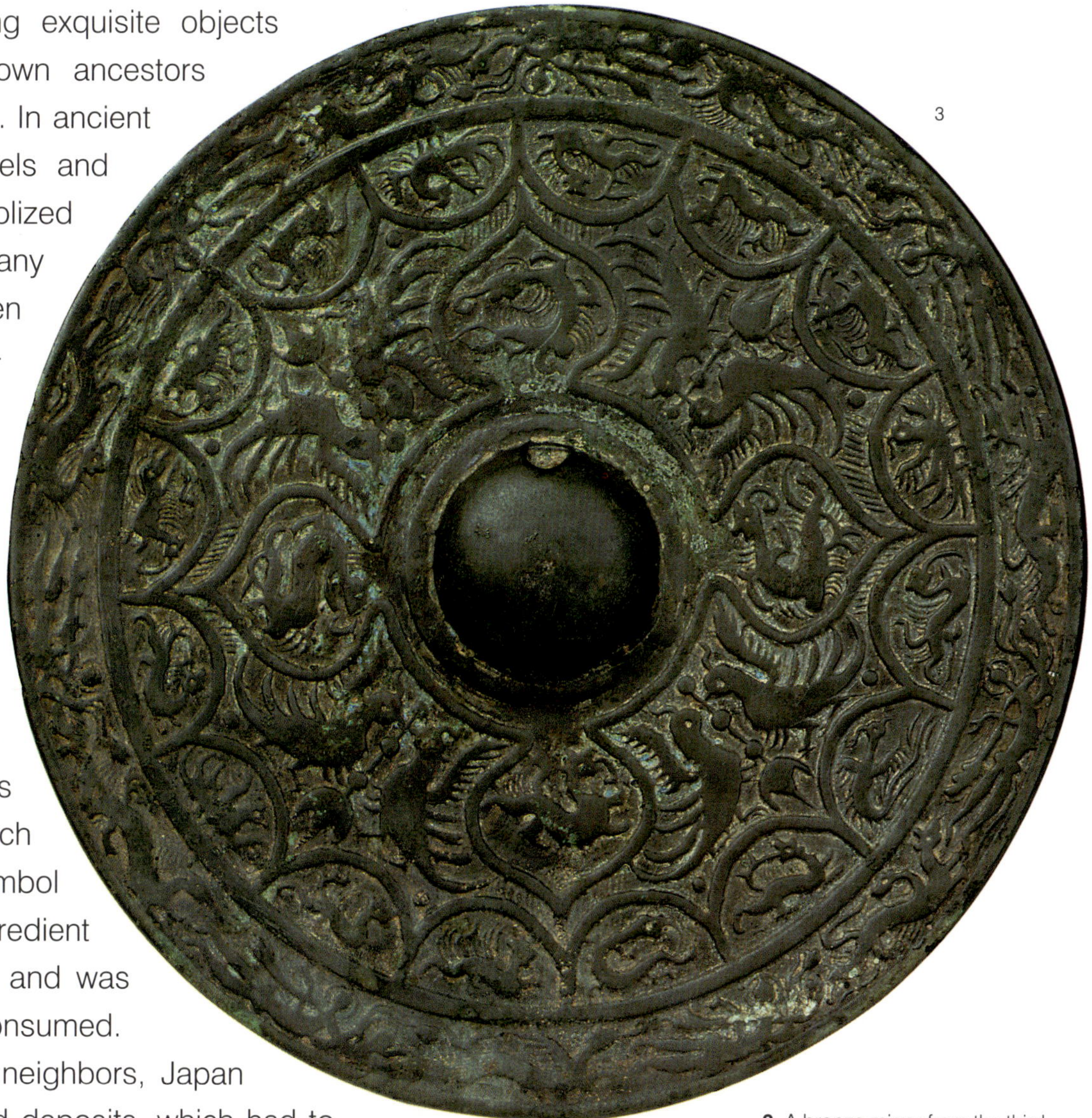

1 Heavy gold decoration on the exterior of a Chinese bronze censer or incense burner, dating from the seventeenth century.

2 A row of brass incense burners from the Forbidden City in Beijing.

3 A bronze mirror from the third century A.D. has a design of dragons, tigers, and phoenixes, and flying spirit figures. Bronze is an alloy of copper, tin, and often lead—one of the "three auspicious metals" recorded in Han inscriptions as being used to produce mirrors.

early pottery

East Asia is synonymous with ceramic art—the Western word for fine wares is "china." The Chinese were the world's first master potters, who jealously guarded the secrets of porcelain for centuries, until its secret was transported to Europe. Trade between the West and China dates back to Roman times, when its ceramic wares were much in demand at the imperial courts of Rome and Constantinople.

2

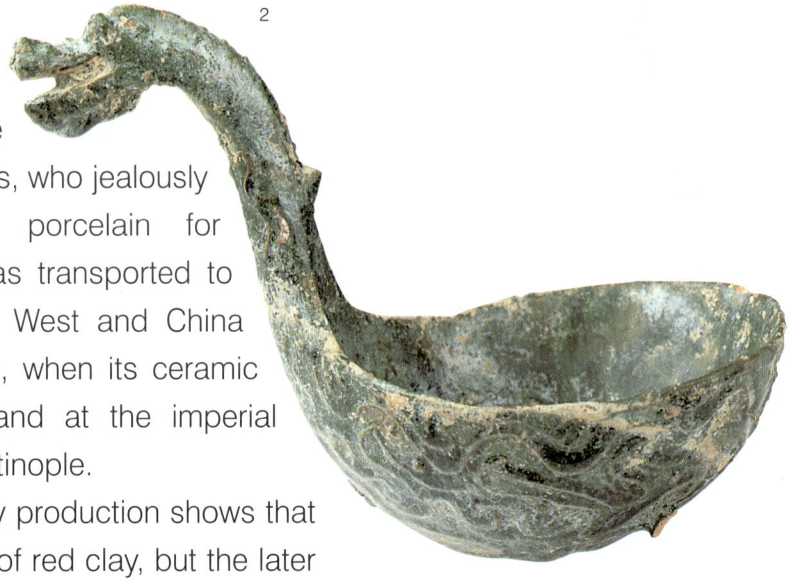

Evidence of early pottery production shows that the earliest pots were made of red clay, but the later development of glazes, using such substances as iron and lead, produced a myriad of beautiful colors ranging from ivory to yellow, red, green, and black.

The first East Asian ceramics were made for mundane uses such as cooking and storage, but clay was also used to model houses and figures, and scenes of everyday life, which were buried as grave goods. The most famous of these is the 7,000-strong terracotta army buried in 210 B.C. to guard the emperor Qin near Xian, China.

1

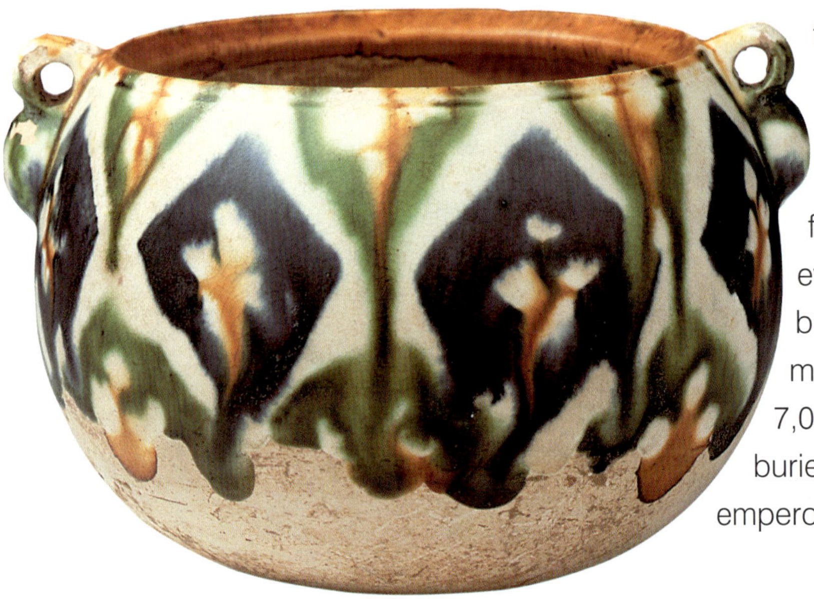

1 An earthenware *Sancai* (three-colored ware) jar is decorated with stylized wax-resist floral and geometric patterns, with blue, brown, and green lead glazes on a white ground. The jar dates from the first half of the eighth century.

2 Dating from the first century A.D., an Eastern Han dynasty, green lead-glazed pottery ladle shows that decoration was already an important factor in early pottery. The ladle has a dragon's head handle, with a pattern of swirling lines.

3 A dramatic *Jizhou* black-glazed bowl with yellowish slip dating from the early thirteenth-century Southern Song dynasty, with an inscription 1225–27. The distinctive abstract drizzling of the glaze is a technique that has been adopted by contemporary ceramicists.

3

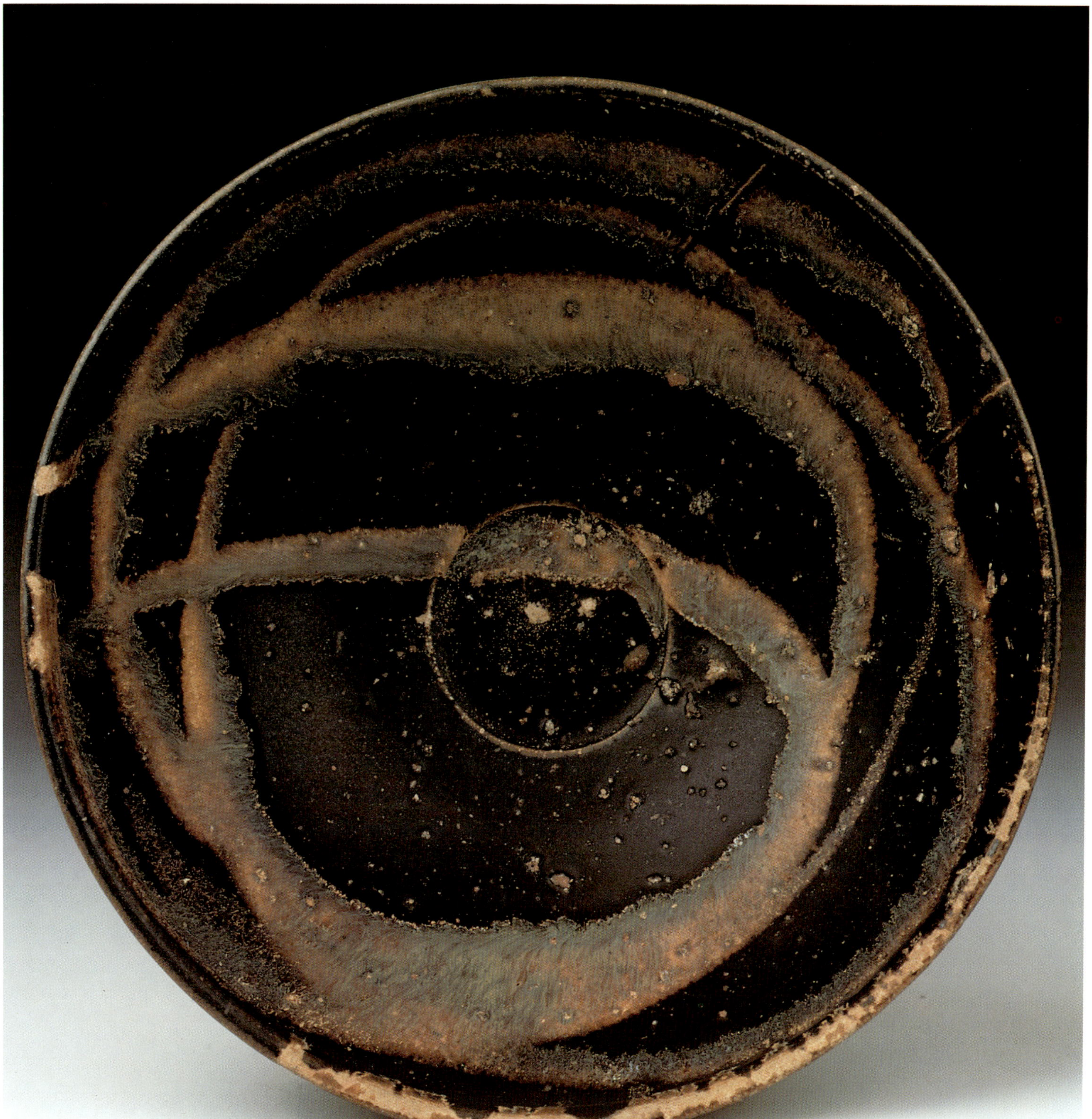

1

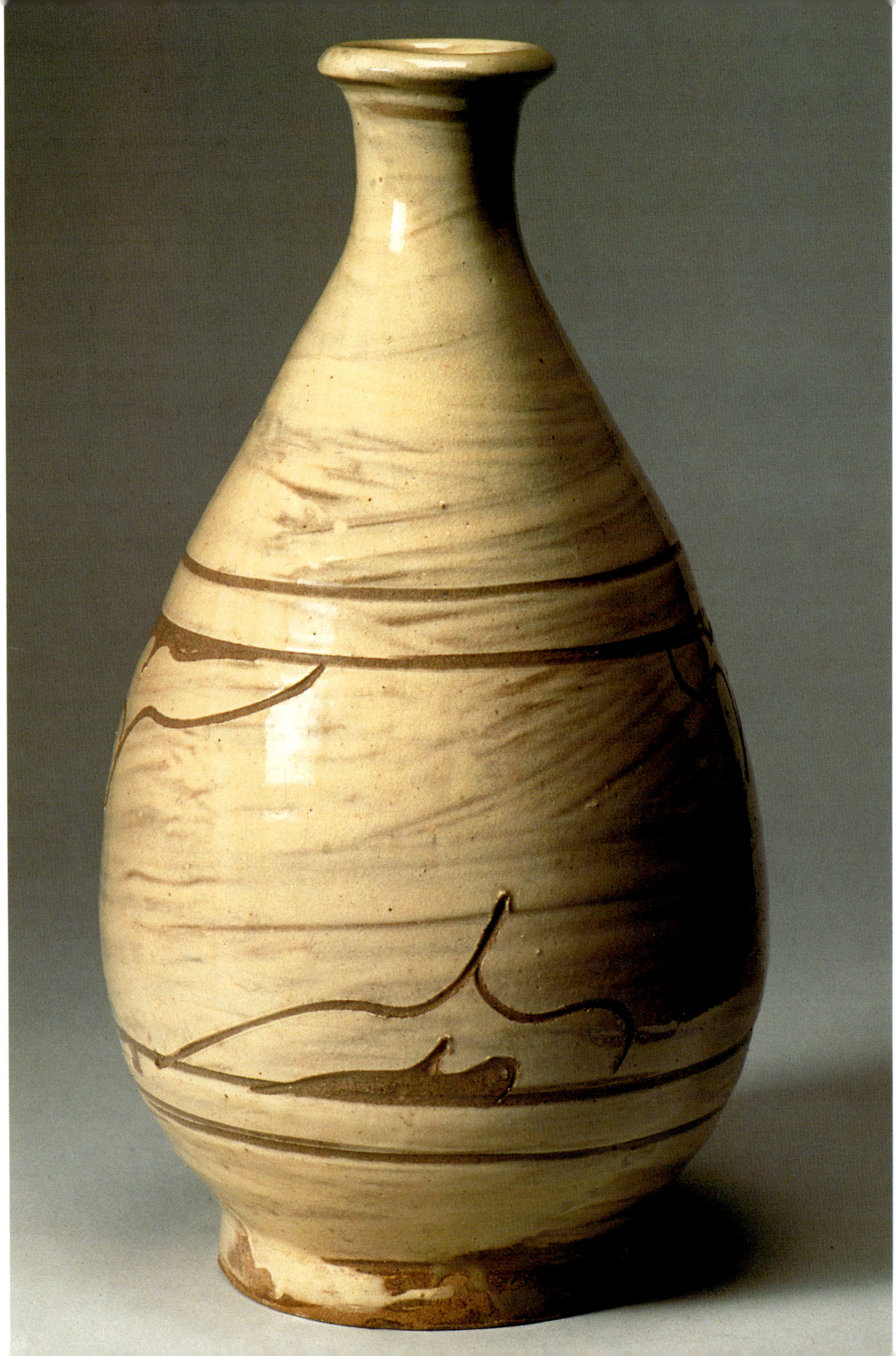

contemporary pottery

East Asia has had a profound influence on the development of ceramics worldwide. The seaborne trade pioneered by the Portuguese in the sixteenth century brought the West the finest Chinese porcelain wares, and led to the discovery of its manufacture in the West.

In the modern period, however, the plain, streamlined ceramics that we associate with Japan owe much to the work of one master potter, Shoji Hamada. He had a considerable influence on British ceramicists such as Bernard Leach, and on the studio pottery revival. In the 1920s Leach and Hamada founded the St. Ives Pottery in Cornwall, building the first Japanese-style kiln in the West. In Japan, Hamada was a pioneer of the *Mingei* (folk craft) movement, which recognized the combination of ancient and modern as a unity.

1 One of the greatest ceramicists of the twentieth century, Shoji Hamada, was known as one of Japan's "living national treasures." His former home and kiln at Mashiko are now a museum. This stoneware bottle with incised decoration was made in the 1930s. The white slip glaze is applied with a brush of rice straw.

2 These fashionable contemporary plates show a strong Japanese influence in their clean lines, high-shine, almost lacquer-like surfaces, and solid colors.

2

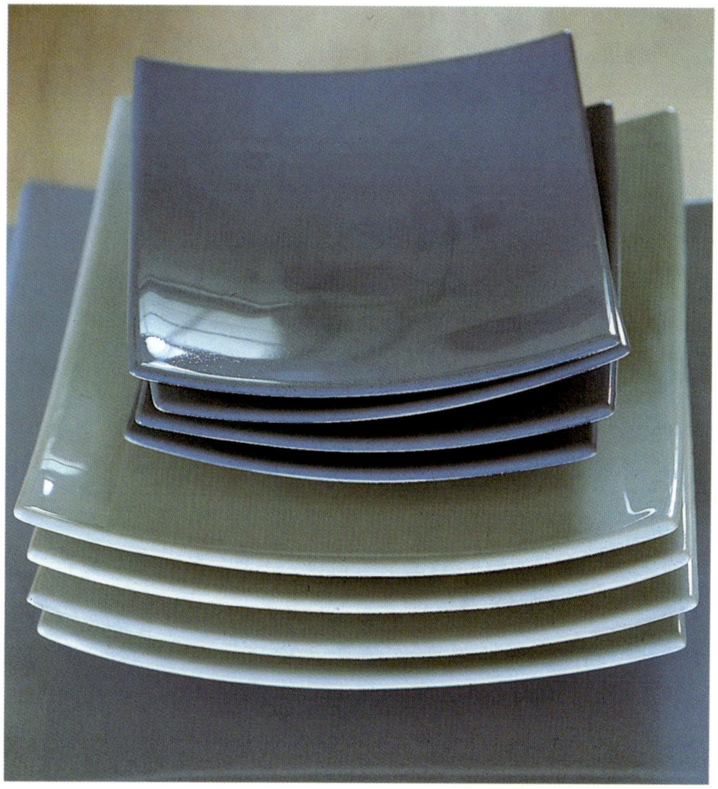

the importance of tea

2

In ancient times, the cultivation and drinking of tea spread from China to Japan, Taiwan, and Southeast Asia. Tea, or *cha* in Cantonese, was first tasted in Europe in Lisbon, Portugal, in the sixteenth century. It was tried in London a century later. But it was only in the nineteenth century, when the British introduced the cultivation of tea to their colonies in India and Sri Lanka, that the beverage became firmly established in the Western world.

Ritual tea drinking was introduced from China to Japan in the late twelfth century at the same time as Zen Buddhism. Initially it was used by monks to ward off sleep during meditation practice, but in the sixteenth century, the ritual of making and drinking tea was codified into the tea ceremony, or *chanoyu.*

1

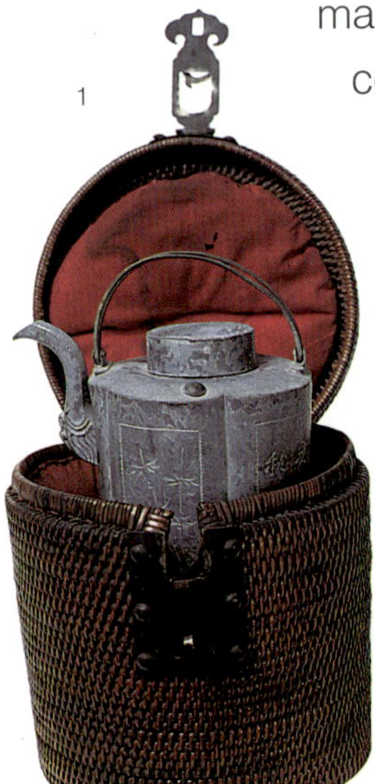

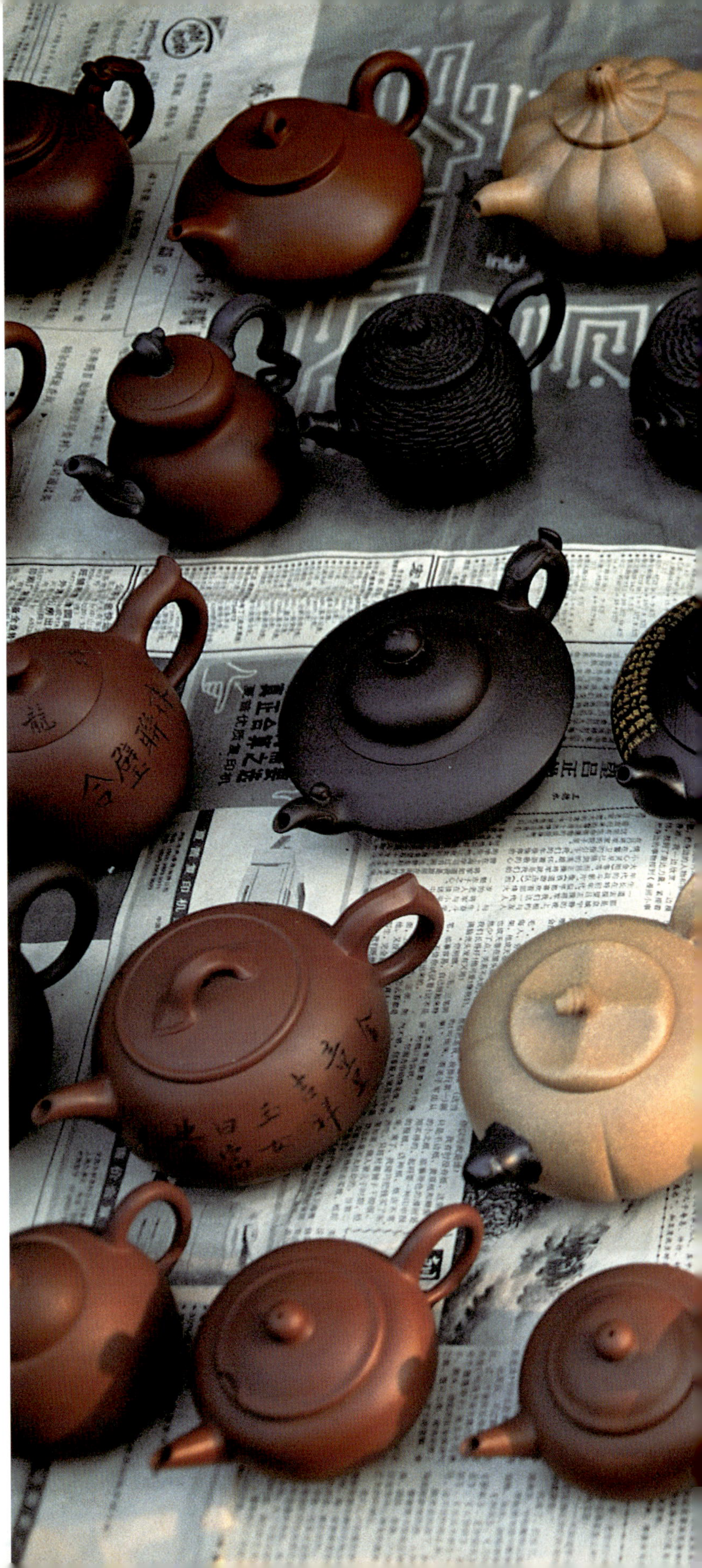

1 A pewter teapot from earlier this century in its original padded woven basket container, designed to keep the tea warm while working outside.

2 Earthenware teapots of varying designs and sizes displayed to their best advantage on daily newspapers in the old city market in Shanghai.

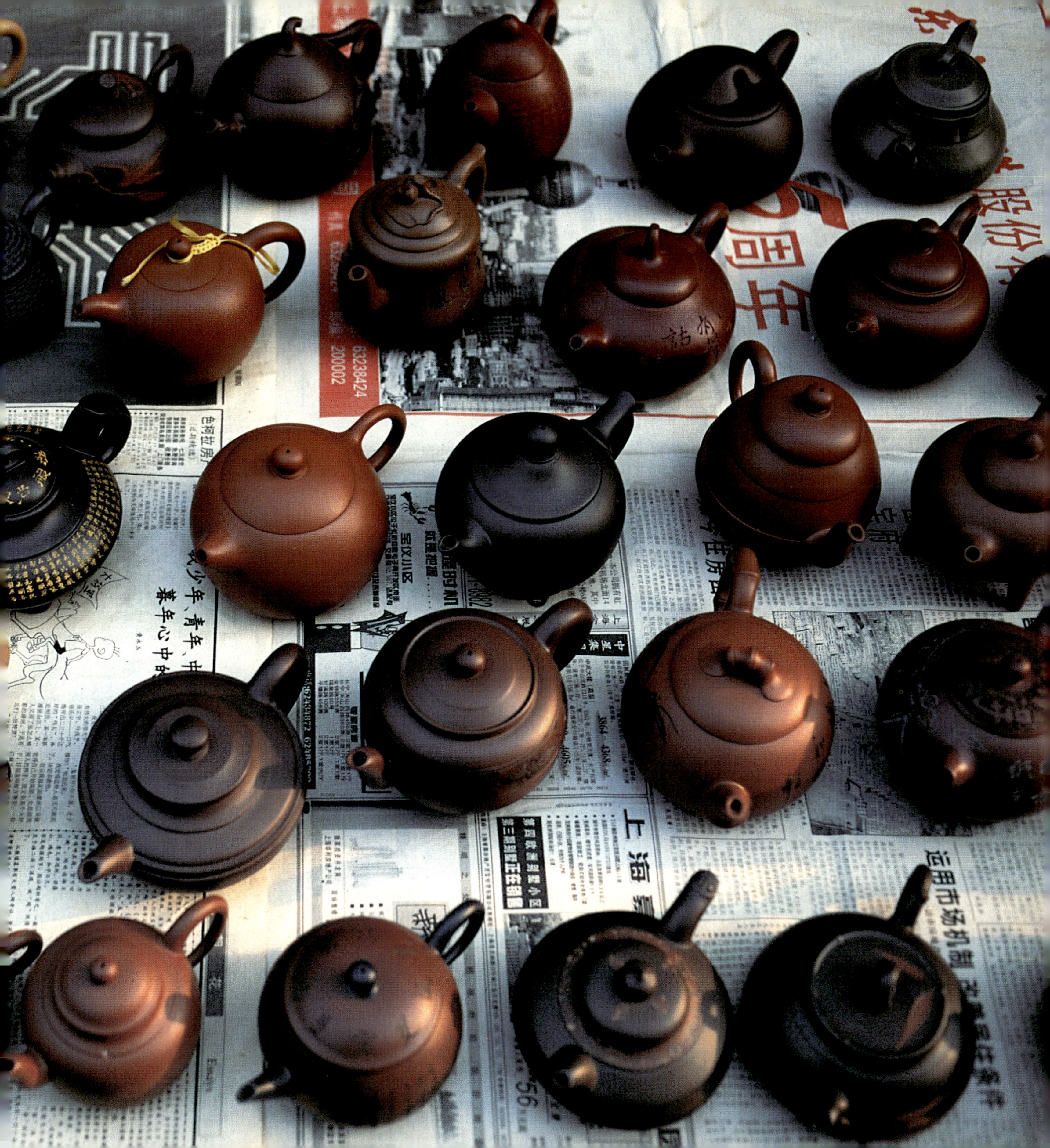
63238424
200002
运用市场机制

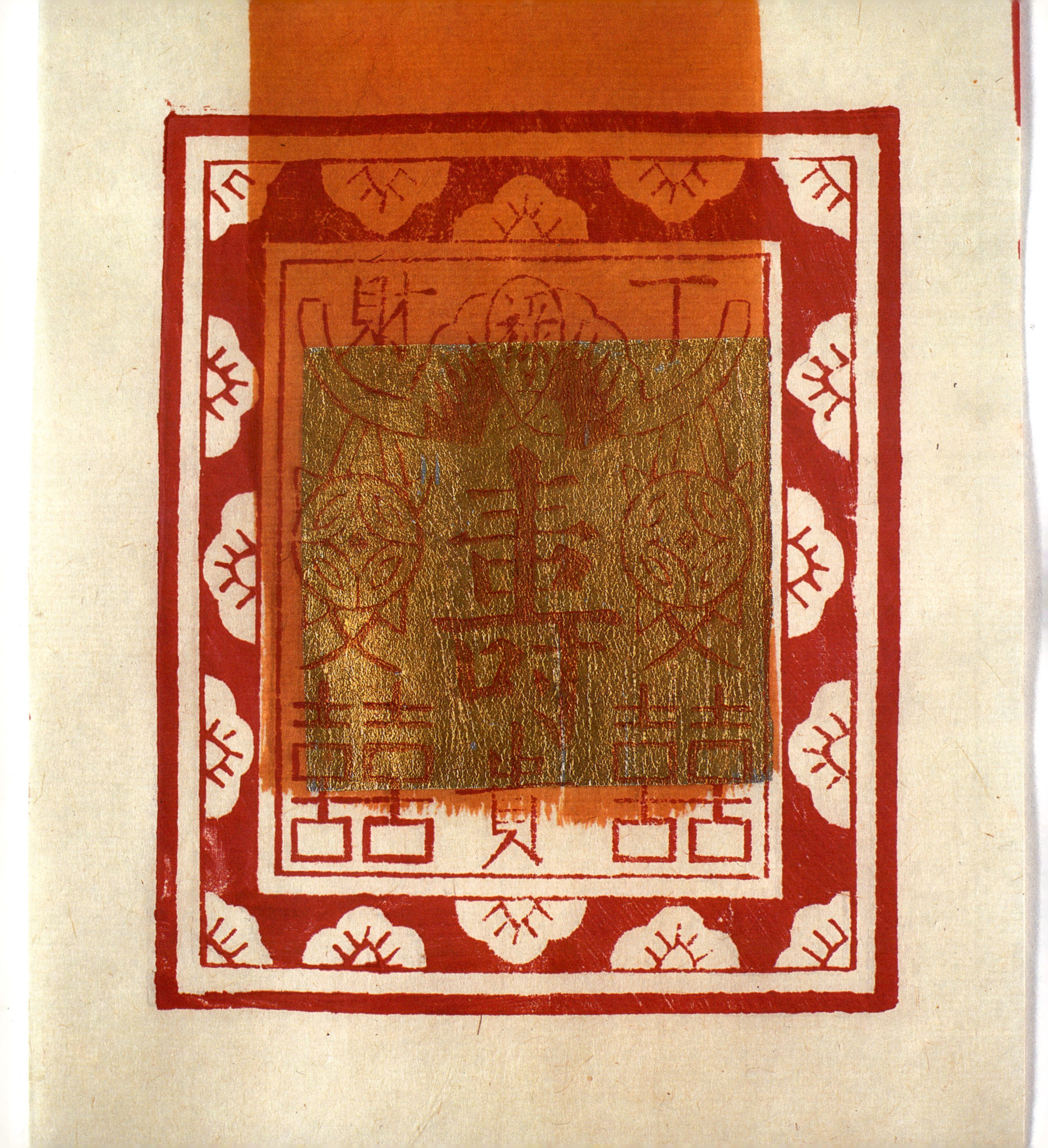

1

2

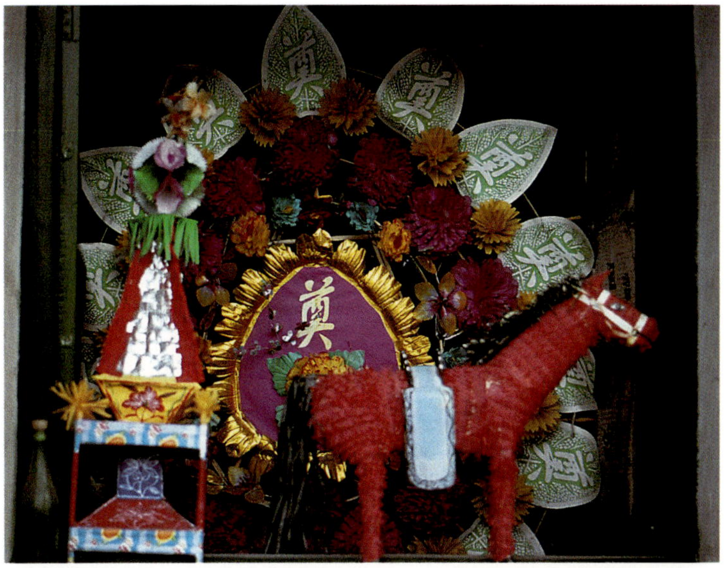

3

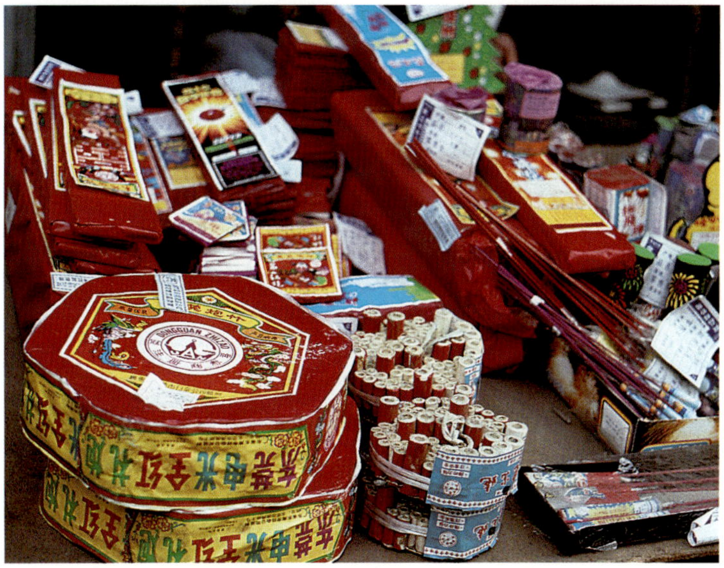

paper
china

In the second century B.C., the Chinese invented paper, which was first made from hemp and other natural fibers. Paper was treated reverently and became fundamental to religious practice. The introduction of Buddhism from India spurred the development of woodblock printing, and one of the earliest books to survive is a copy of the *Diamond Sutra*, printed in 868 A.D.

The traditional art of papercutting, which dates back to the Tang dynasty (618–906), was used to decorate paper windows with delicate cut-out flowers and symbolic animals, such as bats, pomegranates, and lotus flowers.

1 Red and gold "ghost money" is burned at temples, funerals, and on other festivals.

2 A paper horse stands guard over a wreath, also made out of paper, to be burned on a funeral pyre.

3 Even the wrappings for these New Year cakes and fireworks are colorful and decorative.

4 & 5 "Hell Money" is burned at funerals to ransom the soul from one of the eight Chinese hells.

4

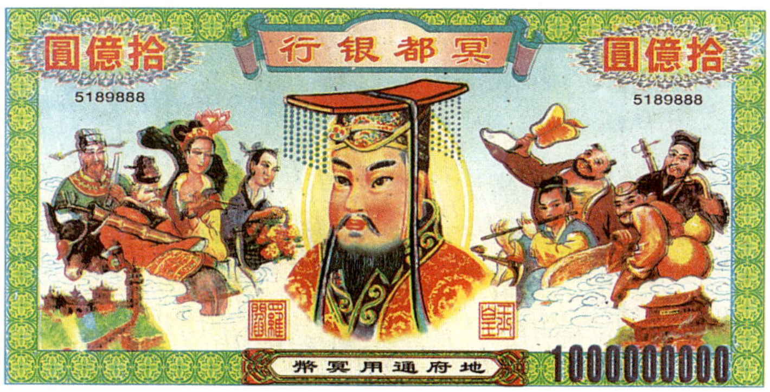

5

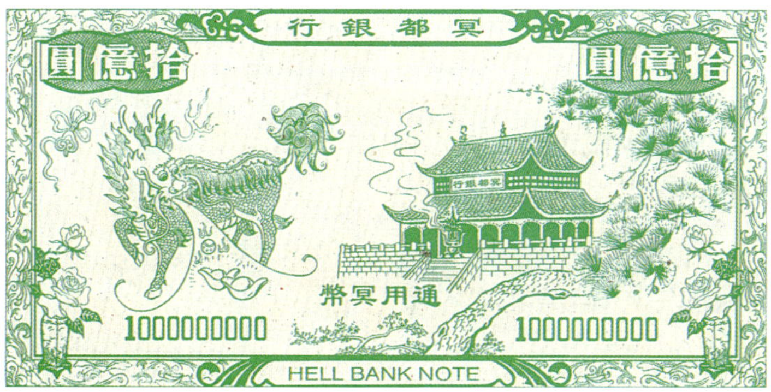

paper
japan

Paper plays a central role in Japanese life and culture, not only as a material for painting, printing, and calligraphy but also as a building material. It is still used in the construction of both traditional and modern houses, to cover sliding doors and screens, windows, folding screens, and light fittings.

Traditional Japanese handmade paper, or *washi*, is among the finest in the world. Its colors, fibers, and textures are inherently beautiful in themselves. It provides the base material for the traditional Japanese paper crafts of *origami* (decorative paper-folding), book-binding, decorative wrapping, and paper marbling.

1 In the grounds of shrines, one can often see sacred trees, denoted by twisted straw rope that is covered in white paper votive offerings.

2 Packaging for traditional Japanese sweetmeats is often exquisite and perfect, as are the contents of the package. Chestnut paste sweets are wrapped in paper decorated in the natural form and colors of chestnuts, and packed in a bamboo box with a decorated lid.

2

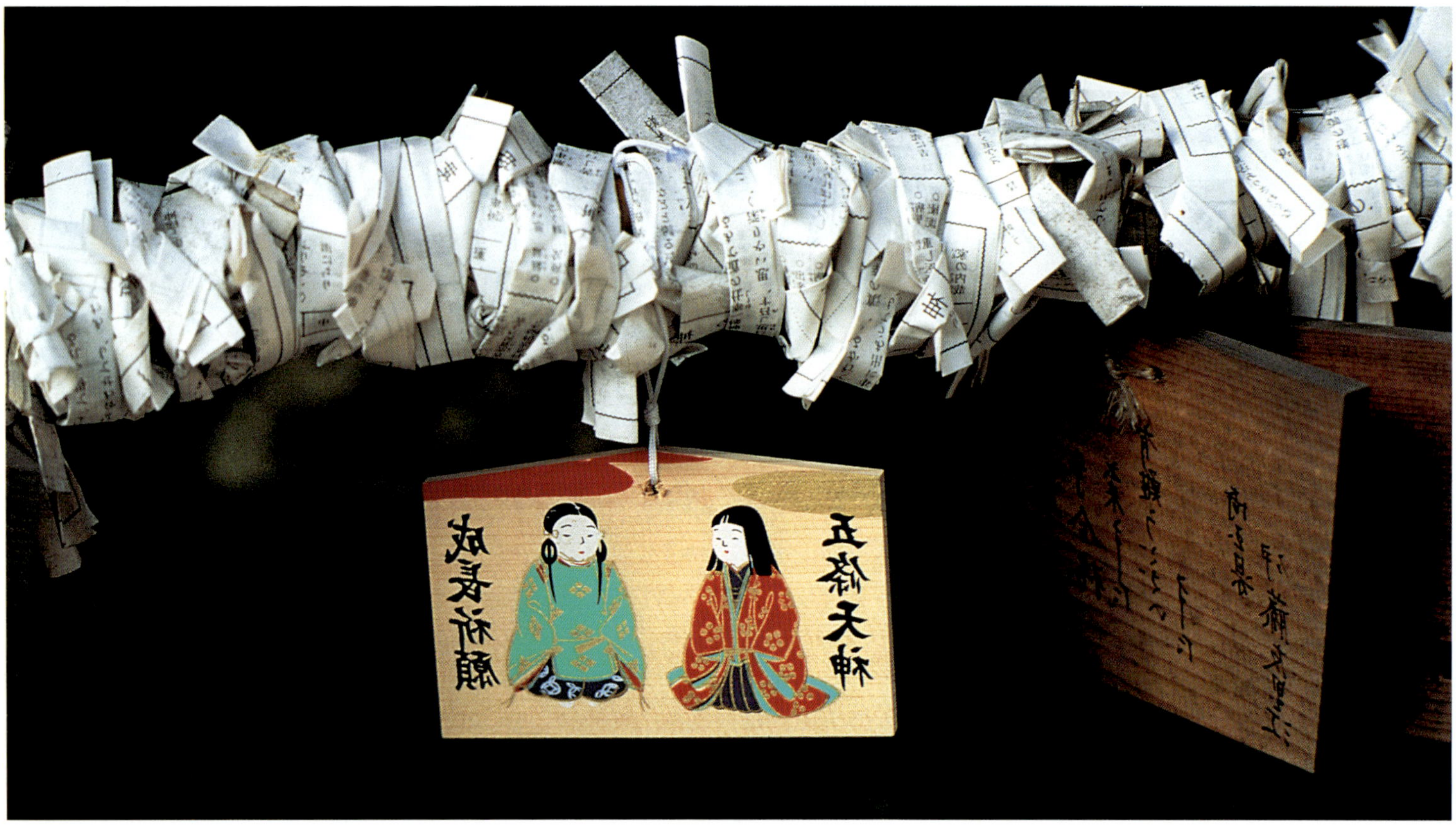

1

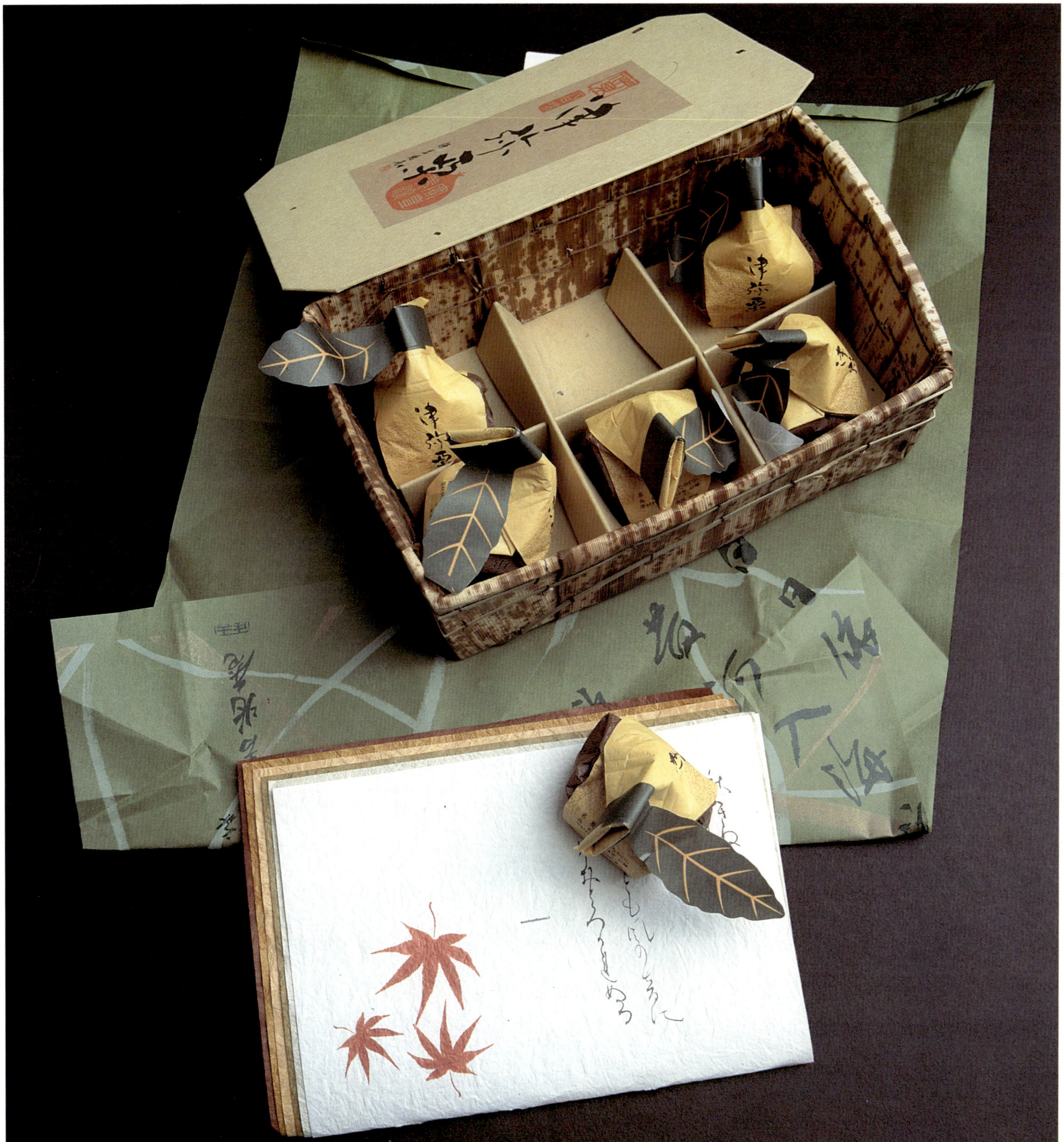

textiles china

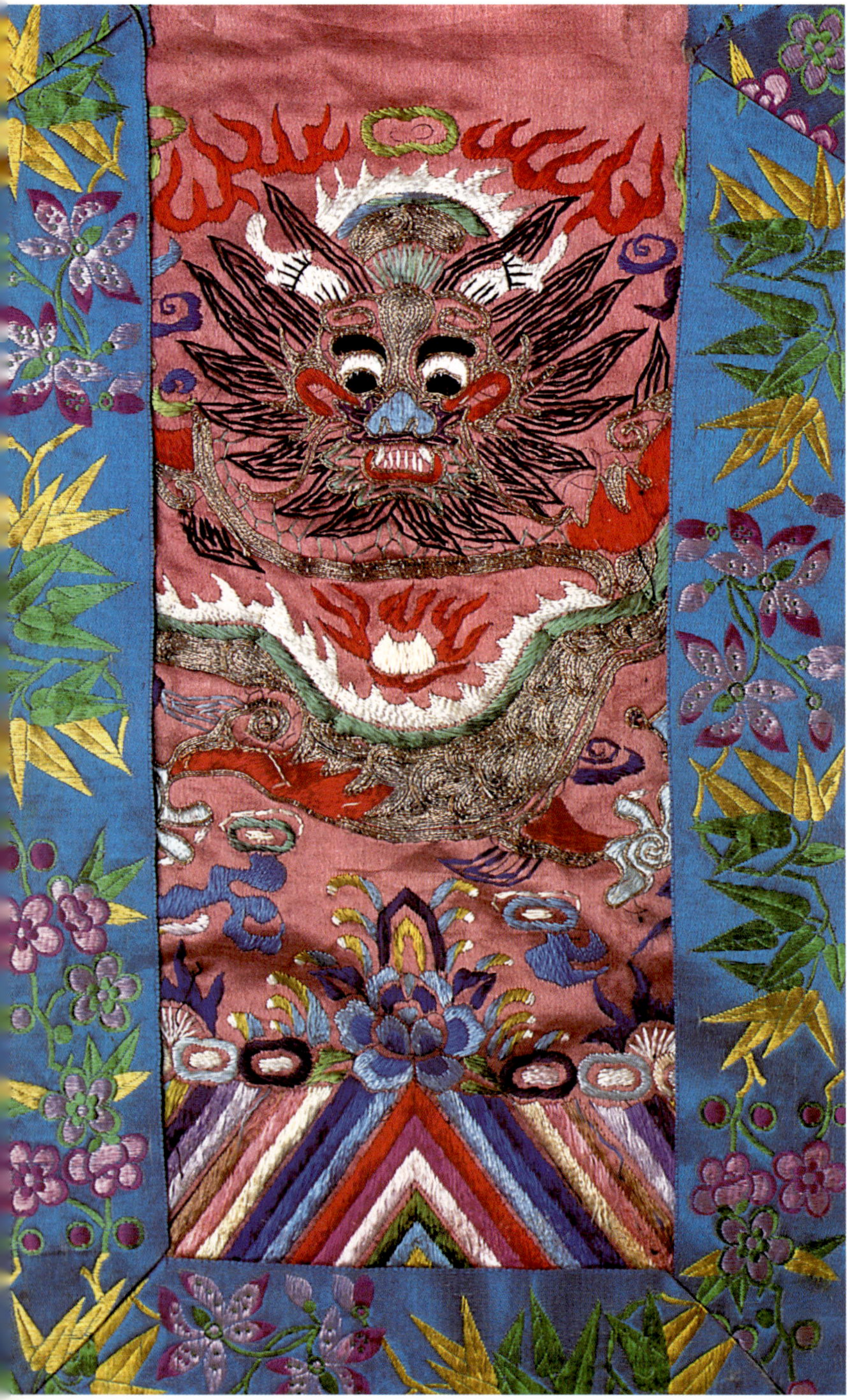

1

Chinese textiles have been a major influence on the world's decorative arts for more than two thousand years. Their designs, the strength and subtlety of their colors, and the texture and sheen of the raw threads are all objects of beauty and wonder. Many of the sumptuous silk robes made for the imperial court and for domestic use by the nobility have survived in remarkably fine condition, as have some fabrics made for religious use.

The Silk Route played a crucial role in Chinese history: silk was traded for Central Asian horses and Indian perfumes. The trade was pursued against dangerous odds by caravans of merchants over some of the most difficult terrain on earth. But by the twelfth century, Europe was producing silk itself, and the heyday of the route was soon over.

2

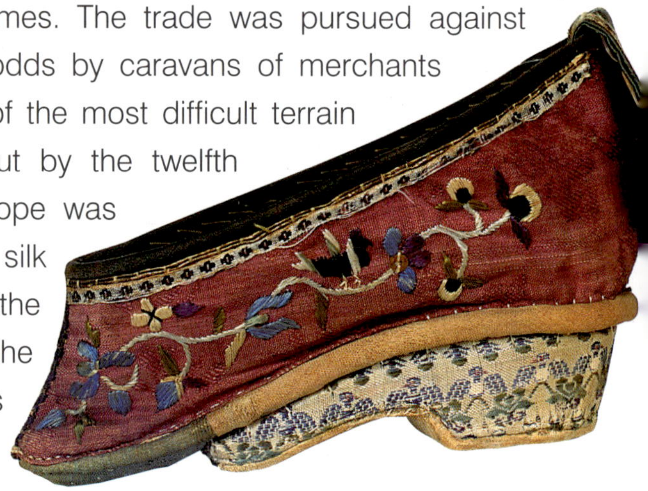

1 Part of a panel of a nineteenth-century concubine's skirt, featuring a simplified version of the cosmic designs of dragon robes laid directly onto the pink sheen of a full satin skirt. Gold threads are mixed with rich silks.

2 A pale purple pair of lotus shoes with delicate floral embroidery.These were used by women whose feet had been bound to make them smaller—an ancient custom finally banned by the first Republican government in 1912.

3

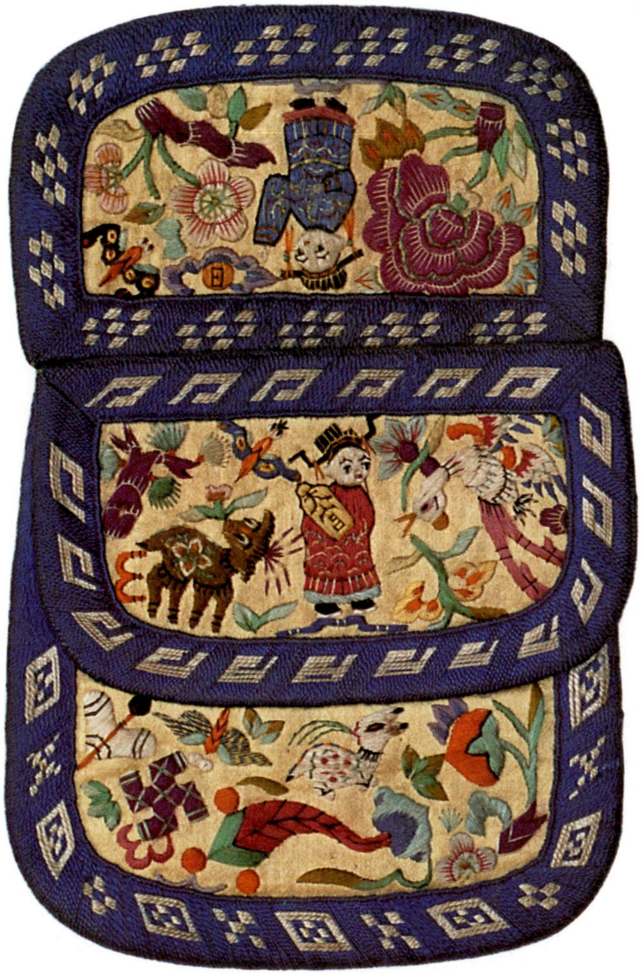

4

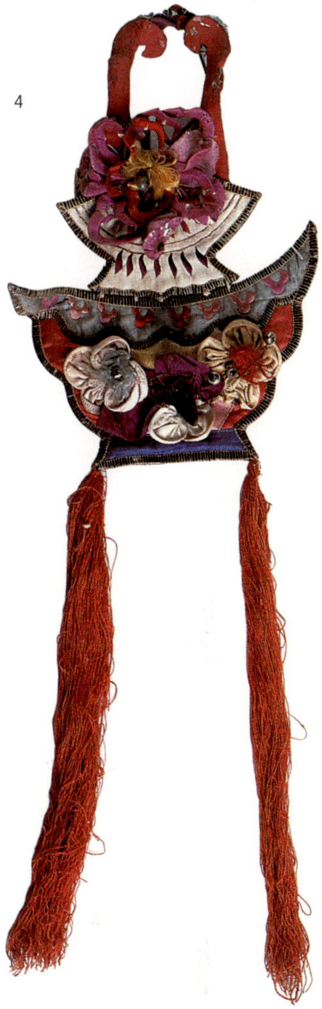

3 Differently shaped purses were made to carry all kinds of accessories, such as watches, fans, and spectacles, or scented cottons. Mandarins also had special ceremonial purses. The patterns could be symbolic, similar in design to court robes, with dragons, bats, water, and wave borders, or they could be floral or narrative. The *da lian* was a flat rectangular purse for carrying money, with a hidden inside pocket in the silk.

4 Headdresses and hair pins were often embroidered or jeweled with auspicious designs including longevity characters, bats, and flowers.

5 Children's footwear, as well as special hats, were made in the form of animals, to ward off evil spirits and to encourage good fortune. Young children's shoes were often decorated as dragons, phoenixes, fish, or deer. They were also fashioned in the shape of dogs, cats, tigers, or pigs, for good fortune and protection. Evil influences were believed to be seen by the prominent eyes and heard by the large ears.

5

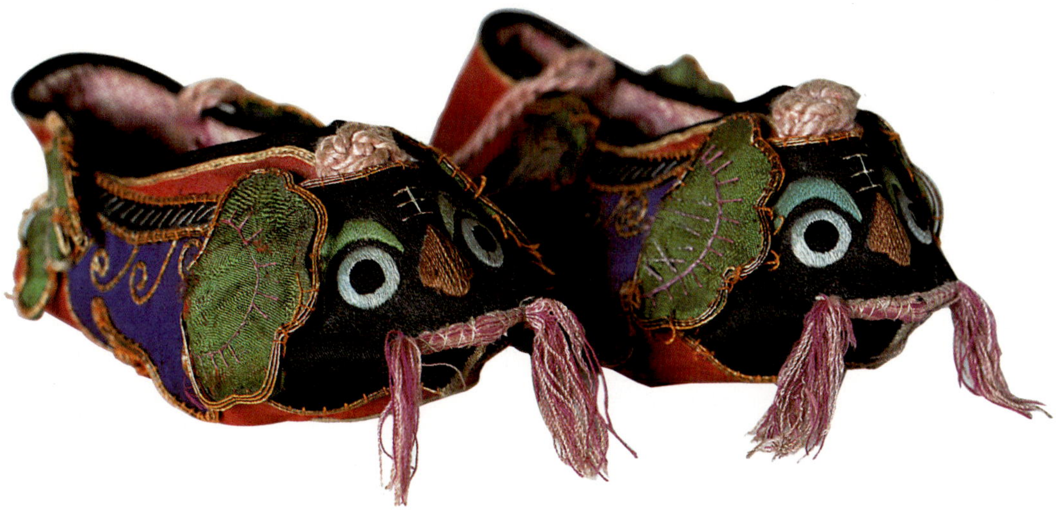

1

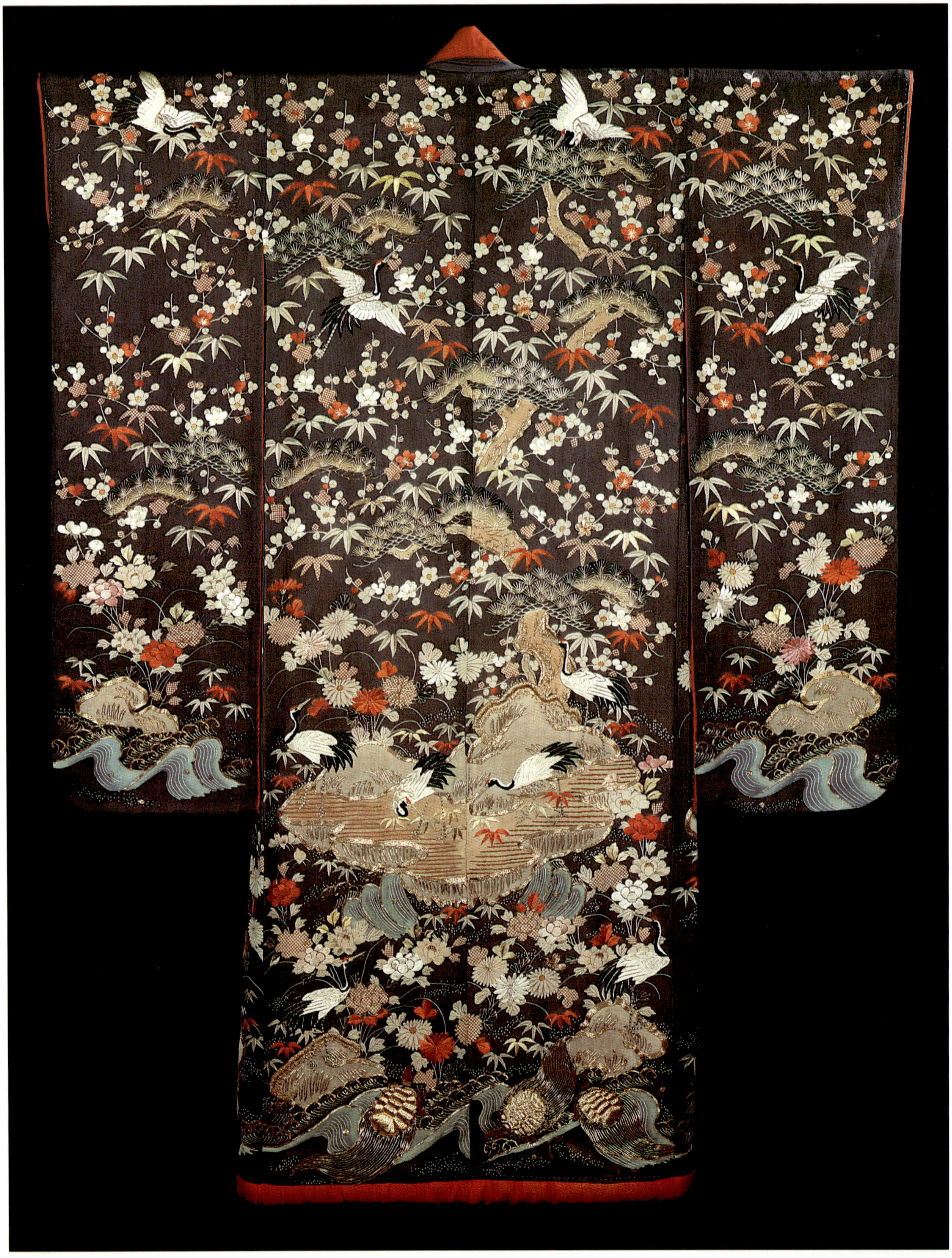

textiles
japan

1 Woman's kimono from the *Meiji* period in the late nineteenth century. The elaborate design of billowing waves and tortoises near the hem and cranes amid trees and flowers above is richly embroidered.

2 The sleeve of an indigo-dyed, heavy cotton Japanese kimono, with a dramatic pattern of waves subtly changing shape toward the hem.

3 Detail of a blue-and-white kimono with a simple floral design.

In the seventh century A.D., the Japanese adopted the Chinese imperial court system, and many of its associated art forms and crafts, including its textile and dress styles. Early examples of these rich textiles, used predominantly for Buddhist ceremonies, are still kept in the *Shosoin* treasury in Nara.

In the centuries that followed, Japan adapted Chinese dress styles and ornamentation to suit its own very different aesthetic sensibility, transforming the heavily ornamented, embroidered Chinese court robes into the flowing, unadorned simplicity of the kimono. A deep blue indigo dye is characteristic of many Japanese textiles. It is often printed on rough hemp, or tie-dyed to decorate cotton *sashiko* quilting and kimonos.

2

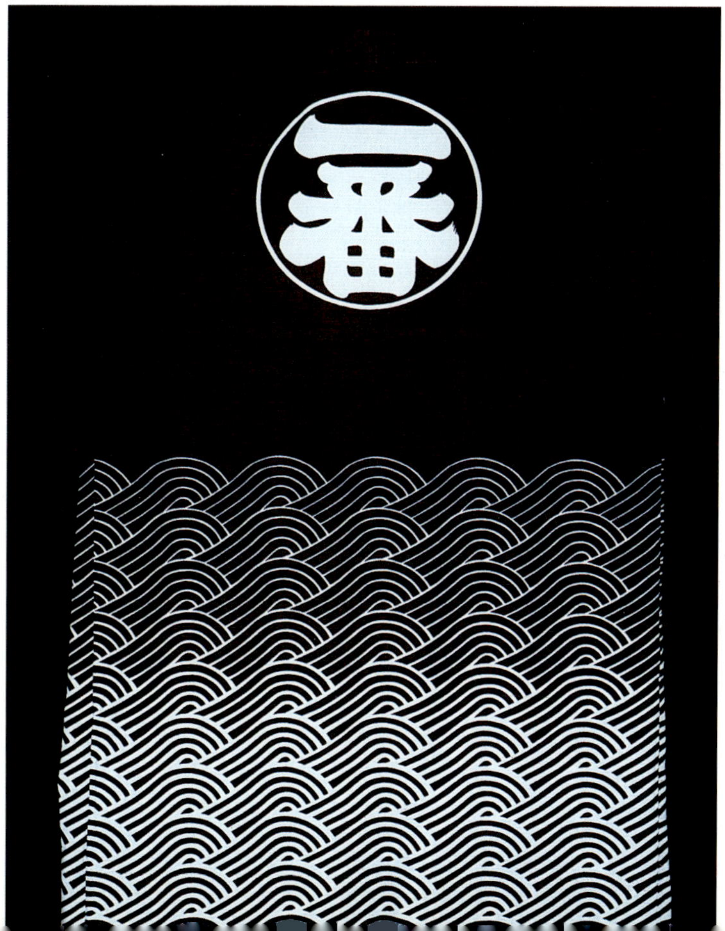

3

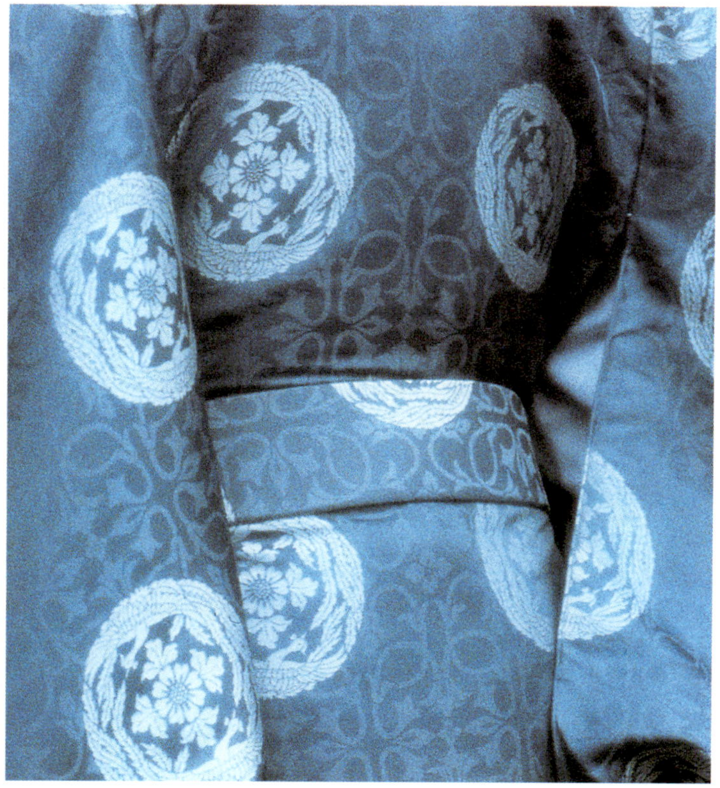

wood

1

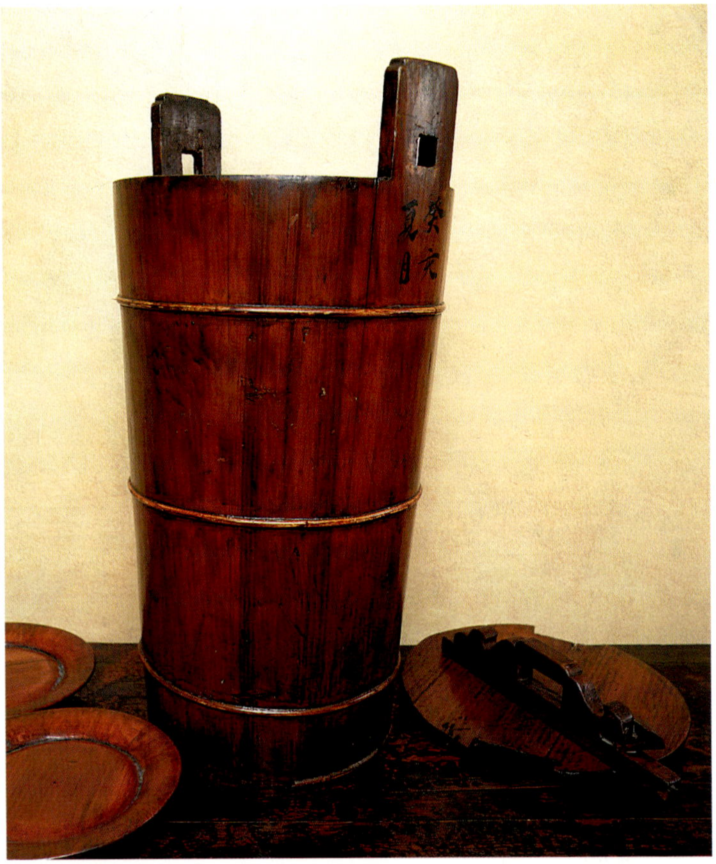

Japan is a mountainous country, blessed with luxuriant forests. With a plentiful supply of timber, the Japanese chose to build in this most adaptable of materials. They developed intricate joinery techniques that allowed them to construct some of the most impressive wooden structures in the world, including the largest, the Daibutsu-den in Nara, which houses a giant bronze image of the Buddha. 3

The Japanese and Chinese have used tree roots and tree stumps to create decorative objects of great beauty. Once polished to enhance the natural grain and color of the wood, they can be made into items such as braziers, brushpots, or vases for *ikebana* flower arrangements.

2

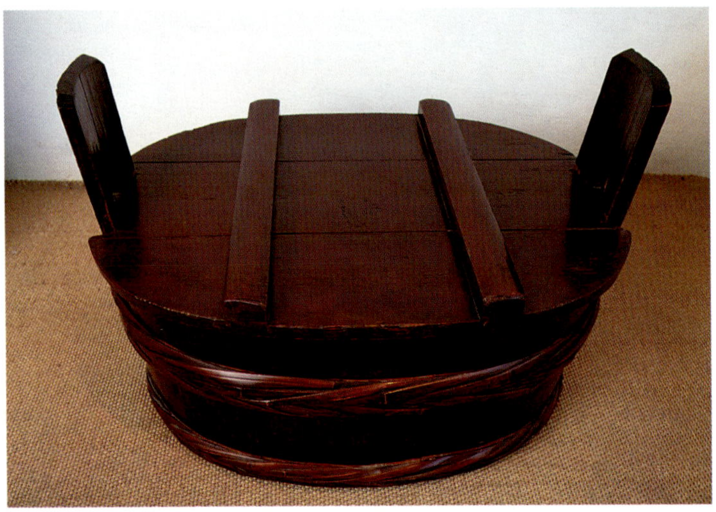

1 A dish carrier that is used for festivals and ceremonies, containing wooden plates—note the dragon-head clasp that holds the lid in place and clicks back.

2 A wooden rice-box from Japan: the gleaming warmth of the wood gives the surface a sheen almost as smooth as lacquer.

3 A pair of Japanese bamboo flutes and a Chinese fly whisk of horsehair knotted onto a bamboo root handle, on a decorative red lacquer document box. In the background is a *tansu* chest, with a natural rootwood carving, probably used for *ikebana* arrangements, and two bamboo scholar's brushpots. The musical instrument in the foreground is a *koto*.

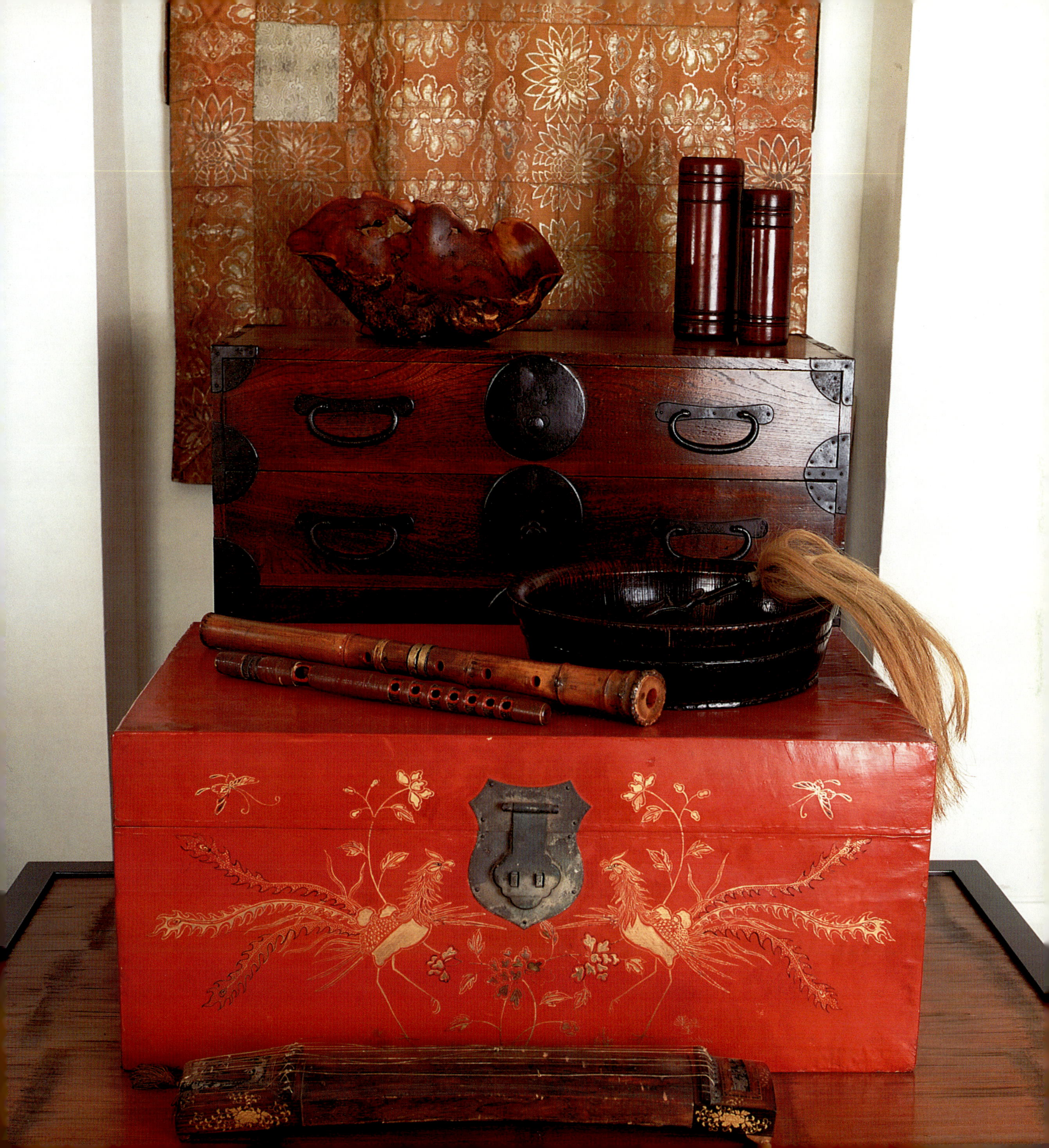

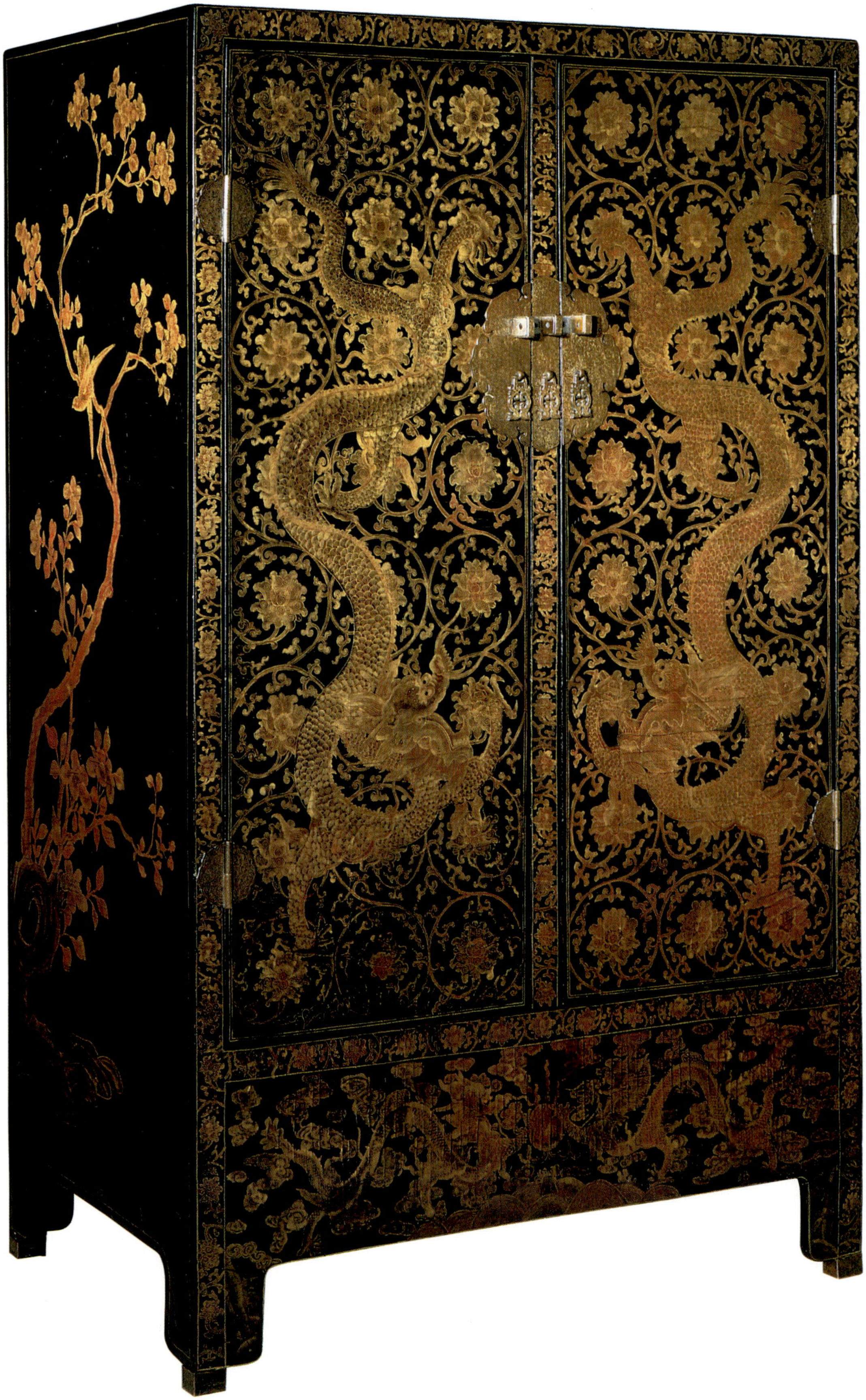

1

lacquer

1 A black and gold lacquer Chinese cabinet (*gui*) dating from the late sixteenth century. Different tones of gold lacquer are applied with a brush and smoothed down after each stage with a pumice. A five-clawed dragon descends through scrolling lotus flowers on each door, and on the side is a design of flowering trees, rocks, and birds.

2 A simple lidded box dating from the Middle Edo period in eighteenth-century Japan. The crane (*tsuru*) is the most popular symbol of longevity, and symbolizes good fortune.

3 A seventeenth-century five-segmented lacquer *inro* with basket by Jokosai, with a silver inlaid iron *manju netsuke. Inro* were used to carry seals or medicines, and were held on the *obi* by *netsuke,* elaborately carved toggles.

The Japanese learned the art of lacquer from the Chinese, but in this instance, the pupil far outclassed the master. Lacquer, or *urushi* in Japanese, is made from the sap of the lacquer tree. Sap taken from different parts of the tree produces the different grades of lacquer that are used to create the intricate shading or raising, or for middle- or background coating. Lacquer was most often stained black, but far rarer early red lacquerwork pieces are much sought after by collectors.

In Europe, lacquerwork, which was first known from East Asian objects, is known as "japanning." Lacquer can be used as a clear protective varnish, or with repeated applications in order to raise a decorative surface.

The Japanese excel in combining lacquer with inlays of precious metals, including gold, silver, and electrum, and natural materials, such as mother-of-pearl, to create lustrous decorative effects on furniture.

3

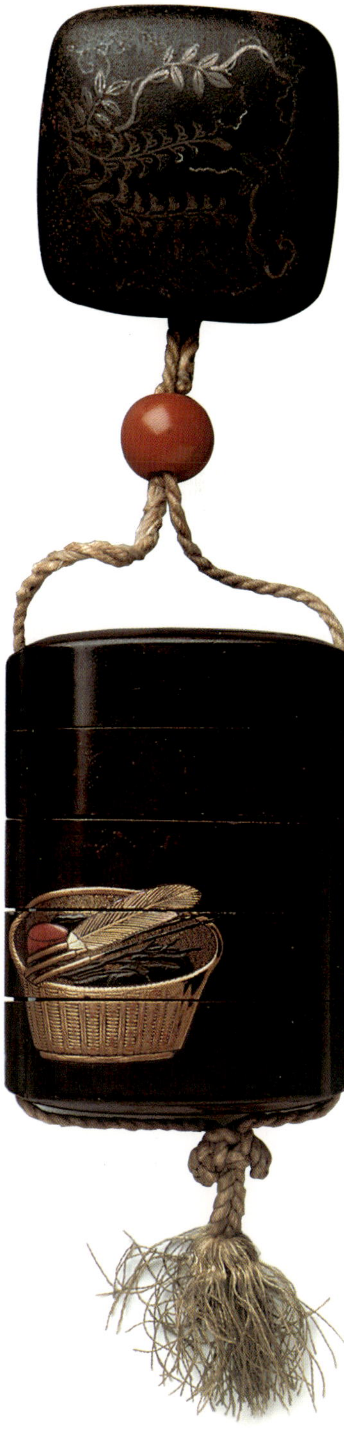

2

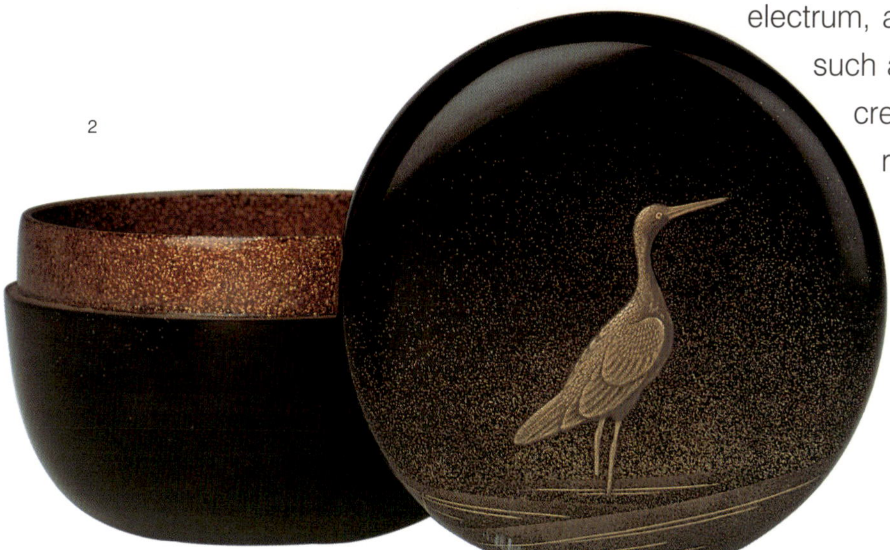

bamboo

Found everywhere in East Asia, bamboo grows quickly enough to be harvested every five years. Its availability and versatility have made it an indispensable material in both China and Japan. Strong yet lightweight, bamboo canes can be woven or plaited into the chairs, tables, wardrobes, and cabinets that furnish the modern East Asian home, or shaped into countless smaller decorative and practical objects, such as baskets, utensils, and hats. 2

Bamboo patterns and cane seating first became popular in Europe during the mid-eighteenth-century craze for *chinoiserie* furniture and mirrors. The popularity of bamboo furnishings for the home continues today, and Westerners often find themselves drawn to the natural feel that it brings to the home, and by its range of neutral golden tones, which can blend easily with any kind of design scheme.

1

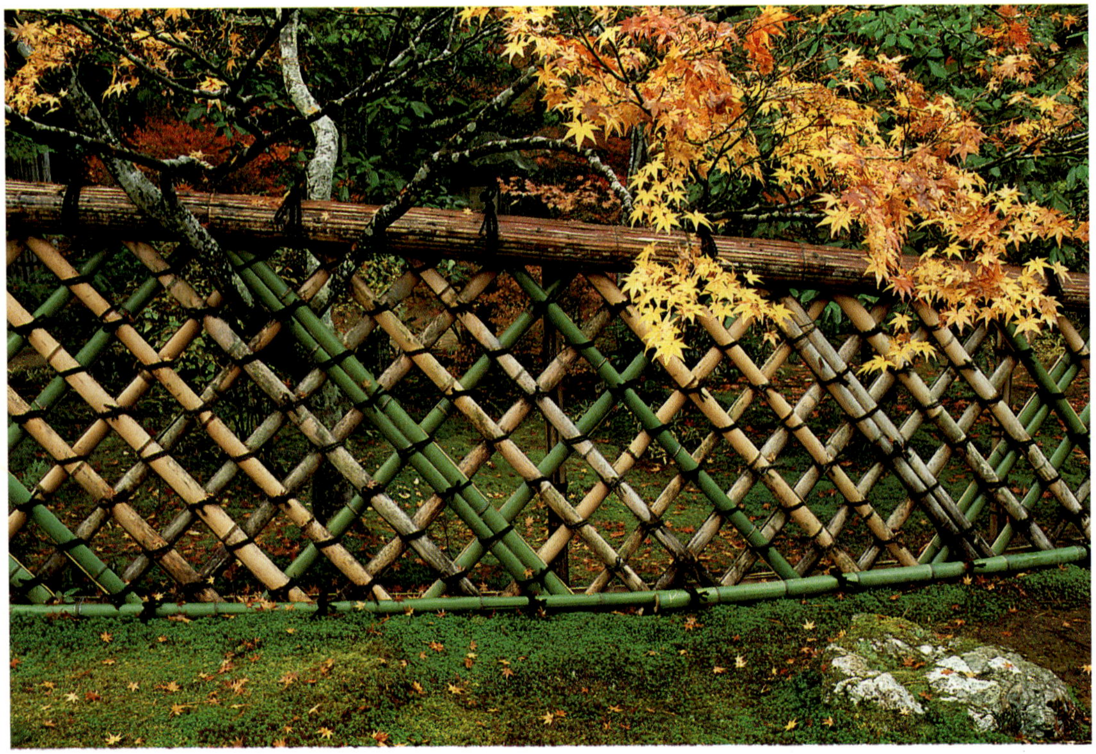

1 Bamboo shoots are malleable and can be woven into screens for fencing. Garden fencing in Japan is a skilled art. This *koetsu-gaki* (*koetsu* fence) is made of a mixture of green and natural bamboo pieces tied in a criss-cross pattern. It can serve as a useful garden partition.

2 This is an example of a Western adaptation of Eastern house-building elements. Bamboo-framed houses are found in both China and Japan, often with bamboo mat walls. Here large columns of bamboo are used as structural supports, with smaller columns and strips of bamboo used to make the roof. Matching materials are used to furnish the interior, including baskets and containers made from other canes and grasses.

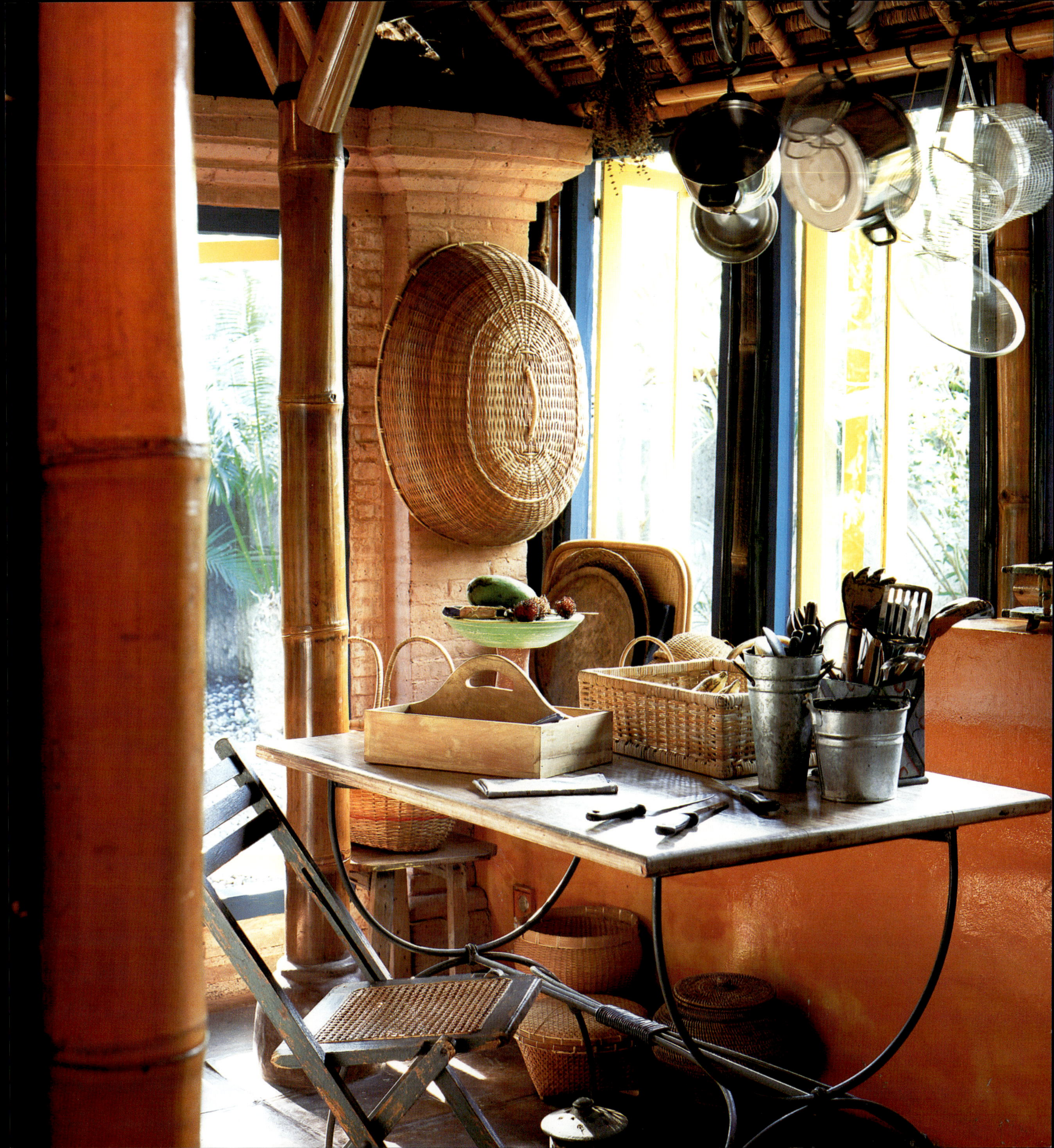

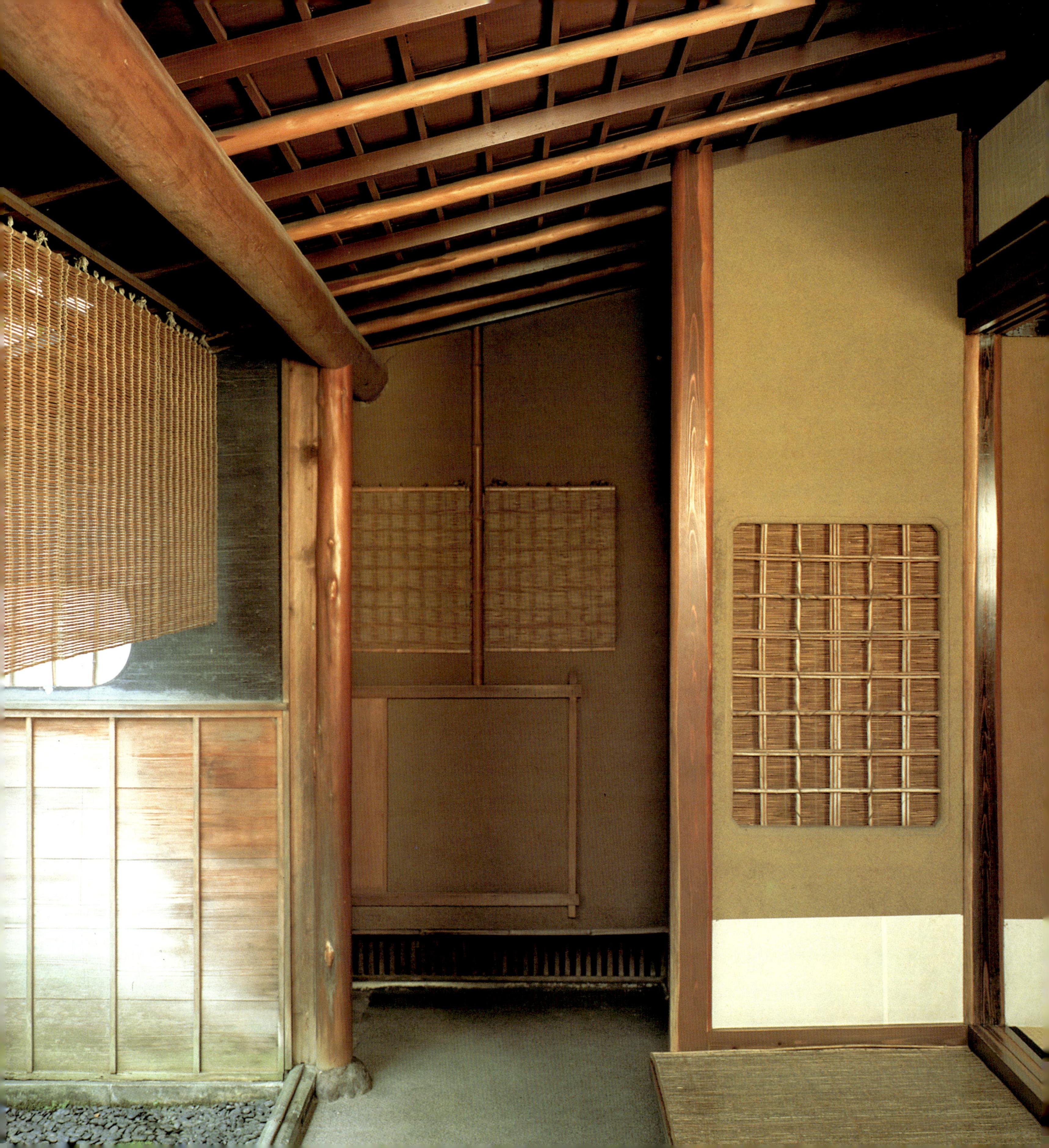

1 Bamboo is used in many different ways, as screens, for walls or windows, or as floor matting. Combined with the stones outside and inside, this combination accentuates the Japanese appreciation of natural textures.

2 The bamboo beading on the cupboards and the delicate set of chairs in this Hong Kong dining room are of spotted bamboo or *Xiang fei* bamboo (weeping bamboo). This owes its name to a legend of two imperial concubines, who were so unhappy when the Emperor Shun died that their tears stained forever the piece of furniture on which they were leaning.

2

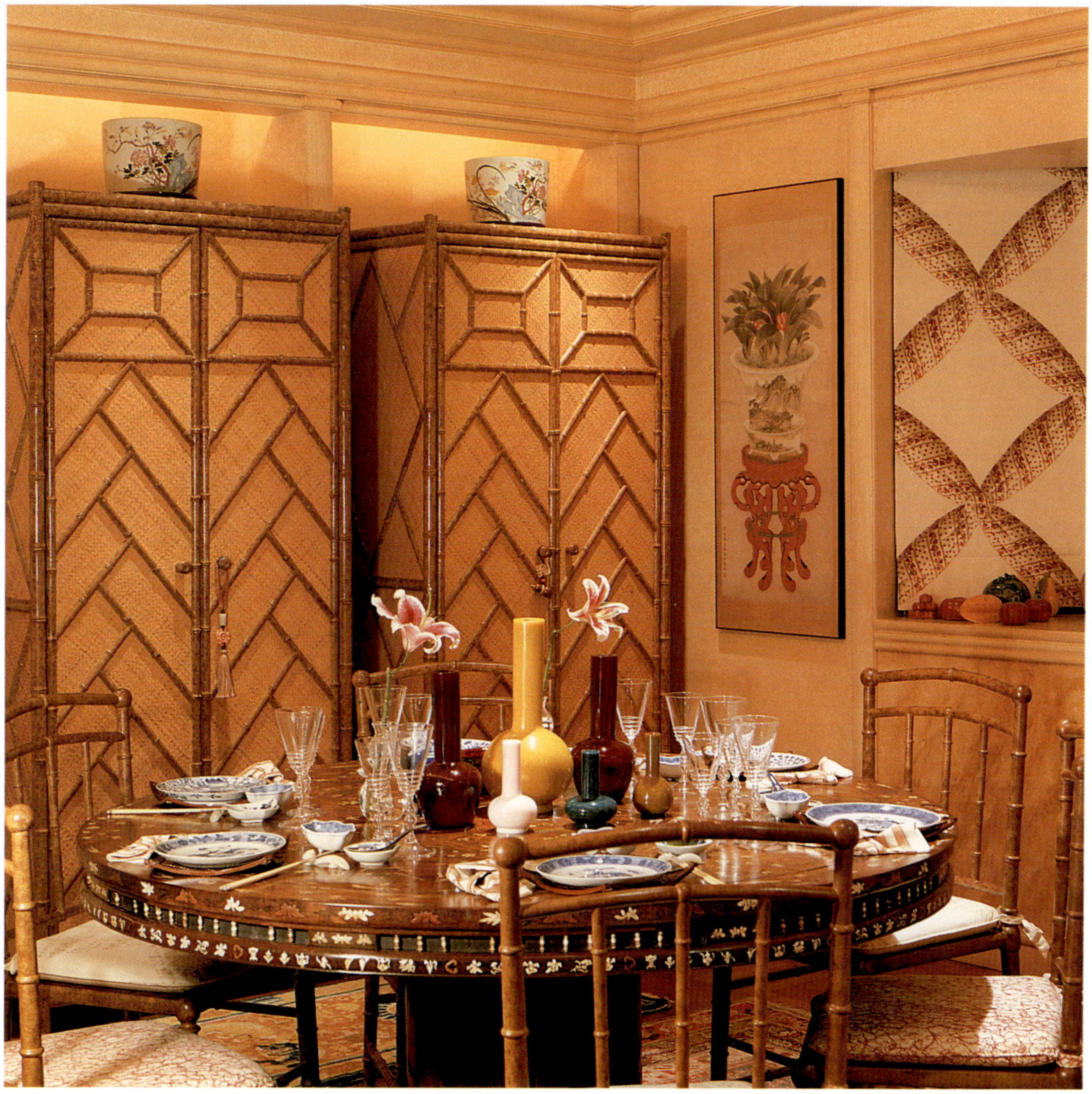

cane and reed

1

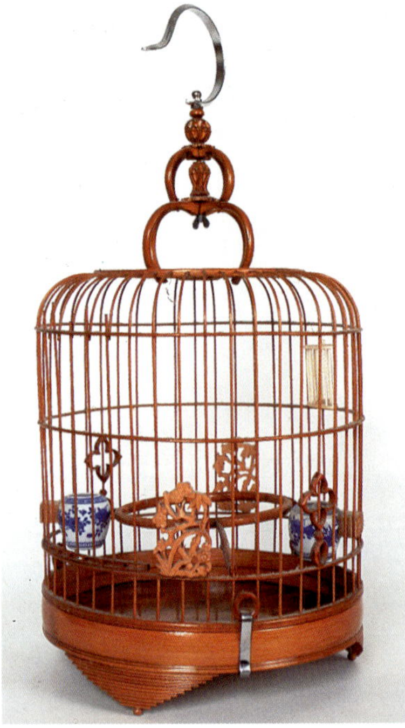

In addition to bamboo, furnishings and decorative objects can be made from a variety of canes and reeds. Even delicate grasses and ferns have their decorative uses, while the resilient fibers of jute and hemp are the base materials for large-scale industrial production. Rope plays an important symbolic role in the native Japanese religion of *shinto*. A hemp rope, often decorated with paper, tied around a natural object such as a tree or rock, denotes that it is the sacred abode of a deity (*kami*).

Natural fibers have many practical uses: in winter, trees sensitive to frost damage are encased in straw and bamboo wrappings to protect them from the extremes of the cold. The art of wrapping and packaging with natural fibers is fast disappearing as new artificial materials find favor, but in rural Japan and China you may still see eggs wrapped in rice straw, dried fish in rope, and rice cakes in oak leaves.

2

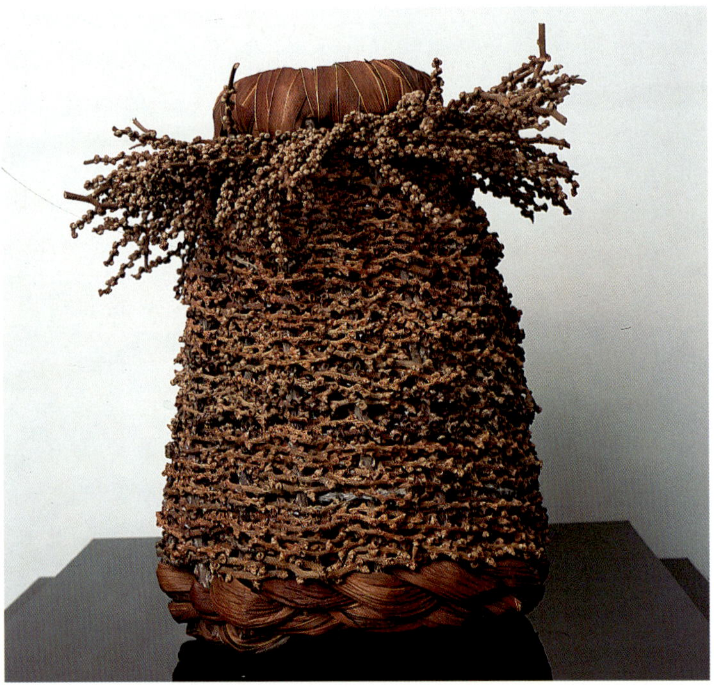

1 The Chinese love to keep pet songbirds, and their sense of decoration extends to the small scale of this miniature bamboo bird cage, complete with blue and white feeder pots.

2 Unusual shapes and textures combine to make this contemporary hand-woven fiber basket by Mika McCann, a Japanese artist working in the United States. To the Japanese, basketwork is a separate art form. The fibers used are Watsonia, cocoseed, philodendron, and palm.

3 A nineteenth-century Japanese basket woven loosely from split bamboo canes, on a tatami mat, made from rice straw. Styles and shapes were adapted to suit tastes, and *ikebana*, the art of flower arranging, popularized the use of baskets in the home.

4 This modern re-interpretation of a traditional three-fold Japanese screen contrasts the solidity of the wooden framework with the delicate lattice of rustic straw panels.

3

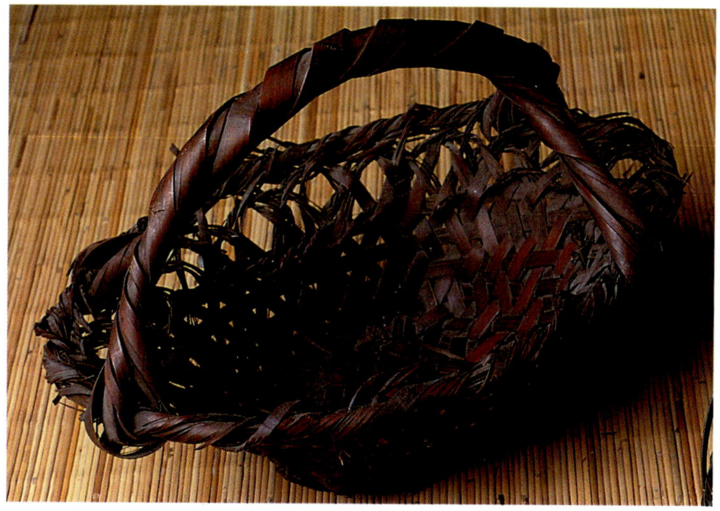

4

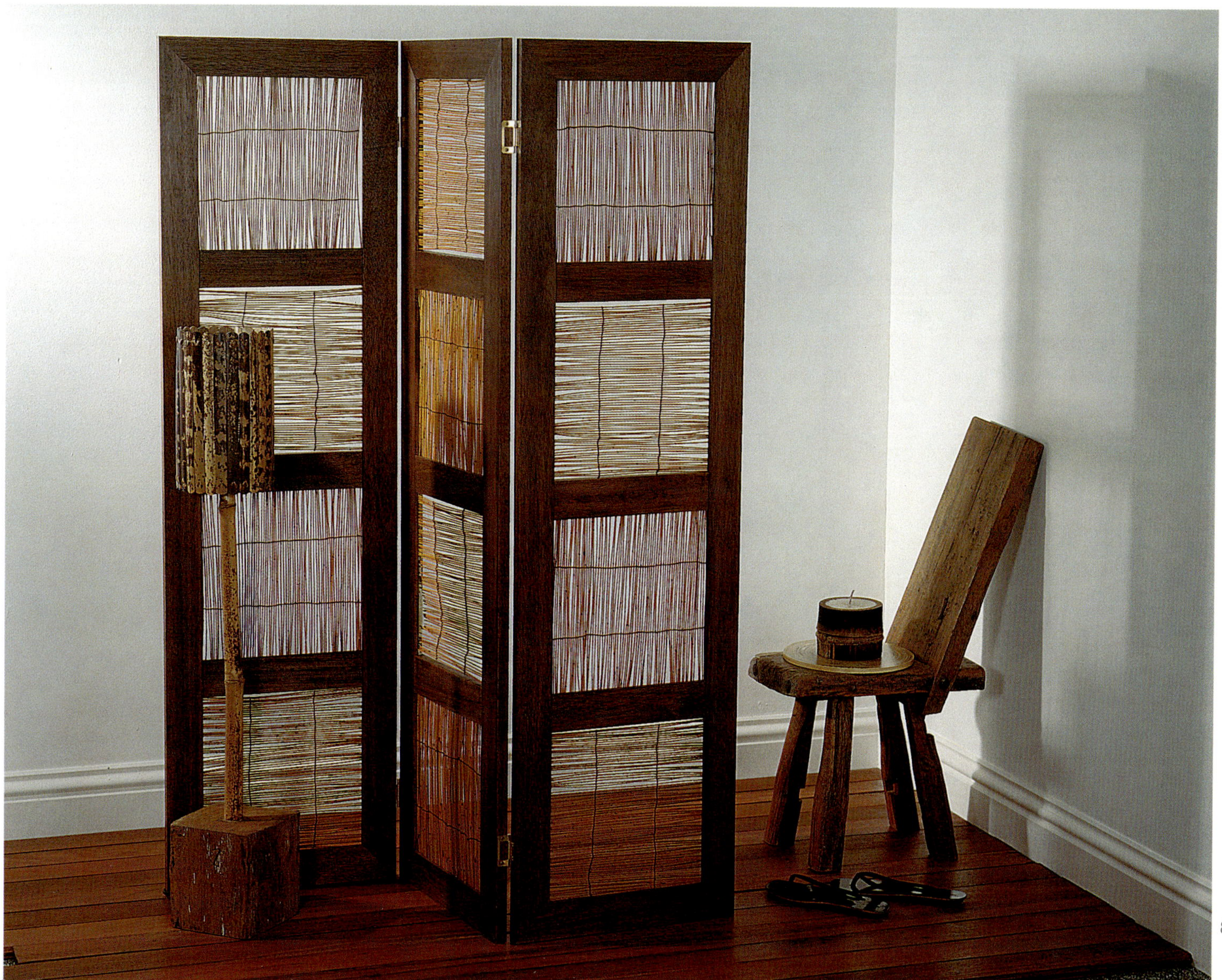

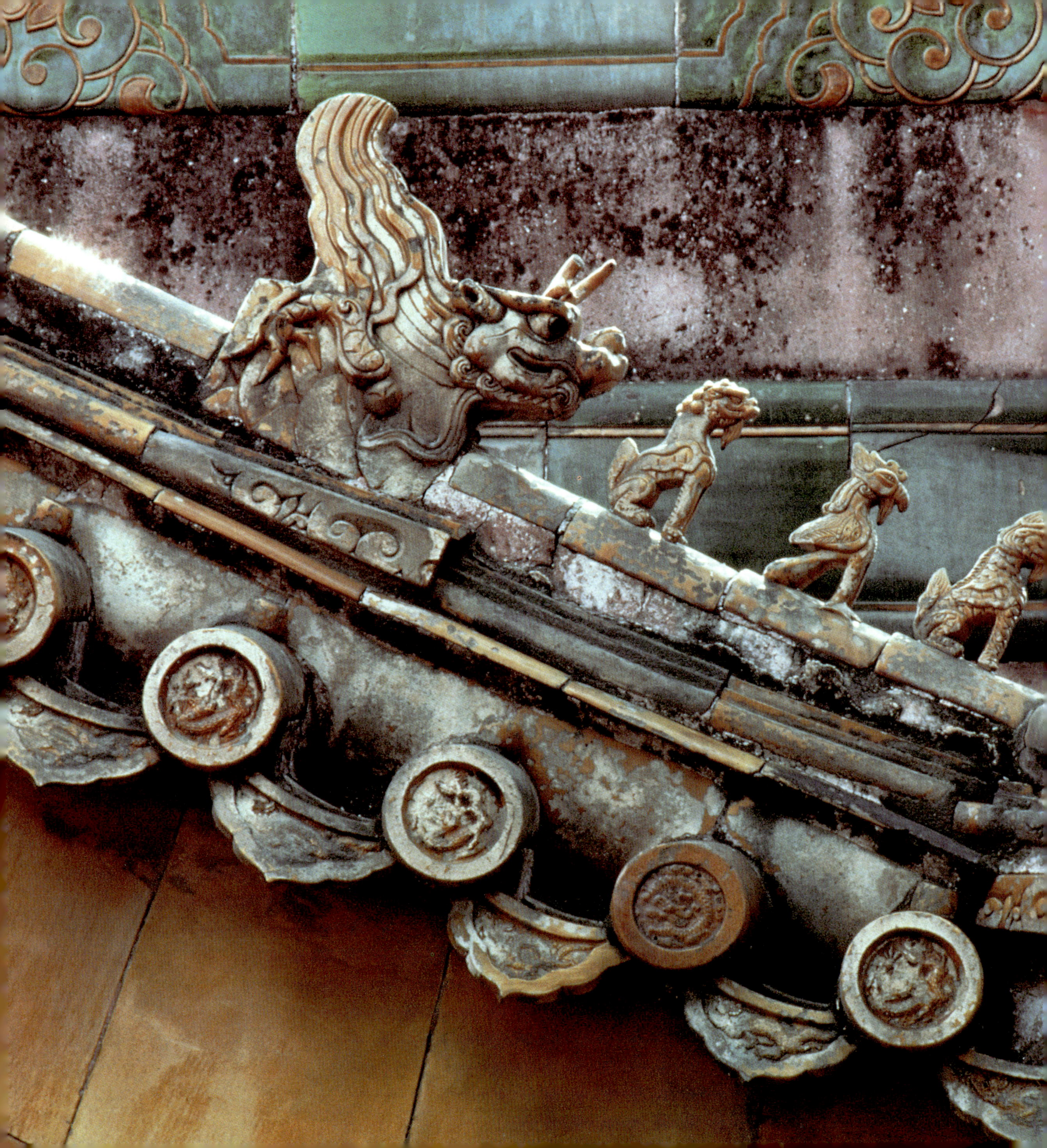

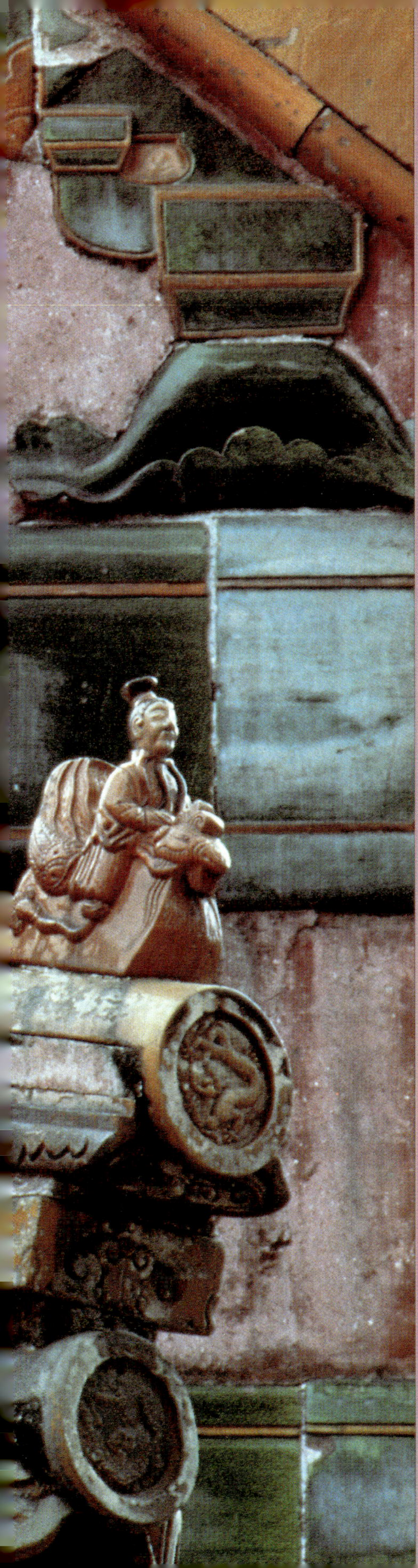

architecture

The key to understanding East Asian architecture is belief. At the height of their power, the Ming emperors (1368–1644) built one of the most extraordinary palace complexes on earth, the Forbidden City in Beijing. In every detail—from the orientation and layout of its ceremonial halls, temples, and avenues, to the design, position, and color of its sumptuous ornamentation—they followed the precepts of the Taoist art of *feng shui*, which aims to channel the beneficial forces of the cosmos to ward off evil and attract good fortune.

Japan, which learned much from China, has also built Buddhist temple complexes, whose design and ornamentation were determined by religious beliefs. In its lay architecture, however, Japan followed a quite different set of ideals, based on the concepts of harmony and simplicity, that reflect a purely Japanese understanding of man's relationship with nature.

The richly colored hues of the tiles theatrically set off a group of mythical creatures on a roof ridge in the Forbidden City in Beijing. As the emperor's motif was the dragon and the empress's the phoenix, these are the most commonly seen on roof ridges and end tiles. Glazed roof tiles were only used for palaces and temples.

exteriors

china

Following the principles of *feng shui*, all Chinese buildings, from palace halls to farmsteads, were oriented on a north-south axis, with the main entrance in the southern wall. China's most ancient constructions were built of wood standing on stone platforms. The high, tiled, hipped roofs were supported by wooden pillars and elaborate bracketed eaves. During the Ming period (1368–1644), these became decorative features in their own right, as can be seen in the carved and painted brackets of the halls of the Forbidden City, the imperial palace in Beijing.

1 The Summer Palace on the outskirts of Beijing where the imperial court escaped the oppressive, humid summer heat. Although built on a smaller scale than the Forbidden City, it consists of several palaces, temples, and lakeside pavilions.

2 A fretwork window frames a romantic view of a waterside pavilion with a tiled, curving roof. Curved roofs were built for aesthetic reasons, but they also had a practical function: they drew rainwater away from the timber frame of the building.

1

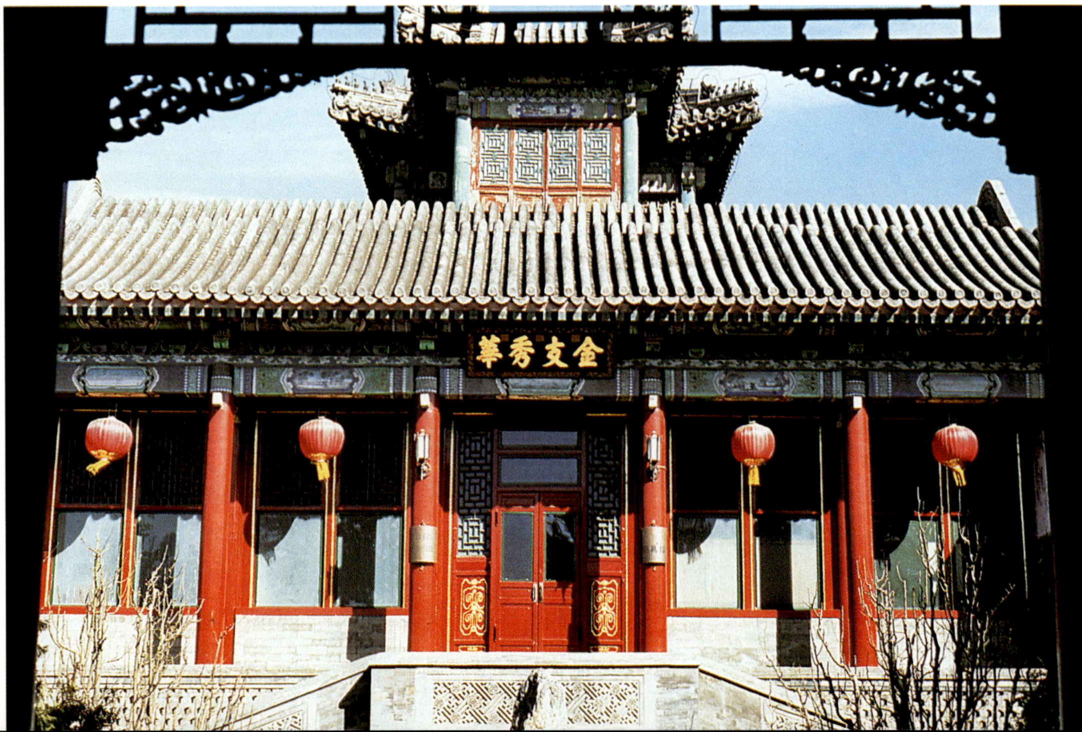

2

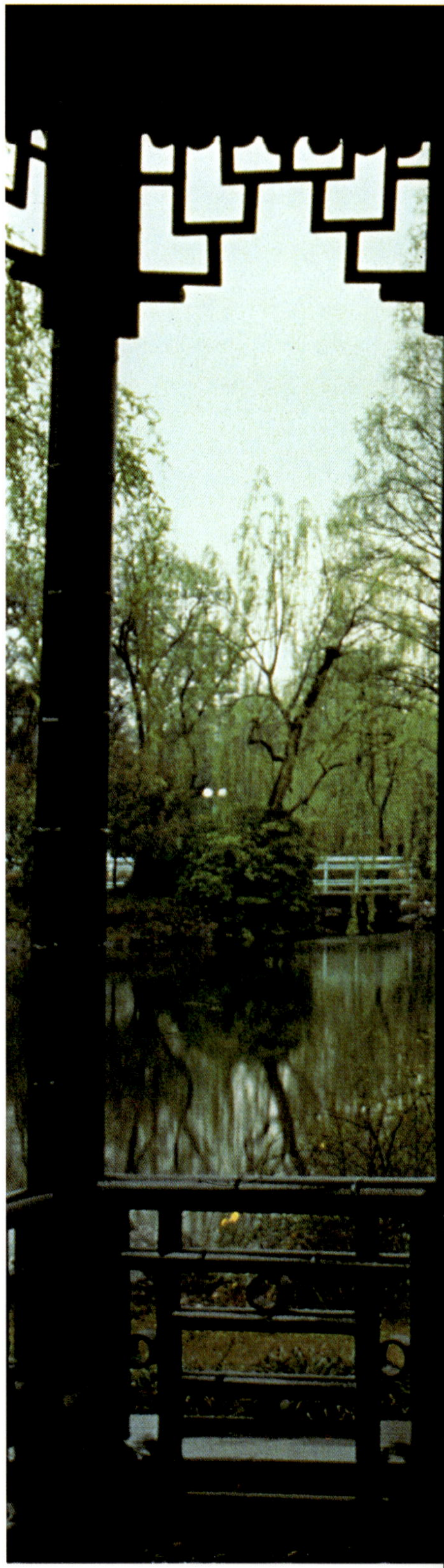

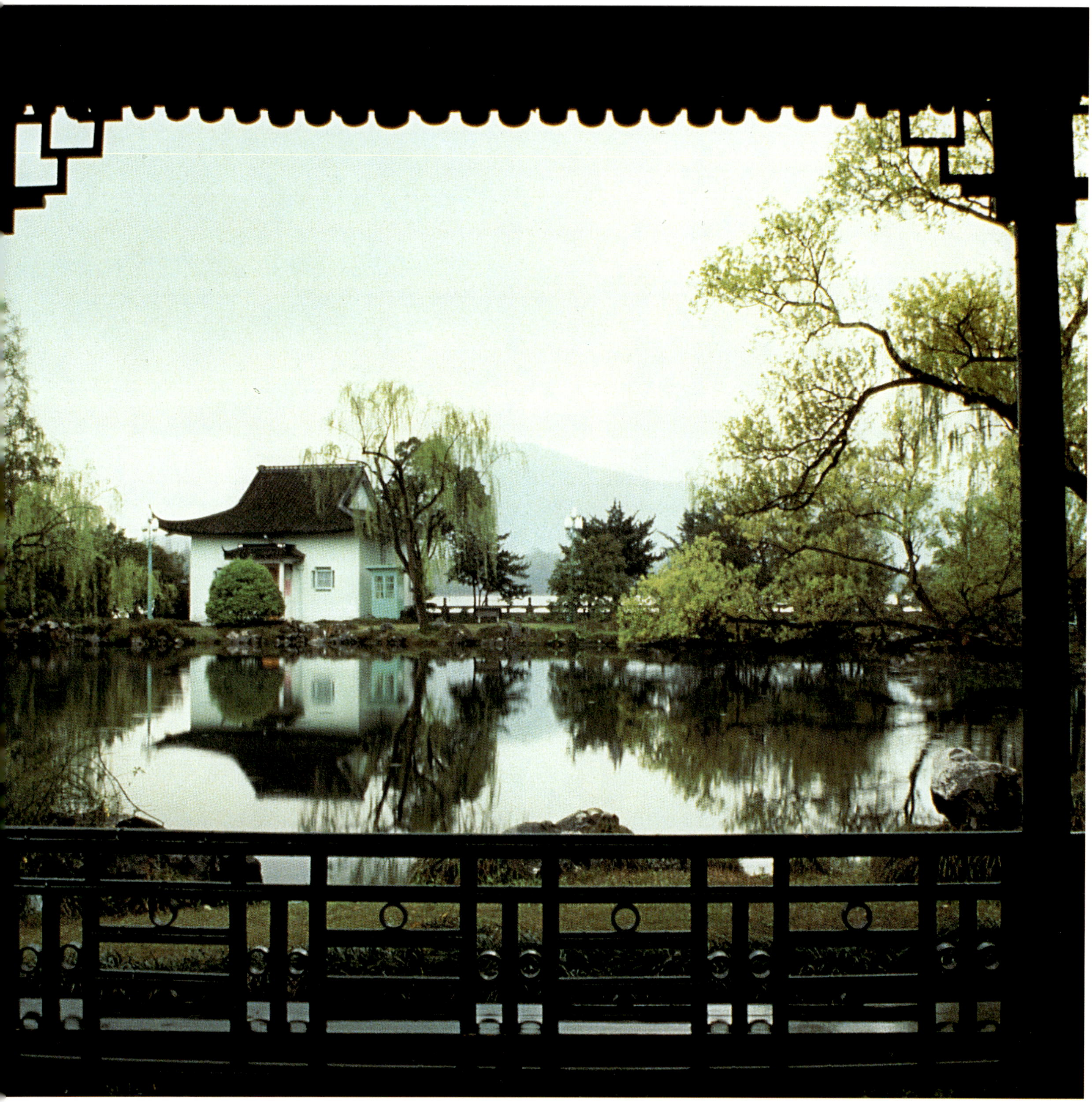

exterior decoration

1
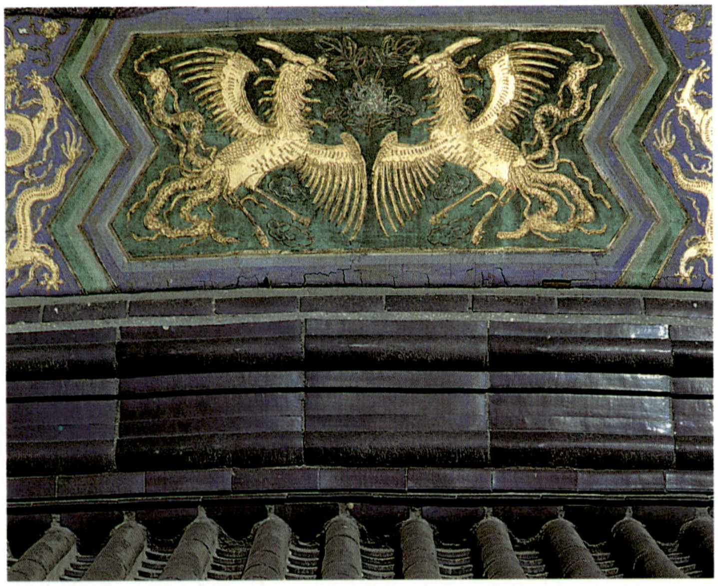

2
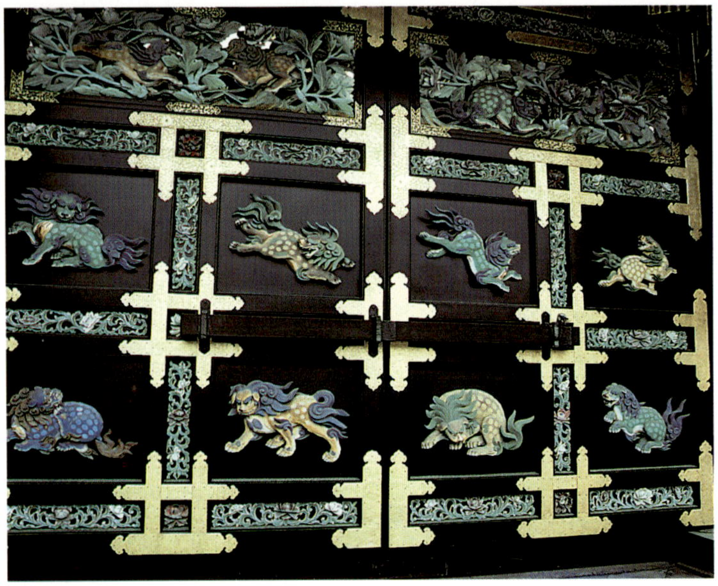

The richness of the decoration of the buildings that have survived from China's imperial past are testament to the Chinese mastery of the decorative arts. Tragically, the political upheavals of the twentieth century have led to the destruction of many masterpieces of China's architectural heritage.

The Japanese have sometimes imitated the splendor of Chinese models, as in the Tokugawa mausoleums of Nikko (pictured right) and in the temple architecture of Nara and Kyoto, but in the intimate spaces of the home and the teahouse, they have achieved a remarkable harmony with their natural surroundings.

1 Detail of the Temple of Heaven in Beijing with two gold phoenixes (emblems of the empress) flanked by two gold dragons (emblems of the emperor) against glazed blue tiles. Chinese temples are usually roofed with blue tiles, unless they were endowed by an imperial benefactor, when they have yellow or green roof tiles.

2 Detail of the elaborate carvings of animals, foliage, and flowers on the Karamon gate of Nishi-Hongan-ji in Kyoto. Two halls of this important Buddhist temple were decorated by artists of the Kano school.

3 The complex of shrines at Nikko, Japan, which combines Ming influences with the decorative style of the early Edo period (1600–1853), was built by the third shogun, Tokugawa Iemitsu, between 1634 and 1636, as the mausoleum of the founder of the dynasty, Ieyasu.

3

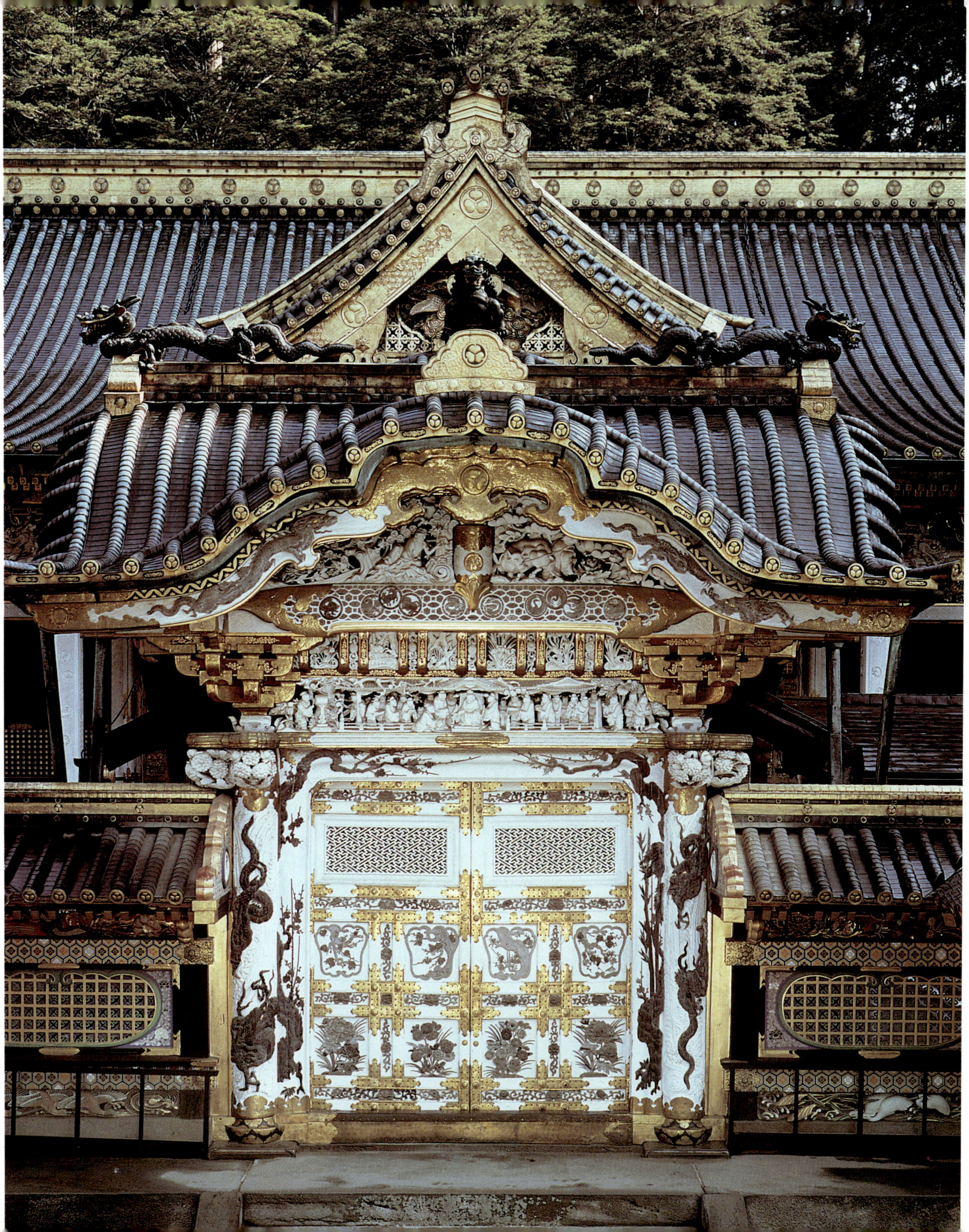

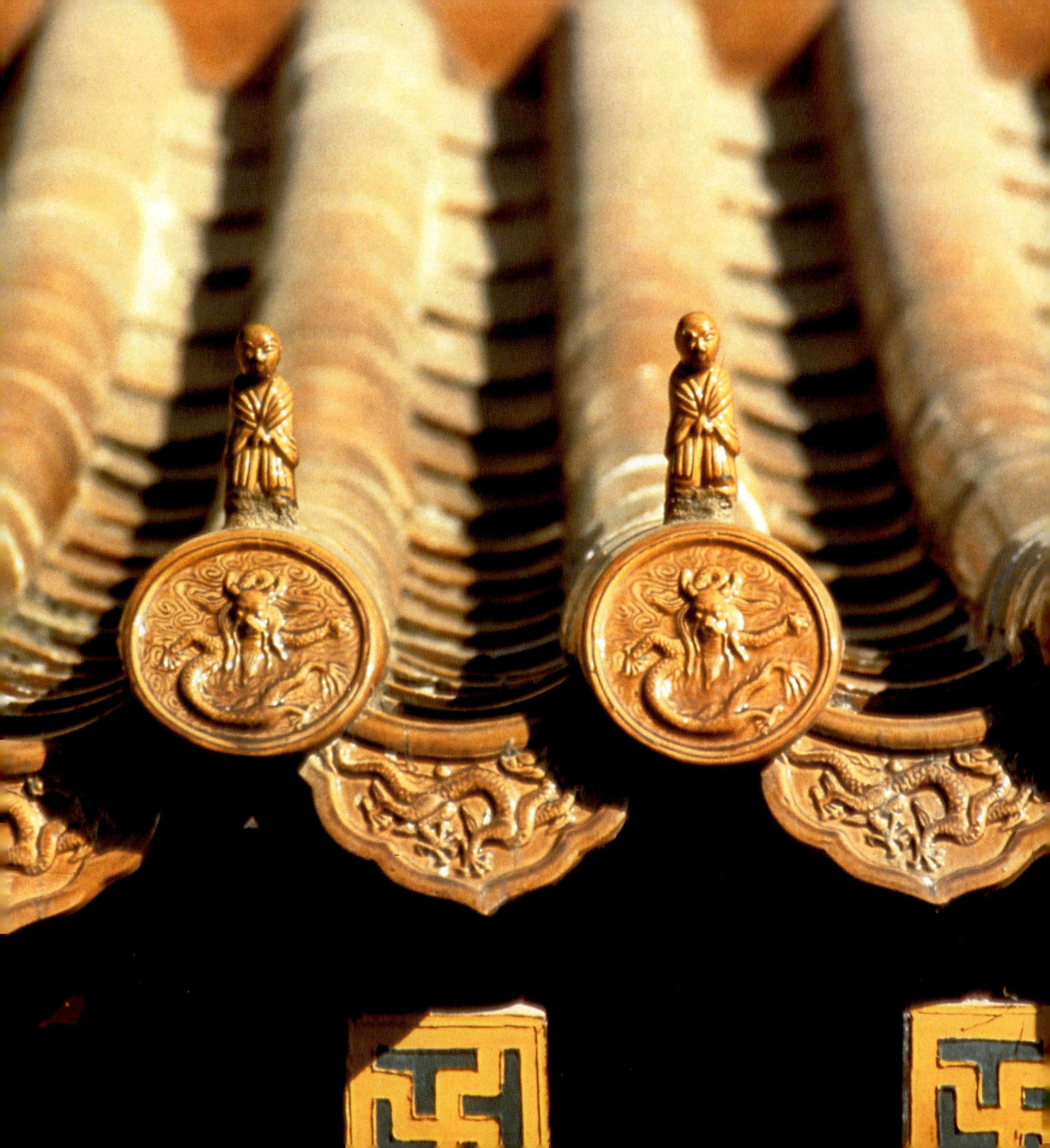

1

roof decoration

Symbolic motifs are a striking feature of Chinese roofs. These are not purely decorative, but serve both social and magical functions, indicating the importance of the building, as well as protecting it from evil influences. In the grandest public buildings the lower ends of sloping ridges were decorated with a series of ten small mythological figures, including the celestial prince on a hen, the dragon, phoenix, lion, celestial horse, and sea horse. In the Forbidden City in Beijing, only the most important building, the Hall of Supreme Harmony, where the emperor was crowned, had the full complement of ten figures on its ridges.

1 This type of richly decorated tile end has been used since the Han dynasty (206 B.C.–A.D. 221).

2 A sixteenth-century Ming dynasty house. A hipped roof with upturned corners could only be used for important halls and palaces.

3 The rows of ceramic animals on roof decorations are usually an odd number. A human-led parade of protective beasts defends each roof end and protects the occupants.

2

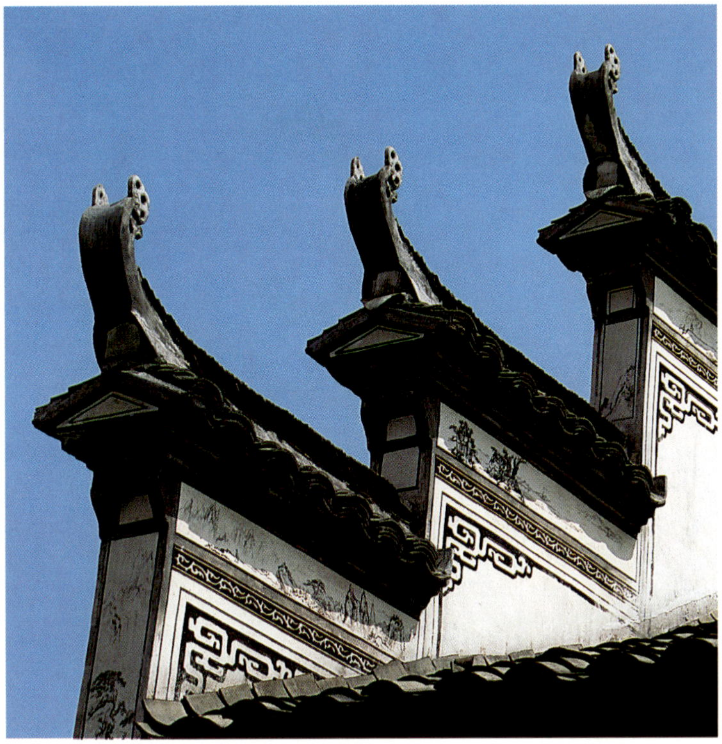

3

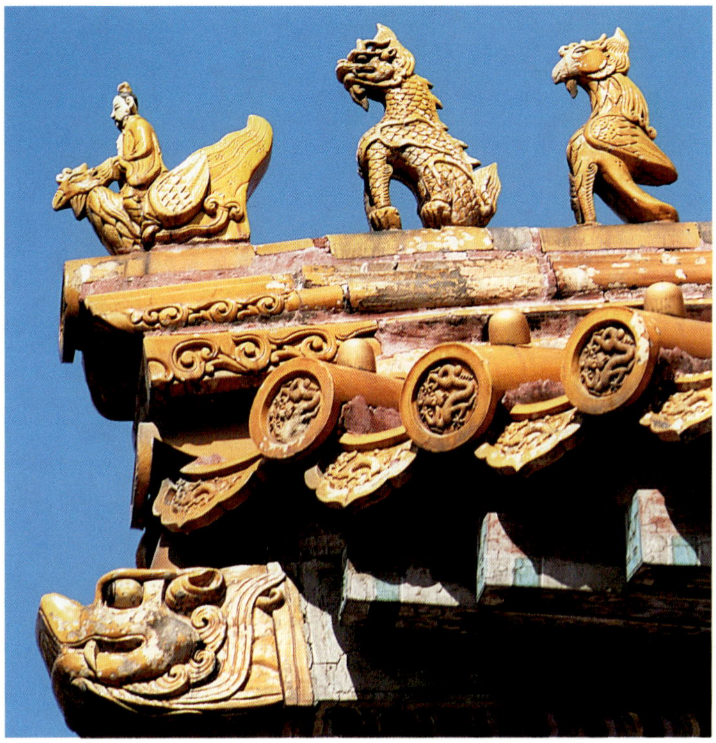

temples

The introduction of Buddhism from China initiated a revolution in Japanese art and architecture. Although rebuilt over the centuries, many of western Japan's earliest temple complexes survive to this day with their original ground plans intact. In the traditional arrangement, a temple enclosure would consist of a central gateway (*chumon*), a pagoda (*to*), and several halls (*do*), as well as residential quarters for the monks, and treasure houses to store and display statuary, books, and relics. The joinery techniques used to construct these temples were built upon the earlier tradition of Shinto shrine buildings, with its characteristic X-shaped interlocking rafters supporting a thatched roof.

1 Detail of the roof and gables of the Byōdō-in at Uji. Famous in Japan as the image on the reverse side of the ten yen coin, this is one of Japan's most venerable Buddhist temples. Its upward-sweeping roofs create a floating structure reflected in the waters of an artificial lake.

2 The most striking shape in Buddhist architecture is the pagoda (*to*), built to house religious artifacts, sutras, or relics.

2

1

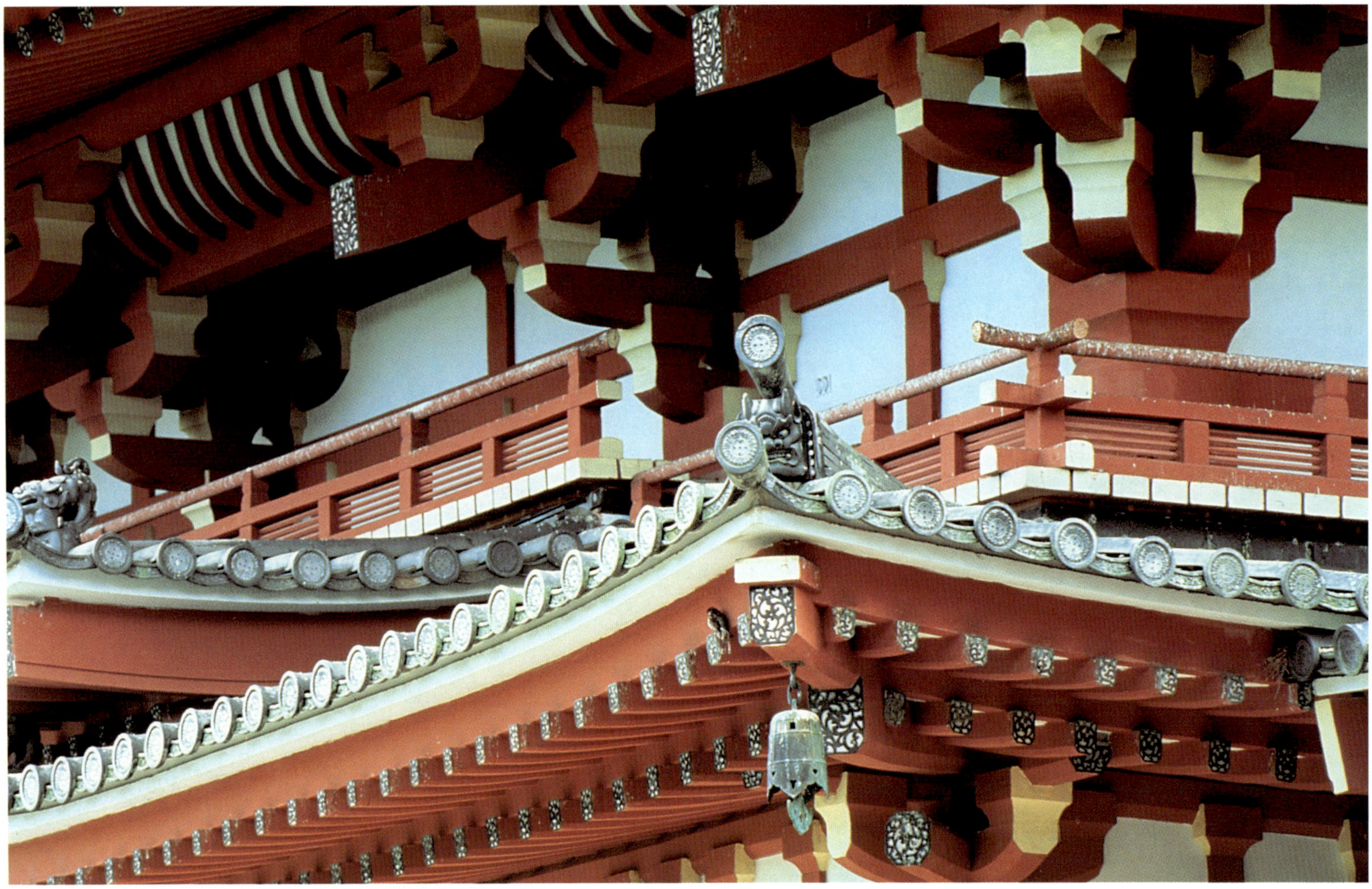

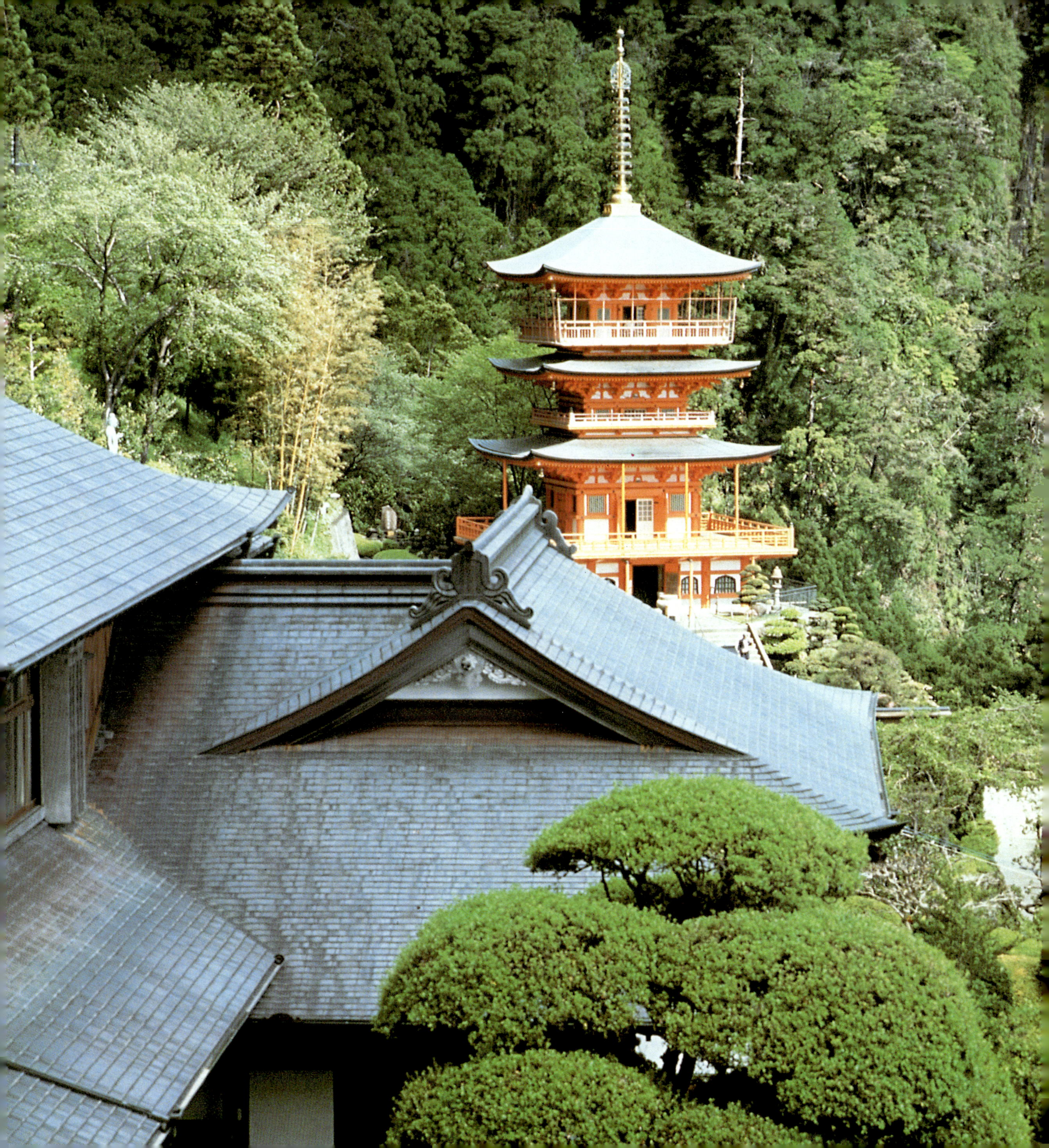

1

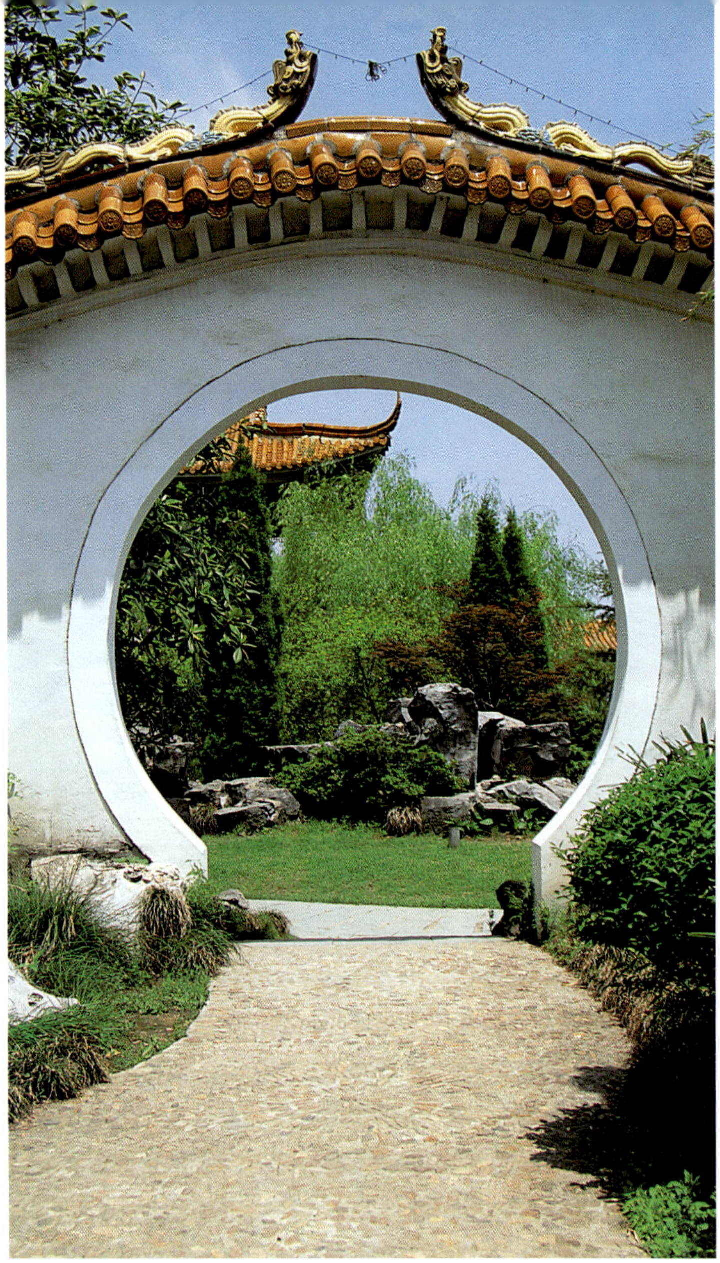

1 A classic Chinese moon-gate creates a romantic vista enhanced by symmetrical perspectives: the carved dragons on the top of the wall echo the curve of the roof beyond. The roof tile ends are decorated in traditional style.

2

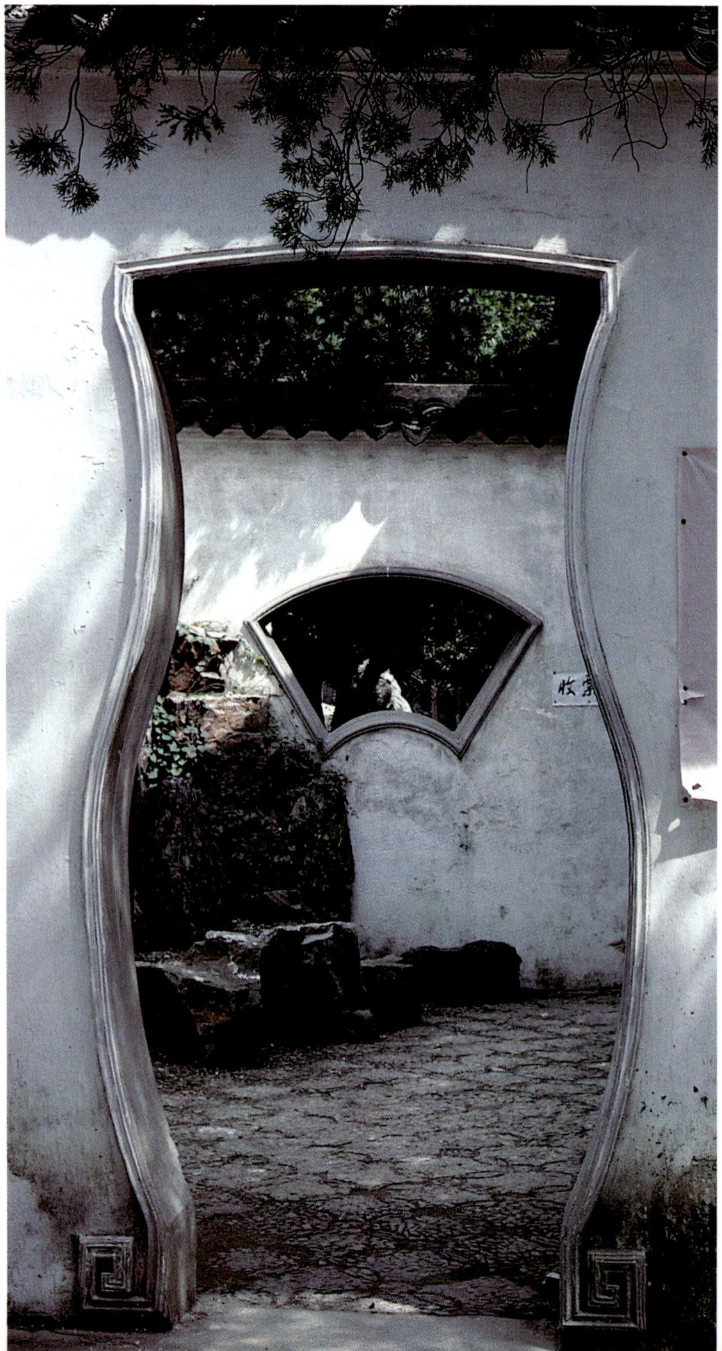

2 This entrance archway in the Ming dynasty Garden of the Love of Attachment (*Jichang yuan*) in Wuxi dates from the early sixteenth century. It frames a harmonious "living picture" of rocks and greenery, which can also be glimpsed through the fan-shaped aperture in the inner wall.

archways and doors

3 Kiyomizu-dera temple in Kyoto is known for the extraordinary wooden platform that suspends the temple over a valley. The use of painted wooden doorframes and windows is no less dramatic—the bright reds and dark greens are highlighted with white.

The doorway has always been imbued with a deep symbolic significance in East Asian culture. It serves as the portal between the human and natural worlds and the boundary between inner private space and the outer public world.

While the entrance hall of the traditional Japanese house, the *genkan*, is often equipped with sliding doors, the Chinese have exploited the full aesthetic possibilities of the doorway, experimenting with form, as in the perfect geometry of the circular "moon-gate." Carefully placed openings create vistas onto peaceful gardens, courtyards, or natural landscapes, all of which change with the seasons to integrate the human living space with the yearly cycle of the natural world.

3

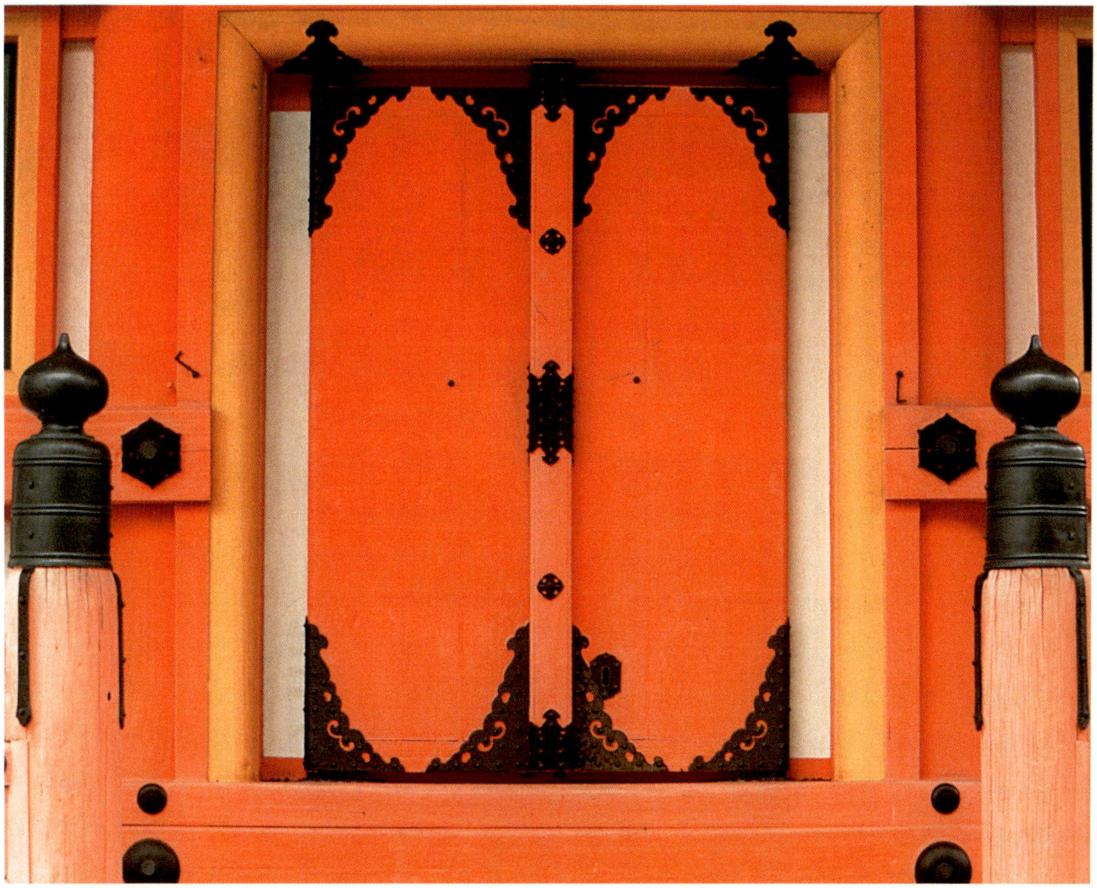

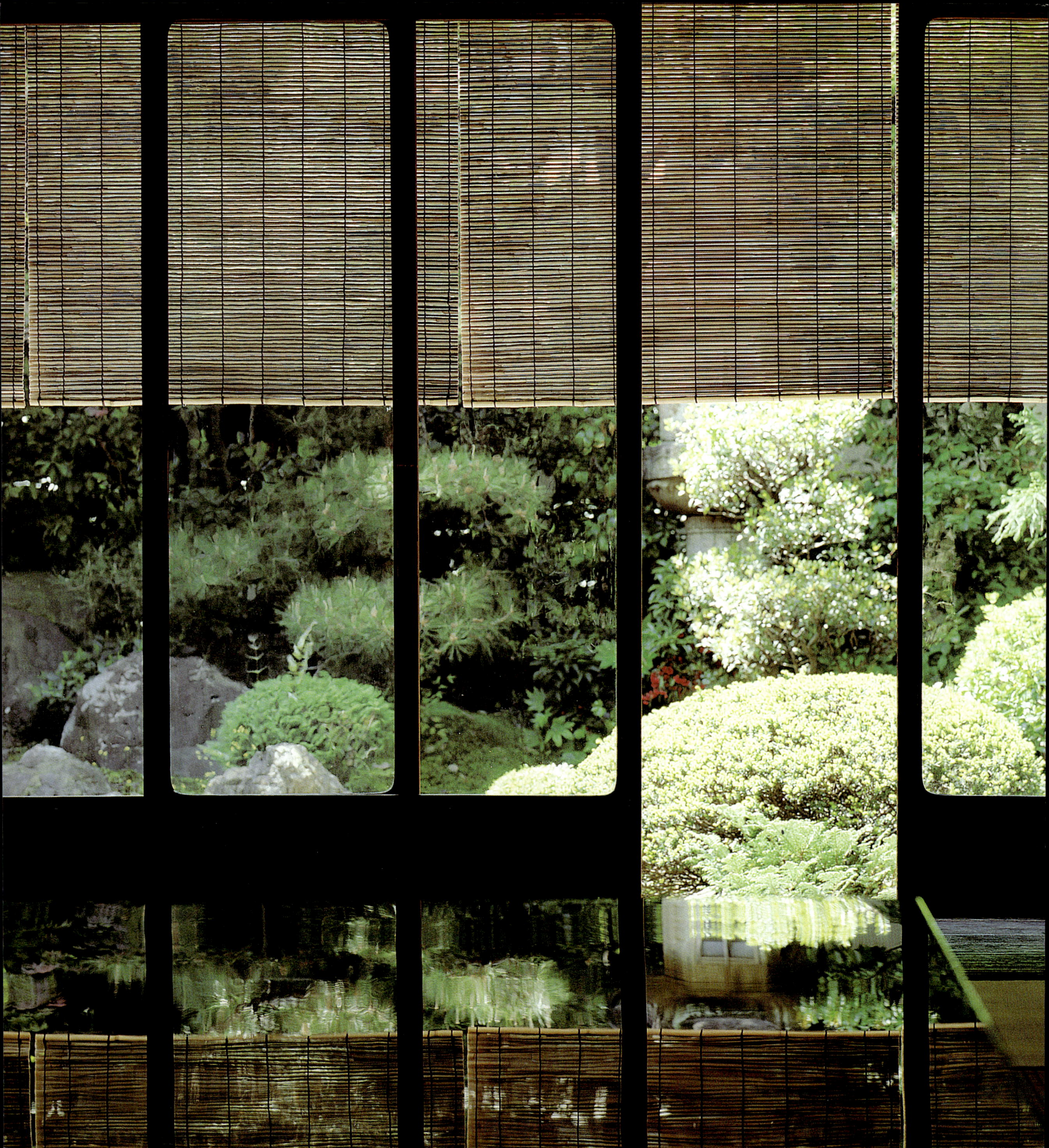

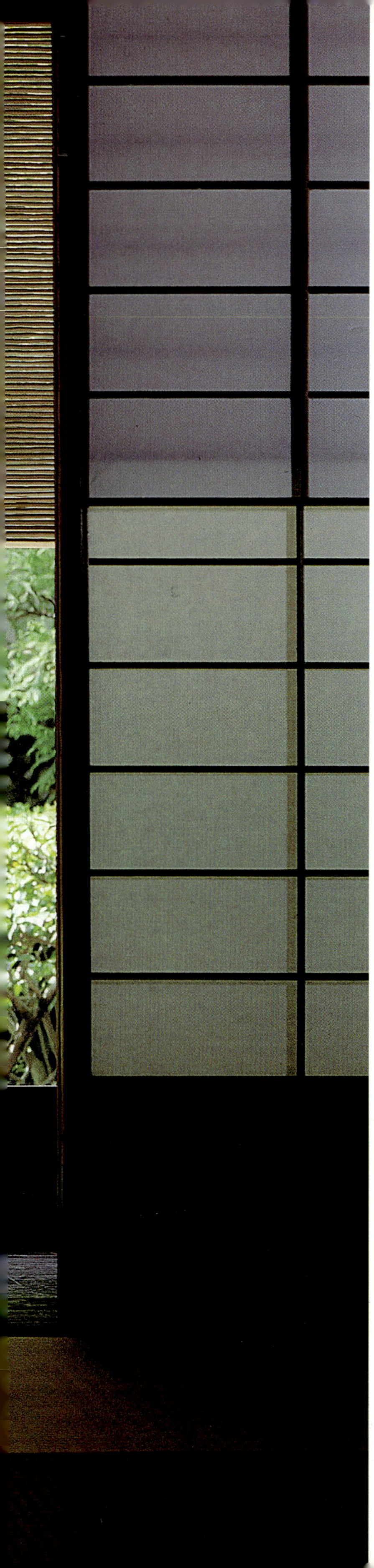

windows

1

1 *Sudare* (bamboo blinds) are hung on the outside of windows or from the eaves of a veranda. Japanese gardens are designed to be viewed from the seated position. *Sudare* can be partially rolled up so as not to obscure the view of the garden while still providing shade.

2 An internal "borrowed" view of rocks in a courtyard, through a window framing a living picture in the Garden of Content (*Yu yuan*) in Shanghai. Windows screened with patterned lattices were not only decorative features but provided links between different areas of houses, pavilions, and gardens.

Window openings in various shapes and sizes, including *marumado* (round windows), are seen in Japan's temple and military architecture. In *shoin*-style houses, however, which lack structural walls, there are no windows in the Western or Chinese sense. Covered in paper until the introduction of glass in the modern period, the *shoji* sliding screens can be pulled back or removed altogether, to open the rear and sides of the house onto the garden around it, and so integrate indoor and outdoor space. This system also provides much needed natural ventilation during the hot, humid summer.

2

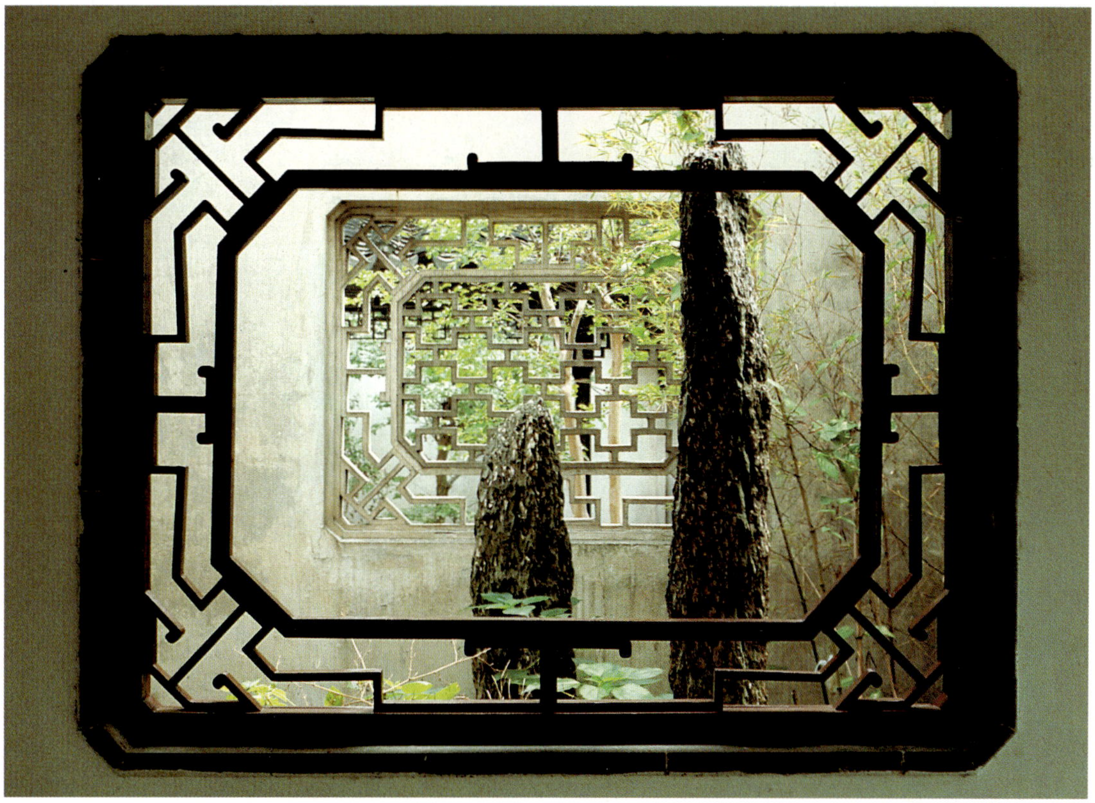

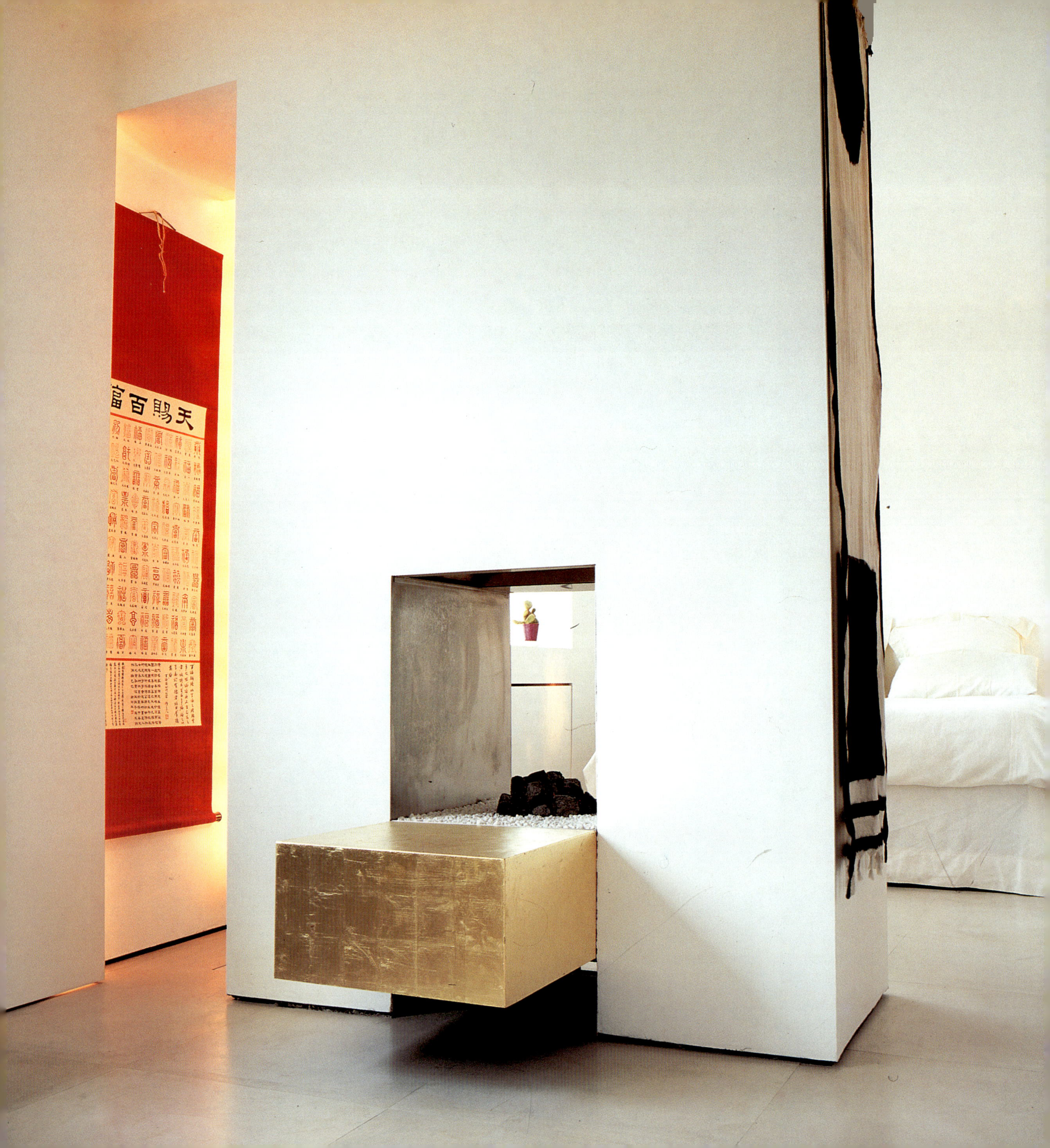

interiors japan

1 In traditional Japanese house construction, the heavy-tiled roof is supported by wooden pillars. With no load-bearing walls, interiors are partitioned by *shoji* (translucent sliding screens), which can be removed to create a single open-plan living space. Whether a room is carpeted or has a more traditional floor covering, the unit of measurement for its floor area is the *tatami* mat (approximately 180 x 90 cm). Large palace rooms measured tens or even hundreds of mats, but in most modern Japanese homes, a room rarely exceeds eight to ten mats.

1 This apartment combines East and West: a large Chinese calendar scroll and black and white Japanese wall hangings are displayed against stark white walls and furnishings.

2 An uncluttered Japanese interior, divided by *fusuma* sliding screens, which are thicker and more opaque than *shoji,* with *tatami* flooring.

2

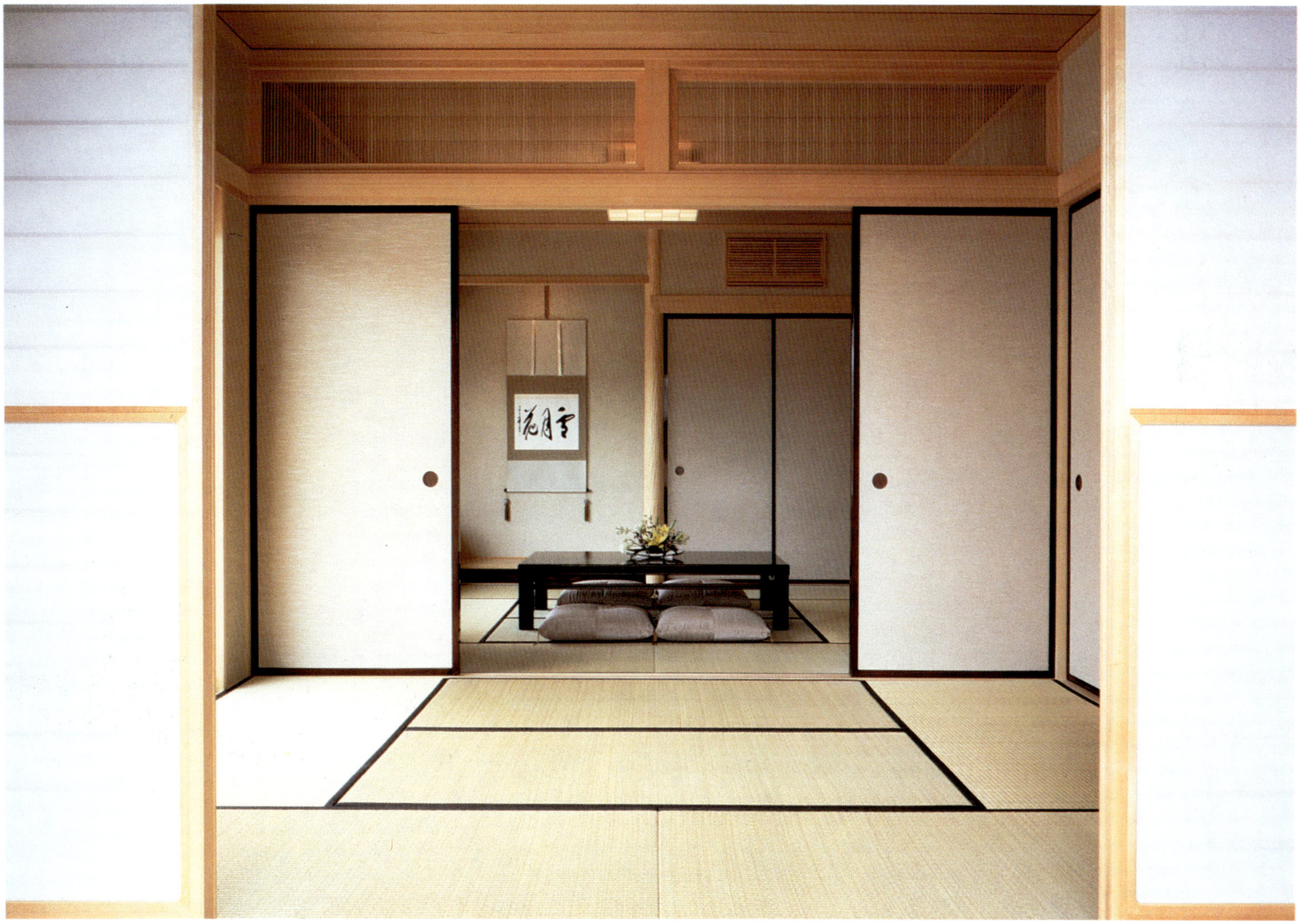

screens

There are two types of screen in use in the Japanese house in addition to the paper-covered translucent *shoji*, which are used as windows at the rear of the house and for internal partitions: *fusuma*, which are usually covered with thicker paper or can be made of plaited materials and are used to screen cupboards and to provide more substantial inner partitions; and *amado*, thick wooden sliding shutters, sometimes reinforced with iron, which fit over the external *shoji* to provide security at night or when the house is unoccupied, and extra protection from the elements in winter and during tropical storms in the summer.

1 The austere elegance of a traditional Japanese interior creates a calming effect, as air, light, and space combine with the natural texture of the materials. The only ornamentation is in the *tokonoma* alcove (center back of picture), usually a flower arrangement and a hanging scroll.

1

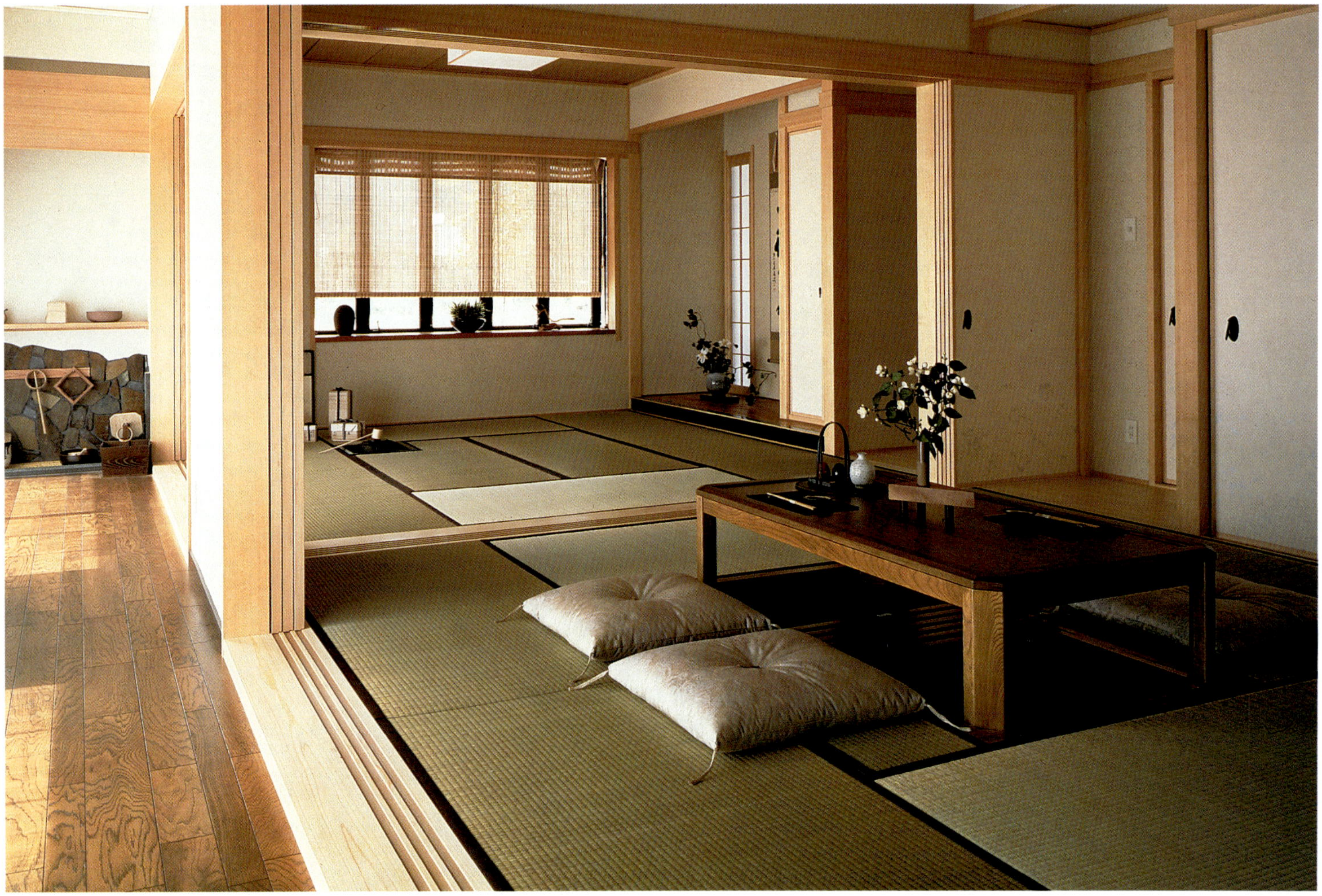

2 Detail of an early twentieth-century traditional reed screen, decorated with incised patterns. Due to the hot, humid Japanese climate, the absence of structural walls and free-standing furniture creates an open-air style, helped by the use of removable sliding screens.

3 Detail of white *shoji* screens. Traditionally covered in translucent rice paper, they create a soft, subdued atmosphere. The paper-covered lattice serves to diffuse the harsh glare of the summer sun.

2

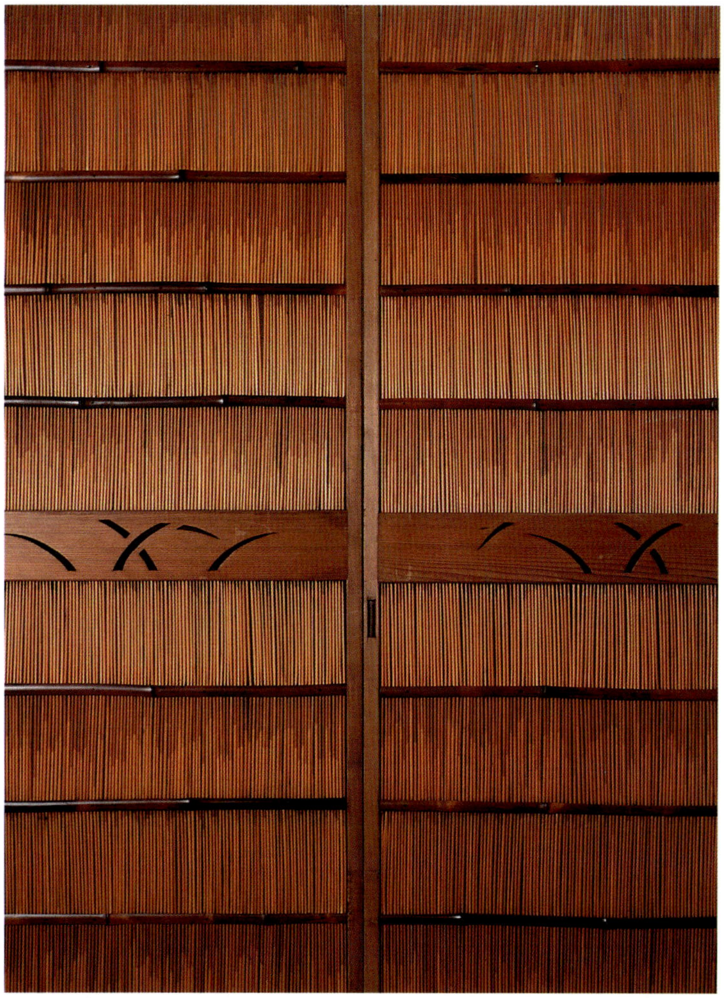

3

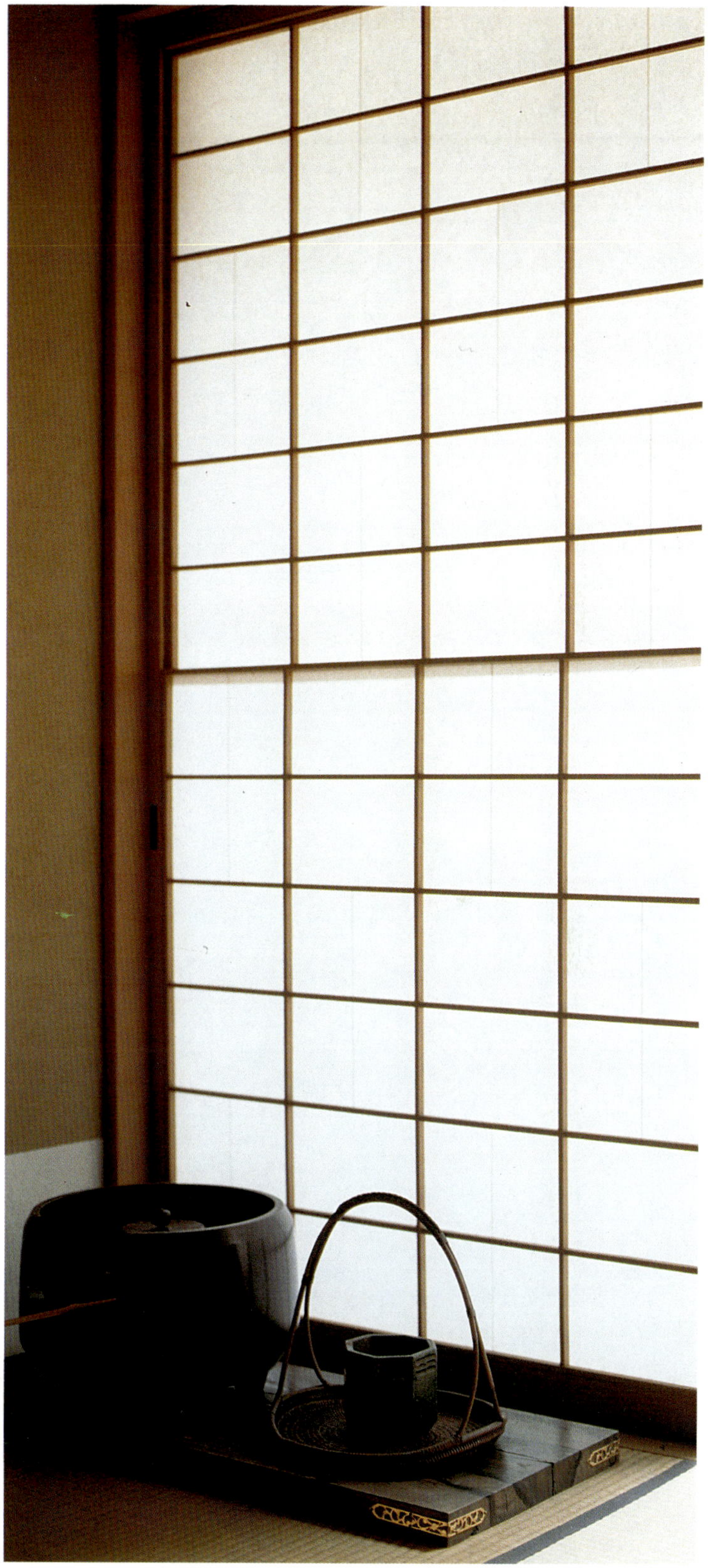

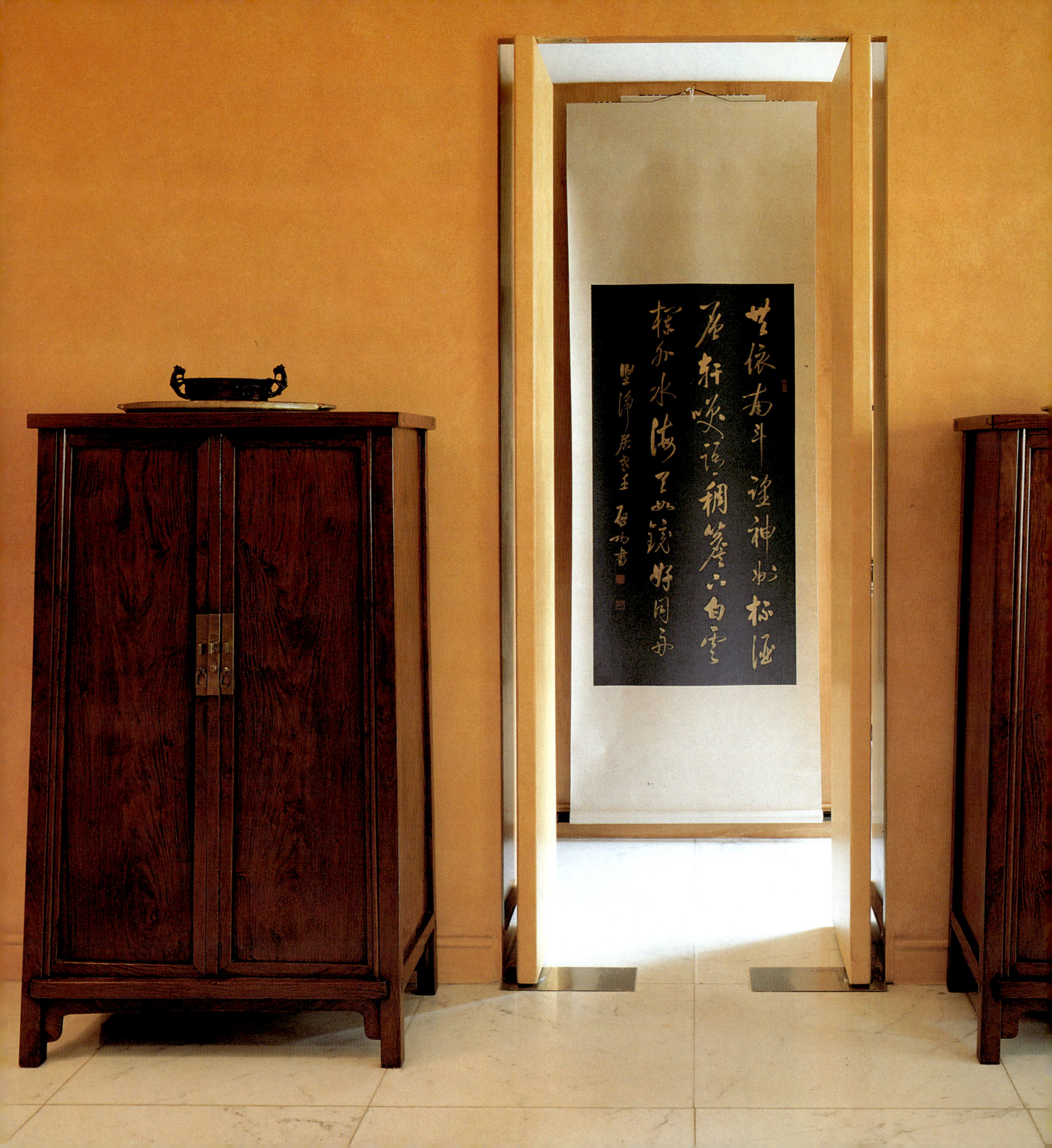

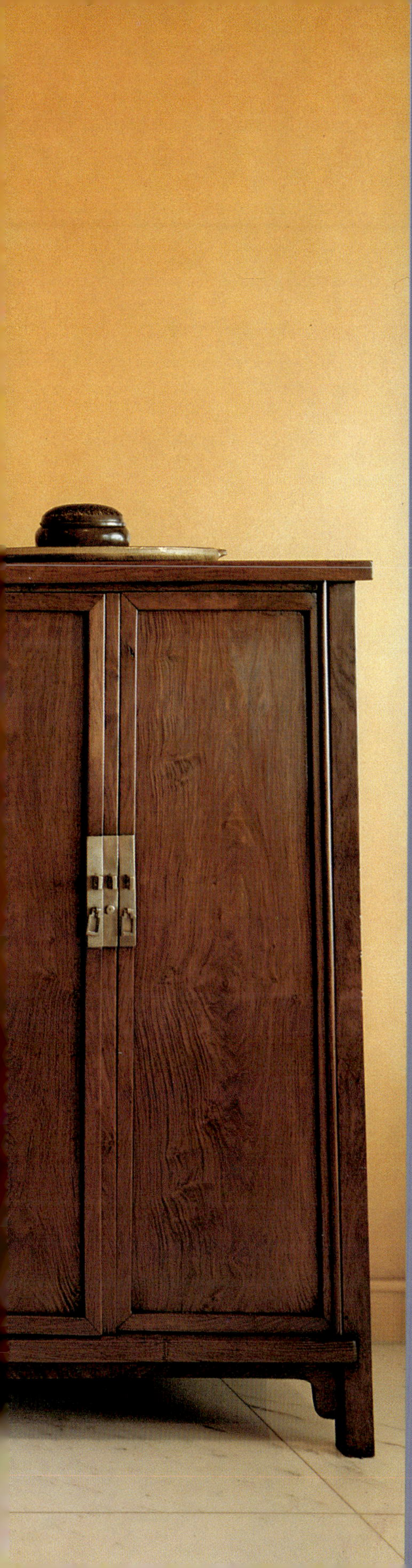

furniture

Domestic life in early China and Japan was lived at floor level. In the colder regions of northern China, houses were equipped with raised, heated brick platforms, known as *kang*. The only pieces of furniture were low tables (*kangzhou*), which served both as eating and working surfaces. While floor-level living is still widespread in contemporary Japan, during the Tang dynasty (618–906) the Chinese court and nobility adopted the lifestyle associated with raised furniture.

The Golden Age of Chinese furniture came with the Ming (1368–1644) and early Qing (1644–1911) periods. The purity of its form and its functional simplicity, and the use of wood textures, lacquer finishes, and ornamental decoration inspired generations of Western cabinetmakers. Furniture imported by the Dutch and British East India Companies started the late seventeenth- and eighteenth-century European vogue for Chinese shapes, materials, and decoration, known as the *chinoiserie* style, which is best seen in the interiors and furnishings of the Royal Pavilion in Brighton, England, which was built for the Prince Regent, later to become King George IV.

A pair of *nanmu* (cedarwood) cabinets frame a doorway in this Hong Kong apartment, taking the eye through double doors to the calligraphic scroll beyond. Gently tapering from the base to the top, the cabinets' single-paneled doors open onto a fitted interior, consisting of a shelf and drawers on each side.

seating china

In the eighteenth century, Europeans were avid collectors of richly decorated lacquer furniture. The Chinese tradition of hardwood furniture was overlooked until the 1930s, when the finely-proportioned pieces of the Ming period were recognized as the perfect match for the minimalist Bauhaus style. In keeping with the overall simplicity of their design, Ming-period pieces had little upholstery; chairs would have been draped with textiles or thinly padded with cushions in colors that accorded with the status of the owner. The Communist revolution of 1949 led to the expulsion of foreigners from China, and the ending of the official trade in antiques with the West. When trade with China resumed in the 1980s, the availability of fine original pieces of classical furniture also inspired a late-twentieth century boom in Chinese furniture design. As our appreciation of East Asian design continues to mature, copies, restorations, and contemporary reinterpretations of classical Ming-period furniture have found a place in Western interiors, as, for a lucky few, have the originals.

1 Nineteenth-century elmwood *yumu* (daybed), with a cane top supported by arched braces on the underside. Daybeds were used both formally and in semi-formal situations, predominantly for daytime napping, or at any time for seating or playing board games. Relatively light to move, they could be easily carried outdoors. Textiles and rugs were added for comfort.

1

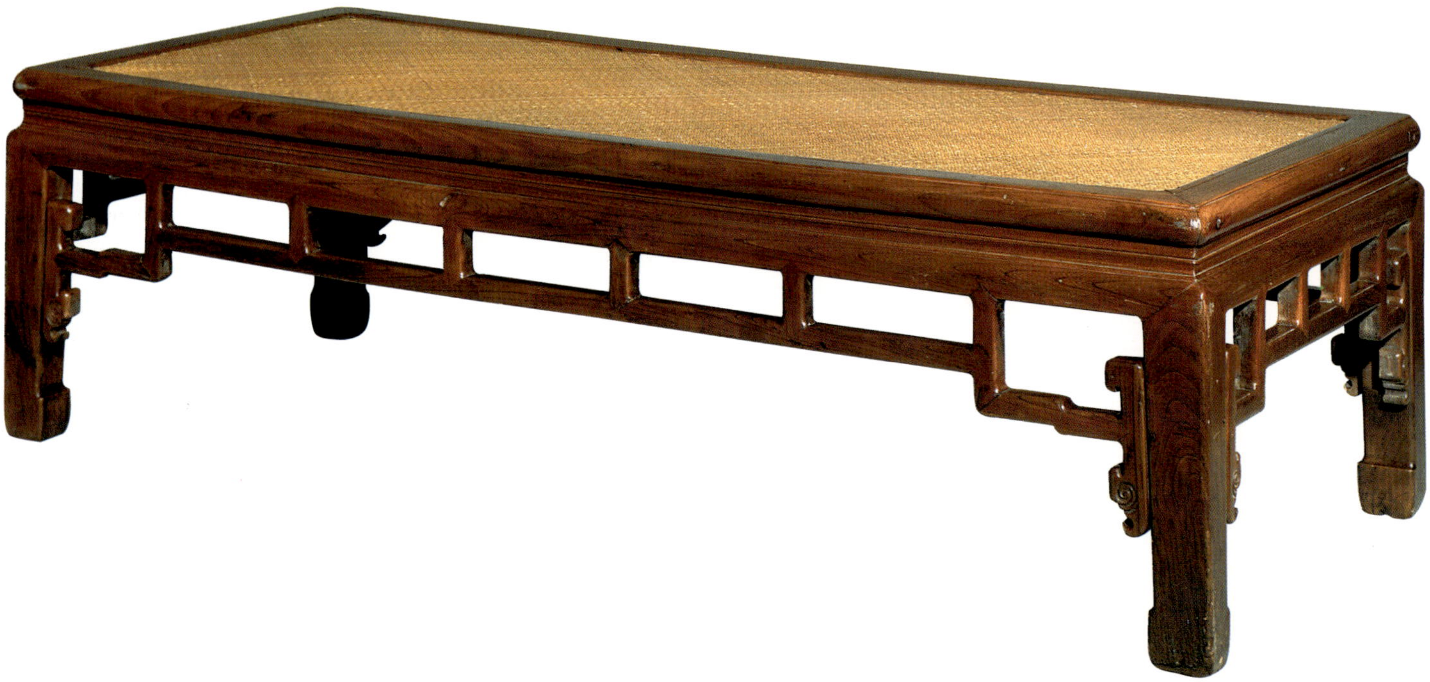

2

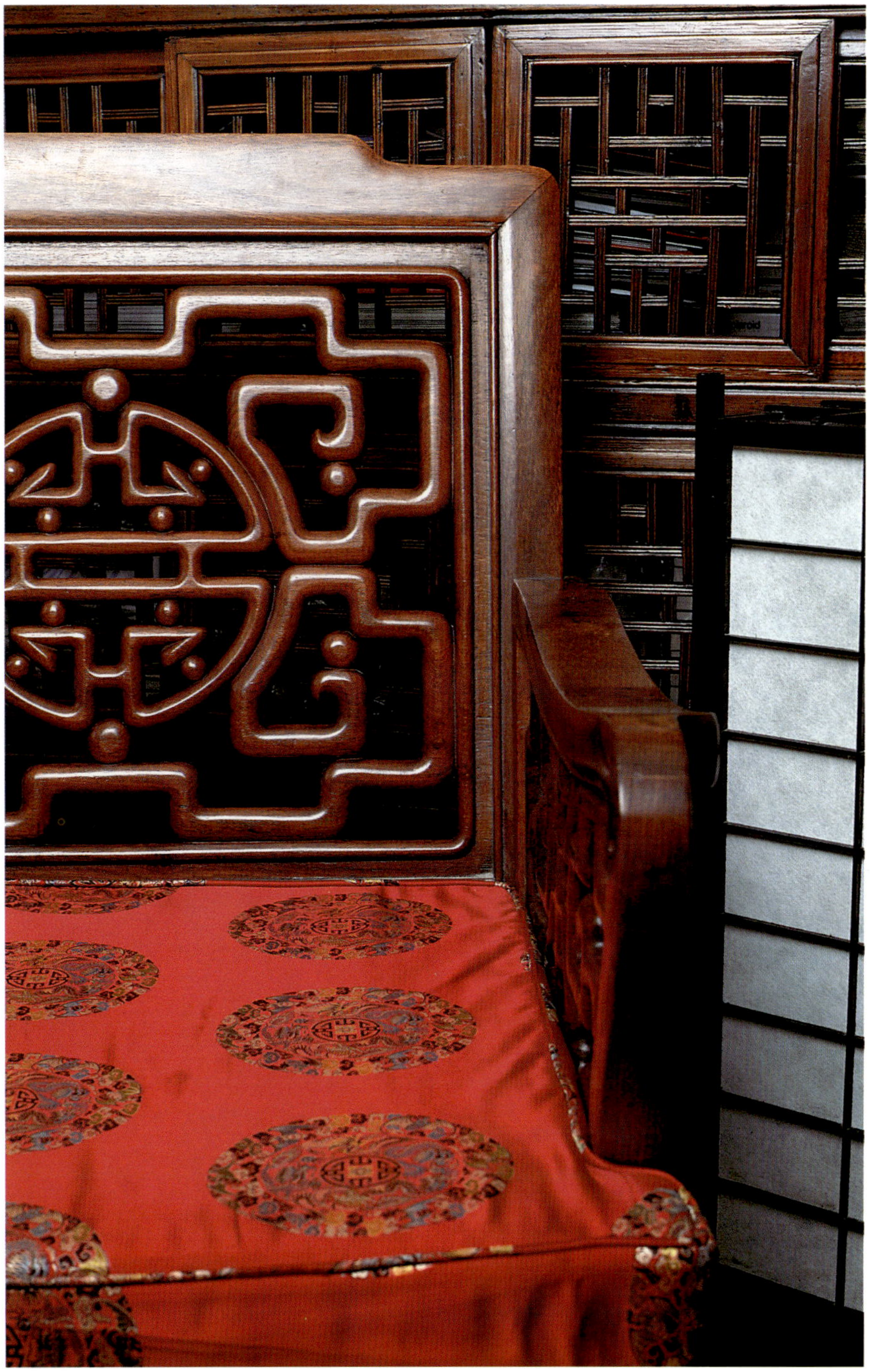

3

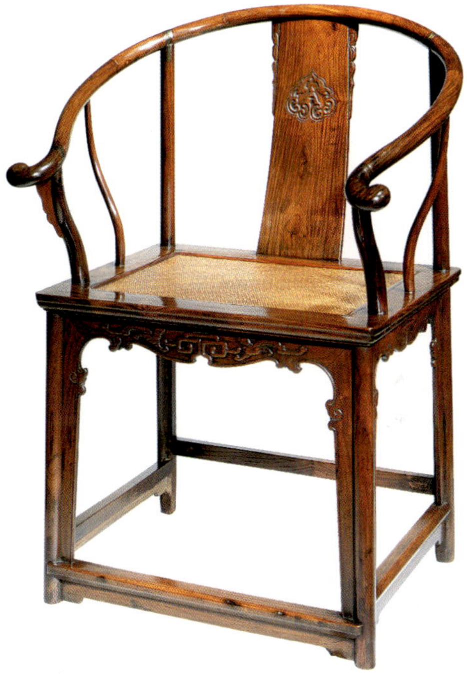

2 This elaborately decorated nineteenth-century fretwork armchair contrasts with the simple aesthetic of Ming-style furniture. It would not have been out of place in a colonial mansion in Shanghai. The carving on the back shows an auspicious *shou* good luck symbol, which also appears in a repeat pattern on the silk-cushioned seat.

3 A *quanyi* Ming chair made of *huanghuali* wood, dating from the seventeenth century. Its curved shape is the origin of its Western name, the "horseshoe-back" chair.

seating
japan

In Japan, the domestic environment is divided into two well-defined areas: "outside," where one is allowed to wear shoes, and "inside," where one must go barefoot or wear indoor slippers. This distinction continues to influence every aspect of home life. Even in modern Western-style Japanese homes, with carpets and raised furniture, it is still customary to exchange one's shoes for a pair of slippers at the front door. In a traditional *tatami* interior, where people will sit and sleep on futons placed directly on the floor, the practice of removing outdoor shoes becomes a necessity for obvious reasons of cleanliness and hygiene.

Although Chinese furniture was adopted by Japan's imperial court in the sixth century, it was only ever used for ceremonial occasions, and for most of the population, life continued to be lived at floor level. As storage in traditional Japanese homes is built in or hidden, free-standing furniture is limited to low tables and display cabinets, supplemented in the modern period by stands for televisions and other products of the electronic age. Seating is provided by flat, square *zabuton* cushions upon which one sits cross-legged, or in the formal kneeling position, sitting back on one's heels.

1

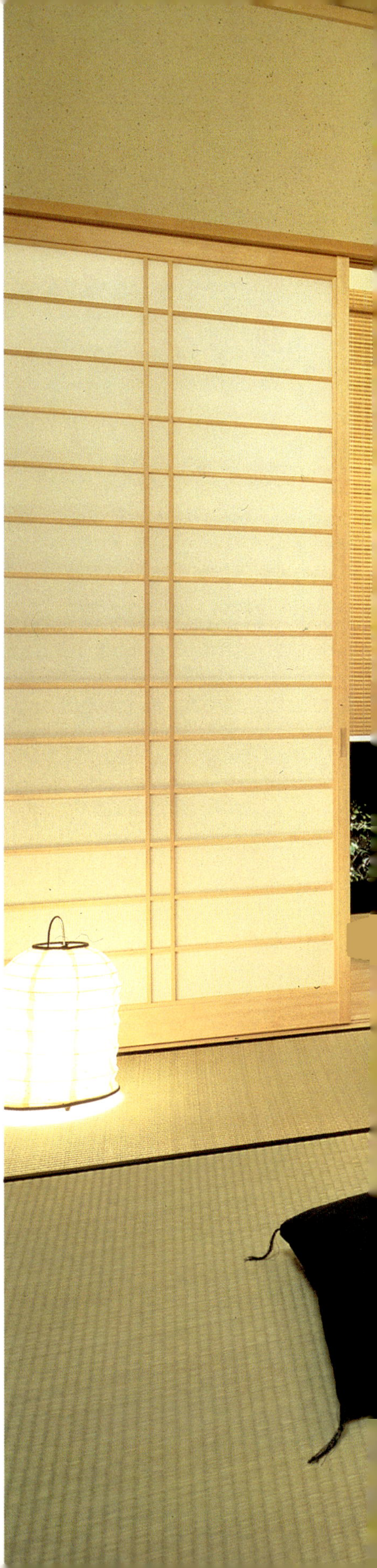

1 In this contemporary *tatami*-floored Japanese interior, a kettle sits in a sunken brazier in the center of a low table. The elegant place settings provide the only hint of color within the neutral scheme of the room. The diners will sit cross-legged or kneel on the black *zabuton* cushions. *Shoji* screens create a partition between the dining area and a smaller room used to view the garden, which can be seen through the rolled-up *sudare* blinds. A small cabinet is used to display treasured pieces of ceramic art and to store personal effects.

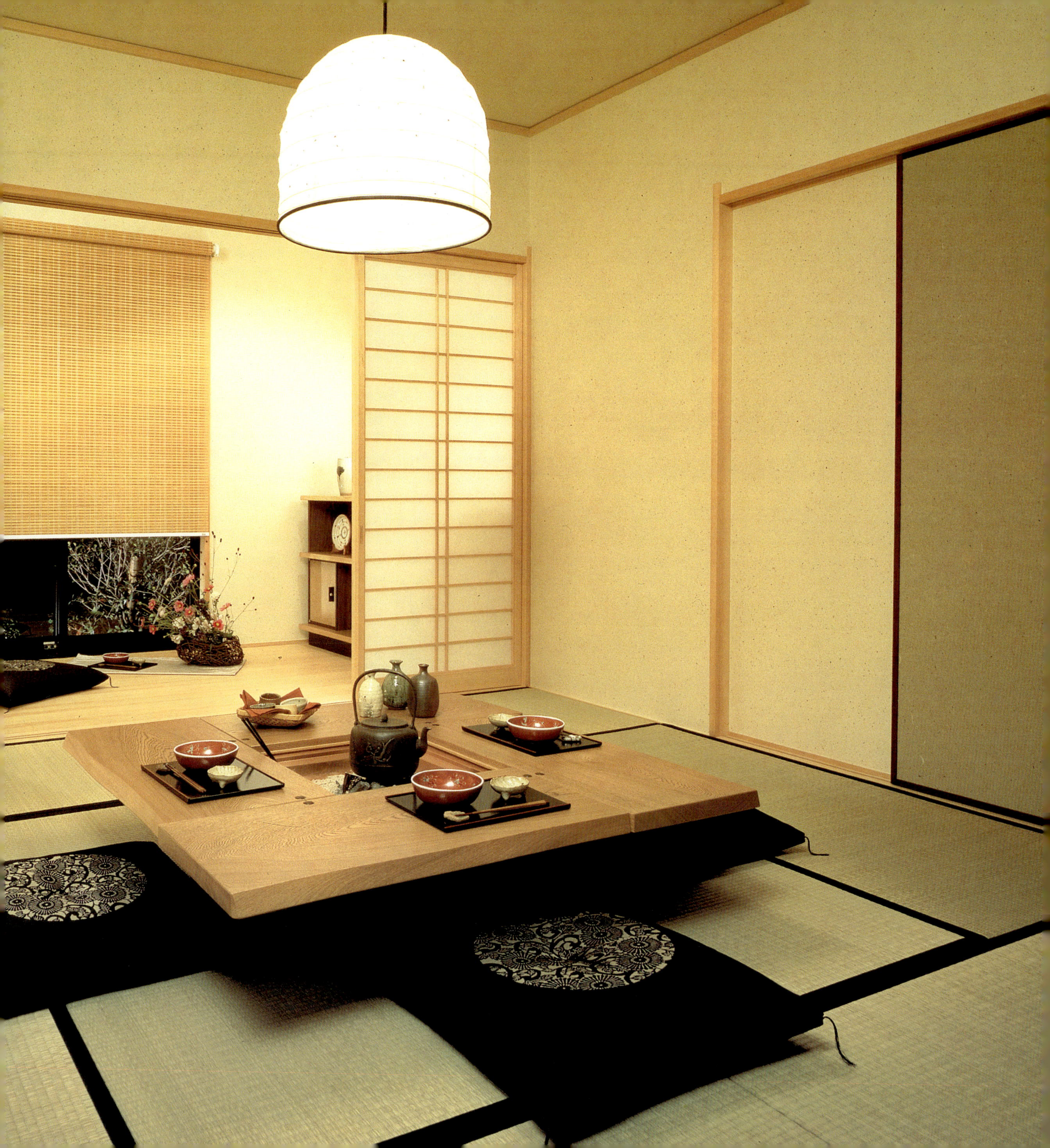

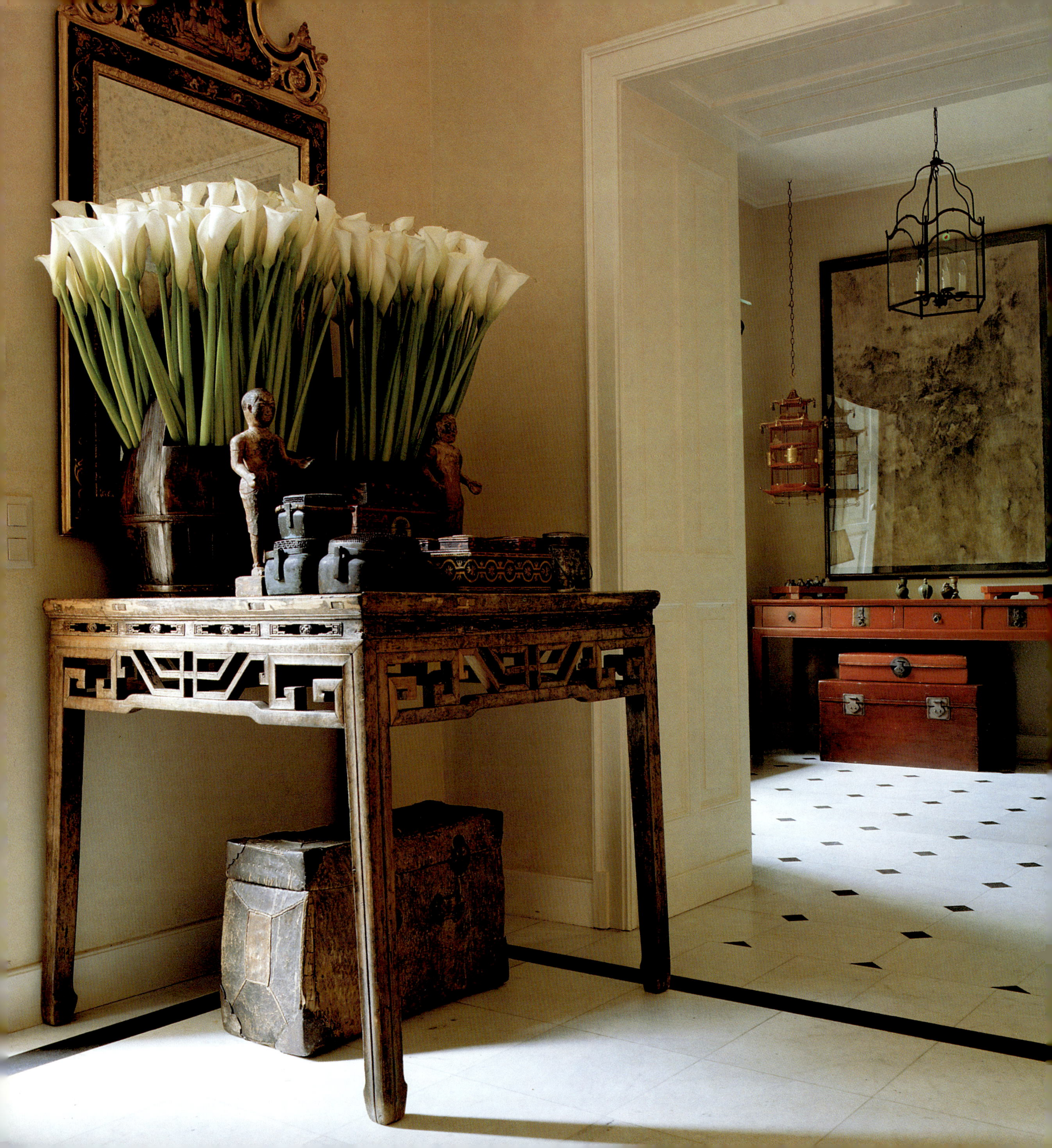

tables

The principal piece of furniture in the traditional Japanese interior is the low, portable table, produced in lacquer or natural wood finishes, which is used for both eating and working. Variants include tables with hotplates or sunken braziers, whose modern versions, known as *kotatsu*, have small heaters bolted to the underside of the table top to warm sitters in winter.

The real treasures of the East Asian cabinetmaker's art are the classical tables of China, which are rightly prized for their purity of line, balance, and proportion. The unique lustrous grain of *huanghuali* wood evokes a bygone age of grace and elegance. Tables were made as scholars' painting and writing desks, and as portable altars. Their manufacture shows some complex joinery techniques: in some instances, tables were held together with a system of interlocking joints, which did not require glue or nails, so that they could be easily dismantled and transported.

1 A collection of Asian antiques and arum lilies displayed in wooden rice pails sits on a table with decorative scrolled carving. A plain red lacquer side table is complemented by the deep reds of the leather cases beneath.

2 Detail of a nineteenth-century scholars' table, after earlier Ming designs, which were usually made of rare *huanghuali* wood.

3 The simplicity of line combined with the richness of the natural wood finish of this modern reinterpretation of a classical Chinese altar table make it the ideal display stand for a piece of contemporary sculpture.

2

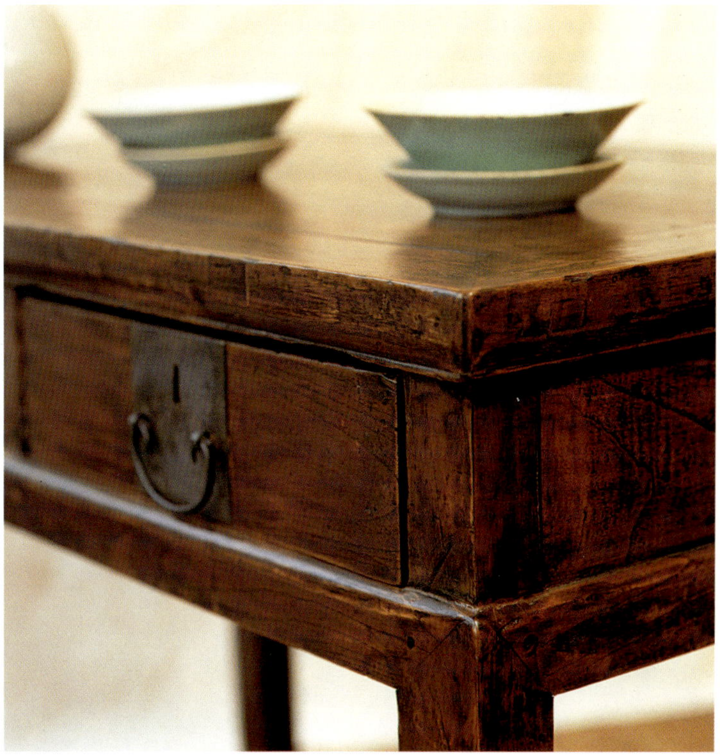

3

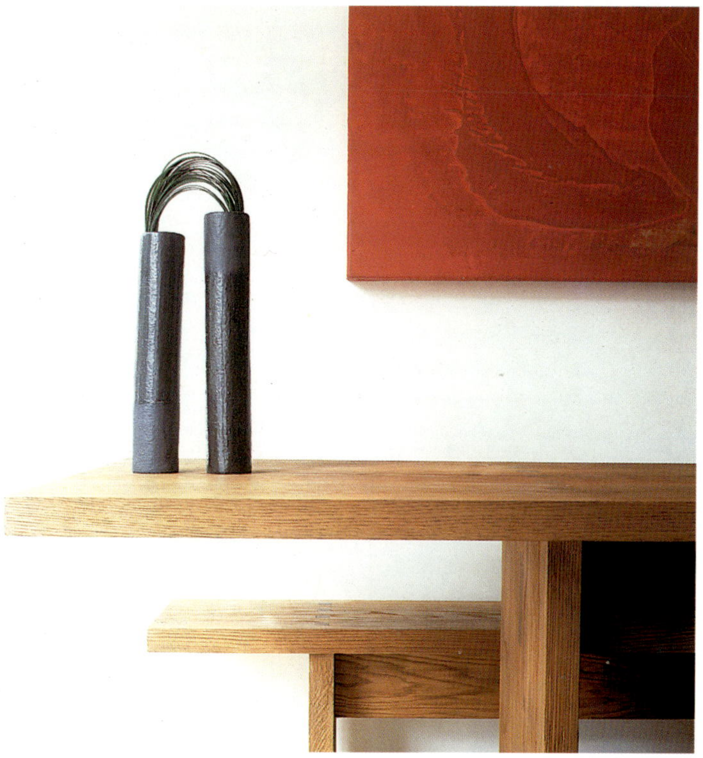

storage

In nineteenth-century Japan, domestic and shop storage was provided by *tansu* chests. These varied greatly in size, design, and finish—from plain kitchen *tansu*, used to store everyday kitchen and eating utensils, to large shop *tansu* used to keep textiles and other goods. Among the most popular with European collectors today are portable *tansu*, used by officials and mariners. These are often reinforced with metal corners to withstand the rigors of travel, and have hinged metal loops on the sides to accommodate a carrying pole. A major feature of these chests are decorative iron, brass, or silver locks, which are engraved with symbolic motifs such as cranes, turtles, pine, plum, and bamboo.

1

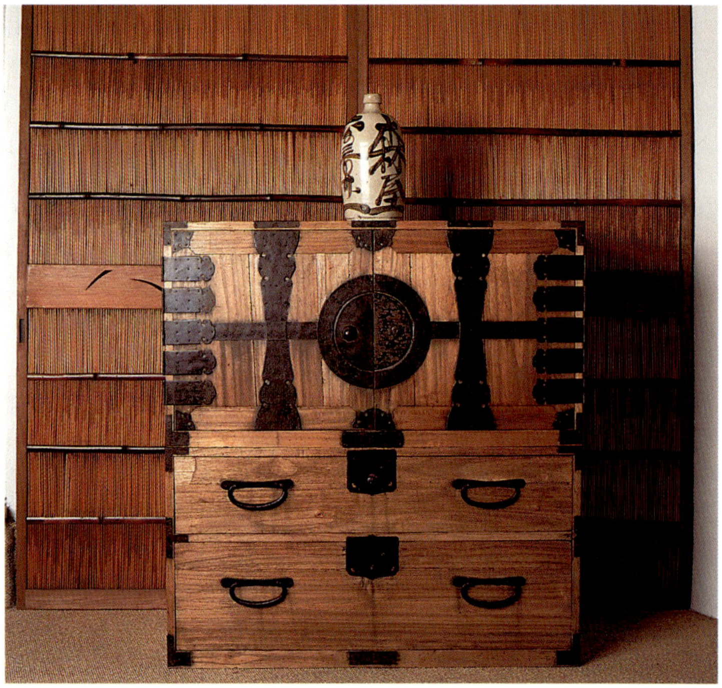

2

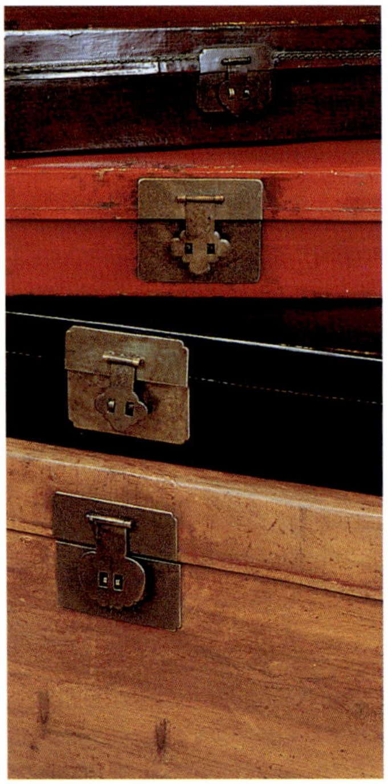

3

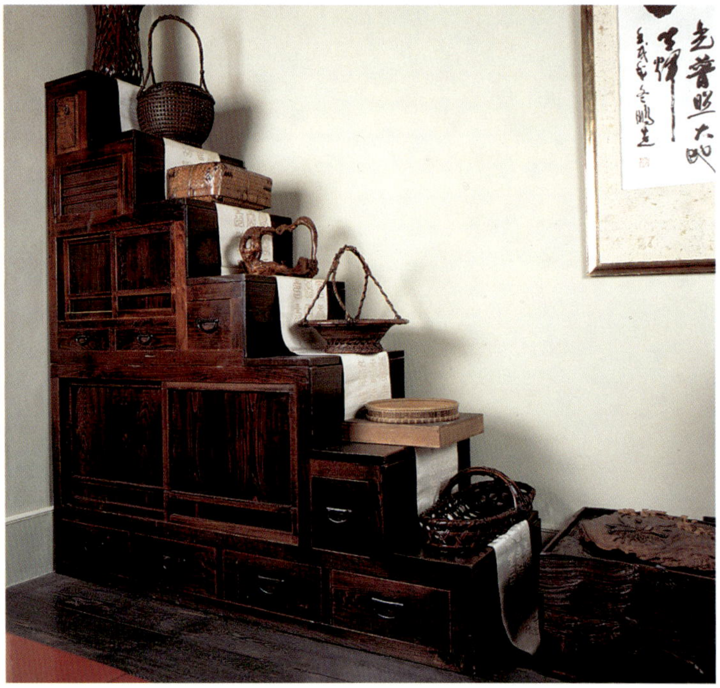

1 *Tansu* clothing chest (c. 1900), made of *kiri* (*paulownia*) and *cryptomeria* (cedar) set against a reed screen. The incised black iron metalwork is bold and graphic, in stark contrast to the wood's grain.

2 Leather suitcases and trunks were made in China after the Chinese saw the luggage of European Jesuit missionaries. The ones illustrated here are made from pigskin stretched over firwood frames.

3 A Japanese step chest, displaying baskets. A small hinged cupboard, drawers of differing widths and depths, and two cupboards with sliding doors, make this a most unusual but nonetheless practical piece of storage furniture.

4

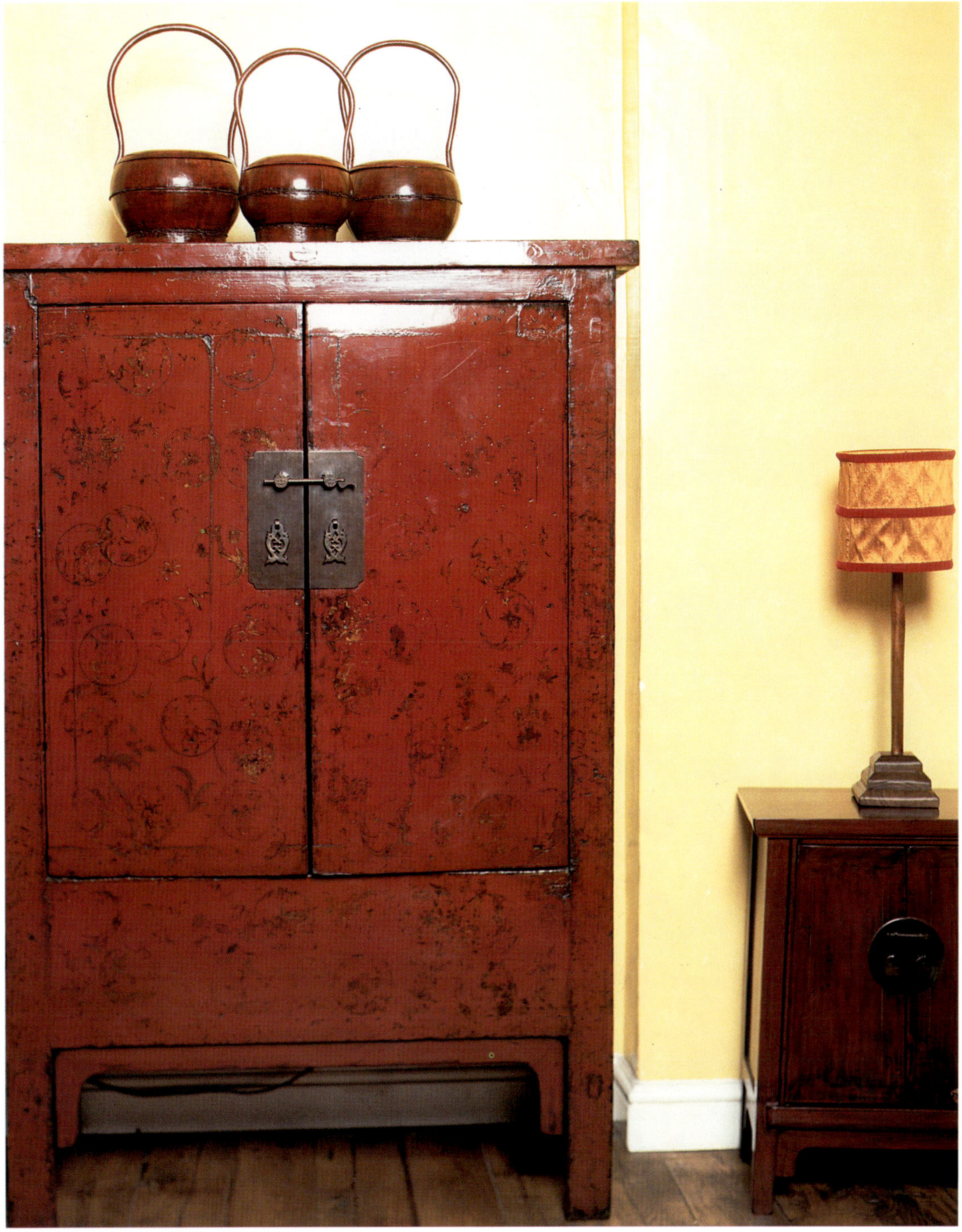

4 Red lacquer furniture adds warmth and color to a room in the coldest of climates. Red lacquer symbolizes good luck and happiness, as this eighteenth-century Shanxi dowry chest testifies. The round dried fruit carriers on top of the chest would have been used for weddings or festivals. To the right of the cabinet, the silk lampshade on a bamboo base stands on a small Ming-period cabinet.

The narrow *tokonoma* alcove is the only purpose-built display space in the traditional *shoin*-style Japanese interior. Instead of leaving several works of art in full view, as in a Western home, the Japanese hang a single painting and calligraphic scroll in the *tokonoma*, which they complement with a seasonal flower arrangement in a carefully chosen container. When they are not in use, treasured possessions, such as scrolls, vases, and teabowls are stored in exquisitely crafted and decorated containers, which are appreciated as works of art in their own right.

The care taken in the design and manufacture of storage and packaging can still be seen today in the packaging of Japanese shops and department stores, as well as the inexpensive bamboo, cane, and rice-paper storage containers and furnishings that are made for the Western market.

1

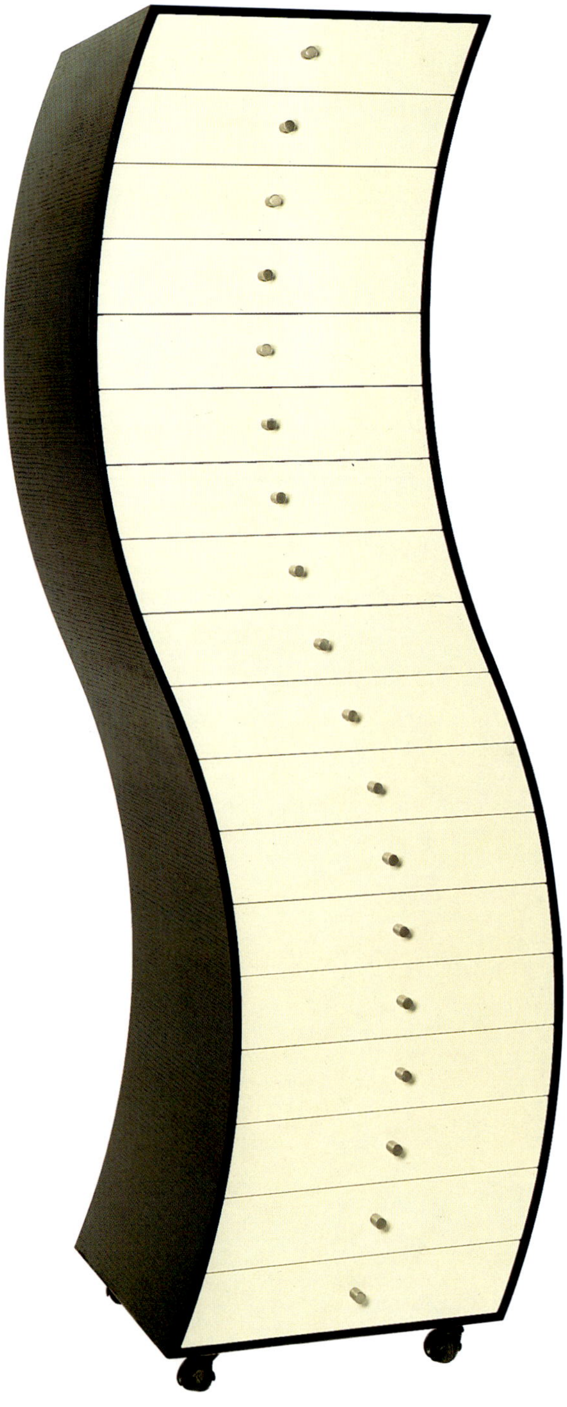

2

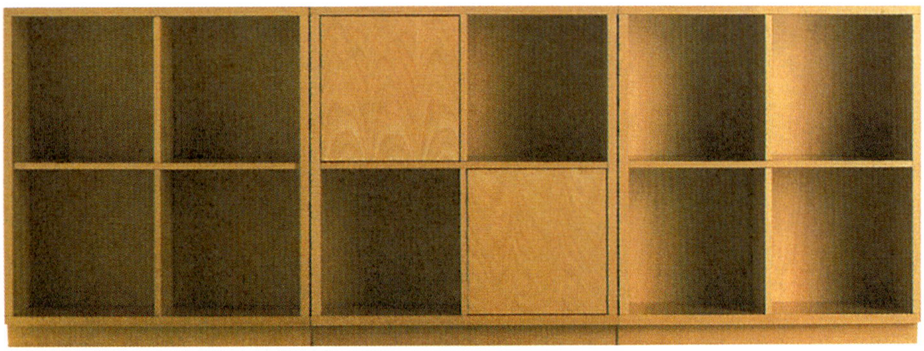

3

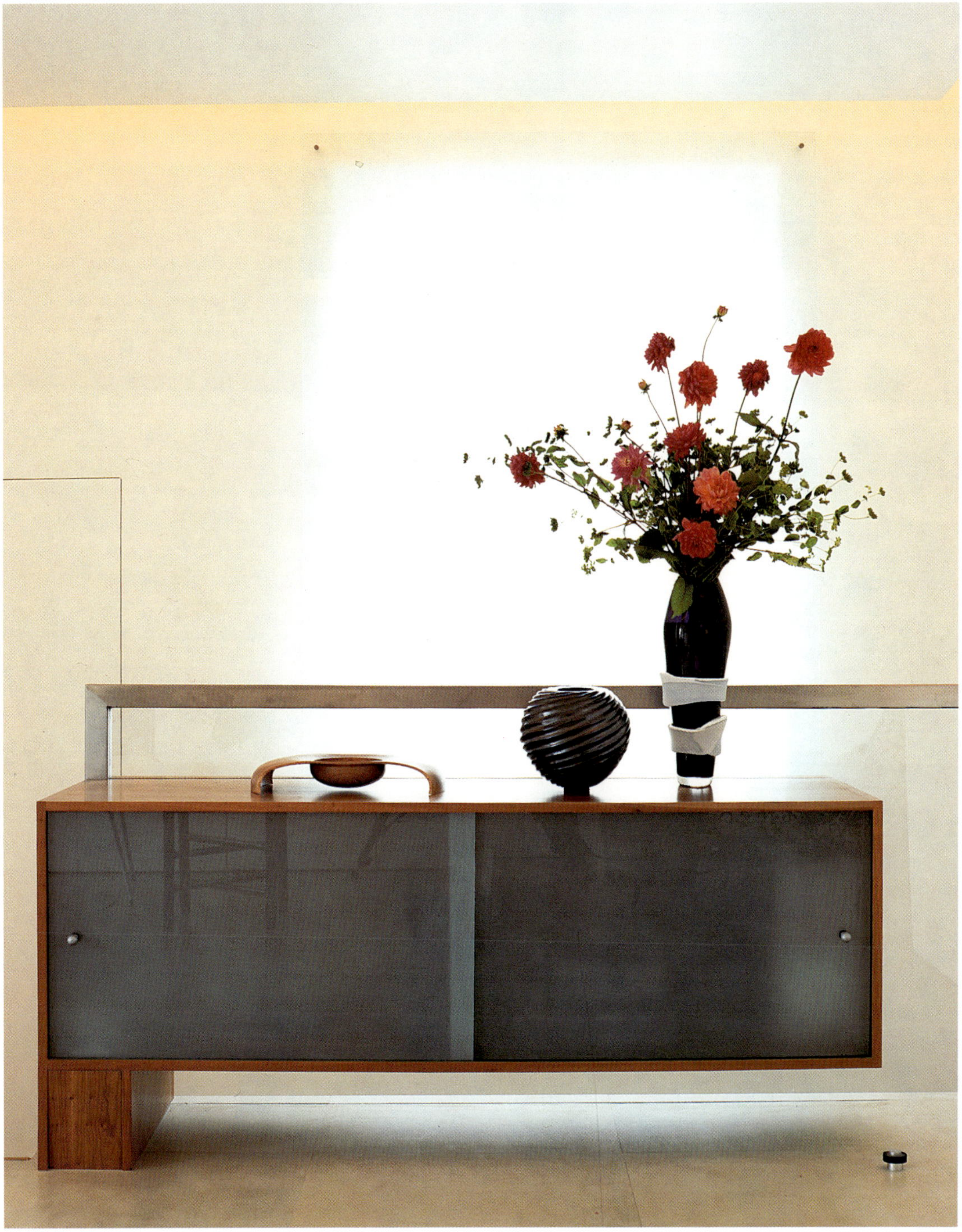

1 Designed by Shiro Kuromata and made by Cappellini in Milan during the 1980s from stained and lacquered ash veneer, this imaginative serpentine chest of drawers is one of the icons of twentieth-century furniture design.

2 A modern interpretation of Japanese storage: simple, low, cube cabinets. Adopting the same principle as the traditional sectional *tansu* chests, these cubes can also be piled up or removed as required.

3 Storage of an even more minimalist nature, this sleek low cabinet is an item of display in its own right.

bathrooms

3

In the traditional Japanese house, the only two rooms that have clearly defined functions are the kitchen and bathroom. Because of the danger of fire, kitchens are often relegated to outbuildings and are not considered to form part of the living space proper, and have stone, tiled, or beaten-earth floors, which require the use of outdoor footwear. The daily ritual of the bath, however, makes the bathroom the most important room of the house. As the water in the heated tub is shared by all the family members, bathers wash outside the tub, using a faucet and wooden hand bucket or shower attachment to rinse themselves.

1

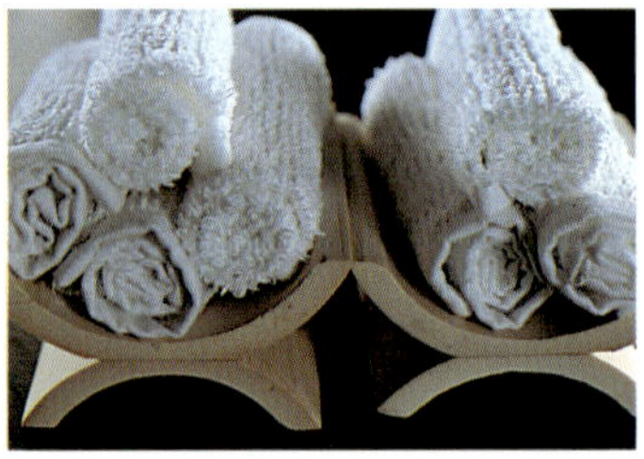

2

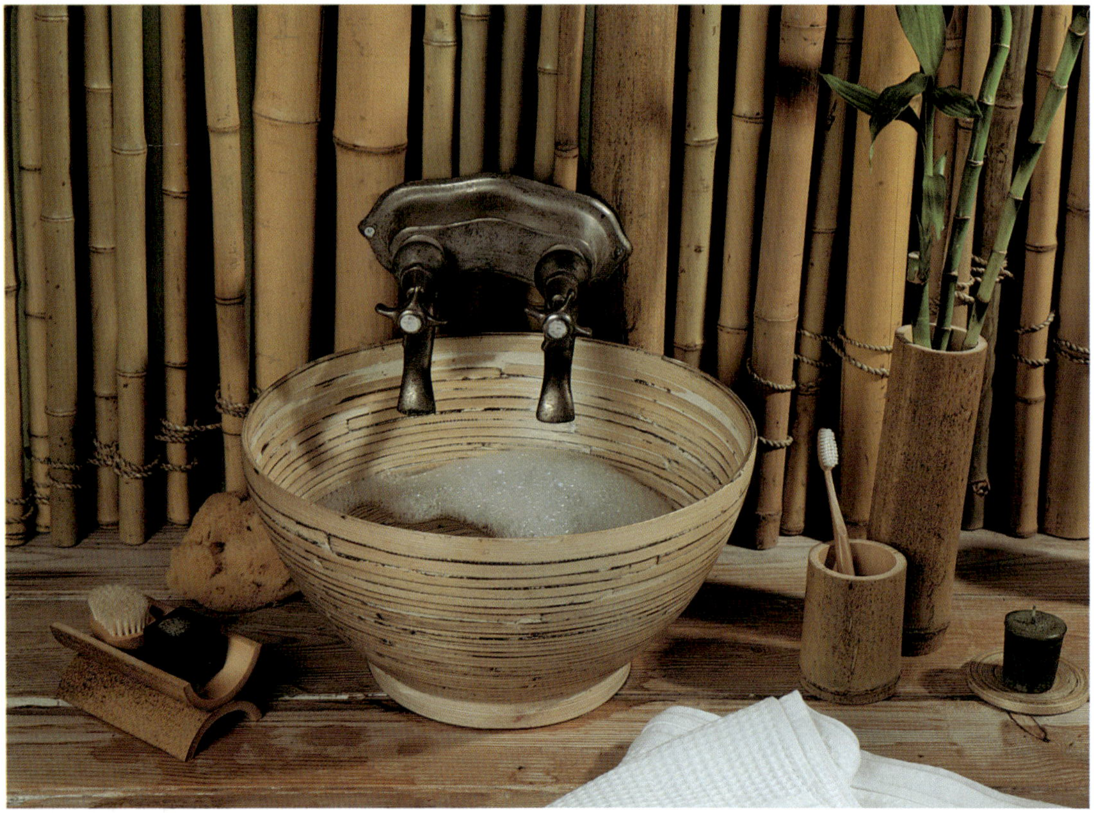

1 The use of subtle natural hues and the combination of hard and soft textures extends to the bathroom: fluffy white flannels are neatly rolled and displayed on curved bamboo stands.

2 Bamboo can be used to great effect in bathrooms, as its dense texture makes it water- and steam-proof. The basin area of this Western bathroom makes heavy use of bamboo, which is actually used more sparingly in traditional Japanese interiors.

3 Wood, usually cypress, is the choice material for a tub, and may also be used to make the slatted platform on the floor of the washing area. This modern interpretation of East Asian style also extends to a round window, but the tiled walls replace the natural walls of wood, rock, or stone that might be used to create the illusion of a hot spring.

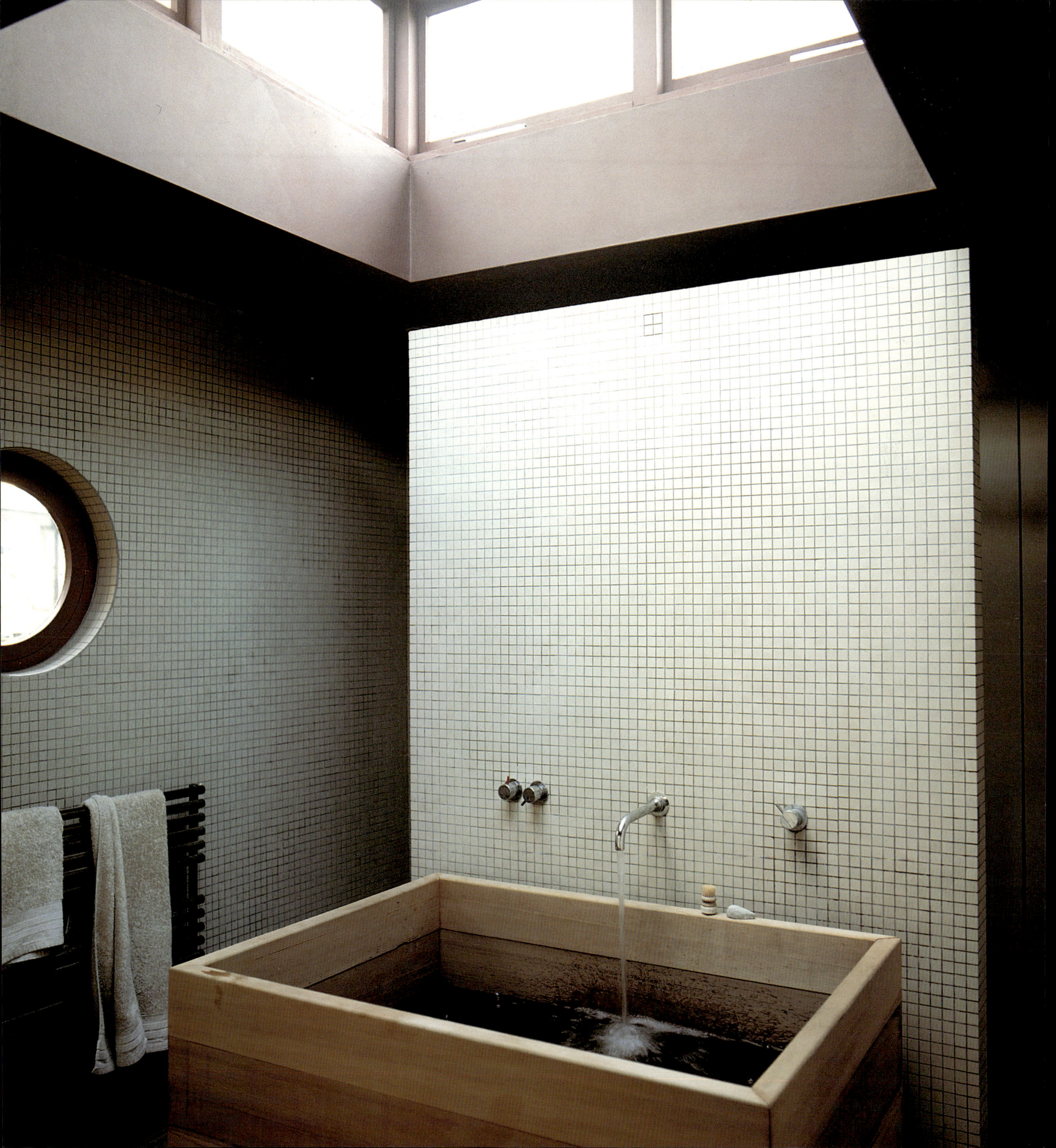

1

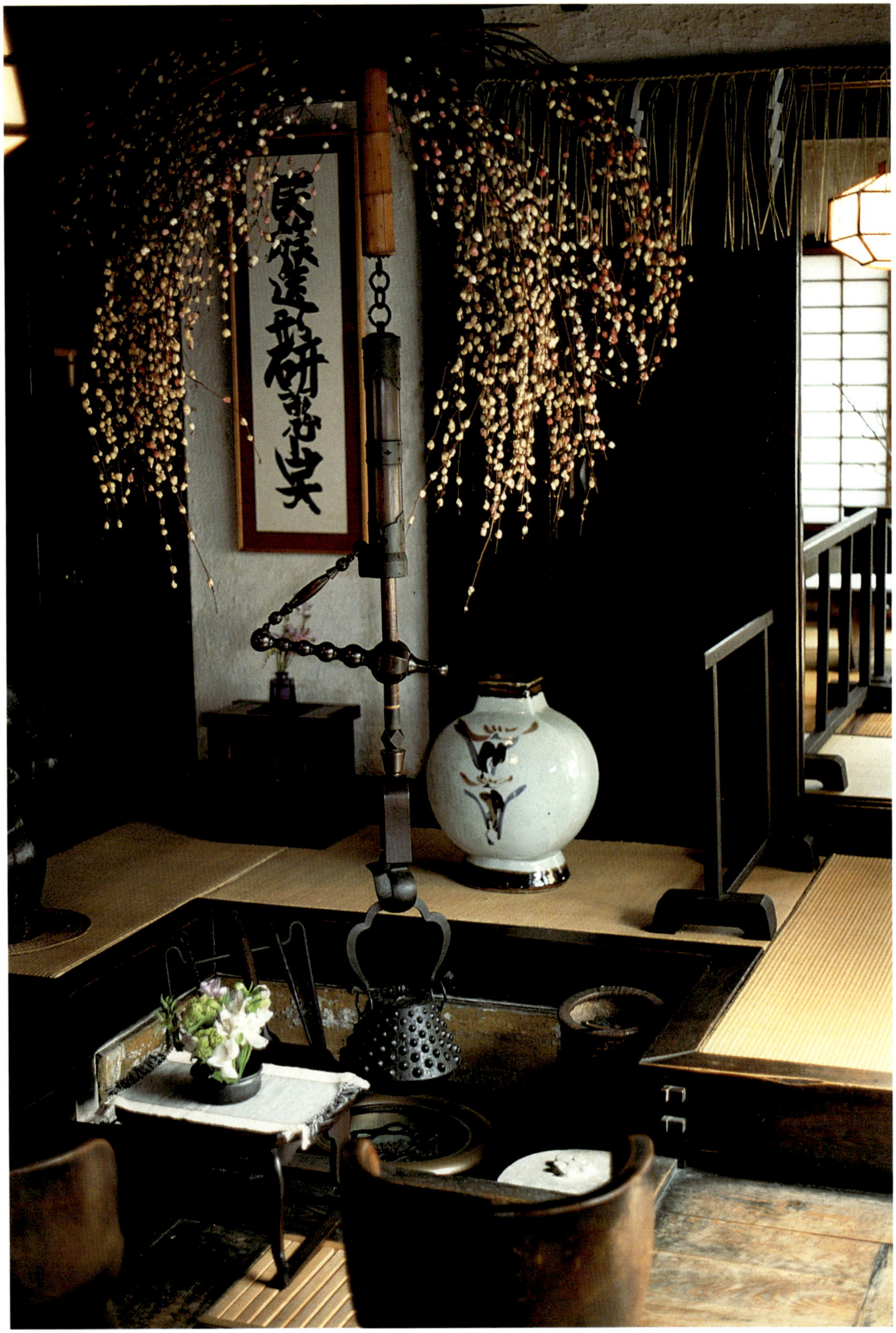

1 The tea ceremony room in Kawai Kanjiro's house in Kyoto. Kanjiro (1890–1968) was a leading potter in Japan and was, like his contemporary Shoji Hamada, an enthusiast of the *mingei* or Japanese folk art movement. He personally designed his house, fashioning it in the style of traditional rural cottages.

2 Japanese 1920s cabinet with teapot and kettle, made of *keyaki* and *kiri* wood. This cabinet would contain all the necessary tea accoutrements, such as teabowls, fresh water pots, waste water pots, tea jars, and tea containers.

3 Contemporary china, consisting of *sake*, rice, and noodle bowls in addition to tea bowls, and a tea jar on display in a slatted wooden cabinet, the natural and the neutral perfectly complementing each other.

tea ceremony

The ritualized drinking of tea was introduced to Japan in the twelfth century by Zen Buddhist monks returning from China. The tea ceremony was quickly adopted by Japanese religious and court circles. In the sixteenth century, tea master Sen no Rikyu (1522–91) transformed the ceremony, and founded one of Japan's most important tea lineages, the *urasenke* school. In this form of the ceremony, which is the most familiar to Westerners, guests dressed in kimonos take tea and a light meal in a small purpose-built teahouse, erected in its own garden. All the items used are selected for their beauty and rarity. The purpose of the ceremony is not the drinking of the bitter, frothy green tea, but the appreciation of the experience and the environment on the aesthetic level.

2

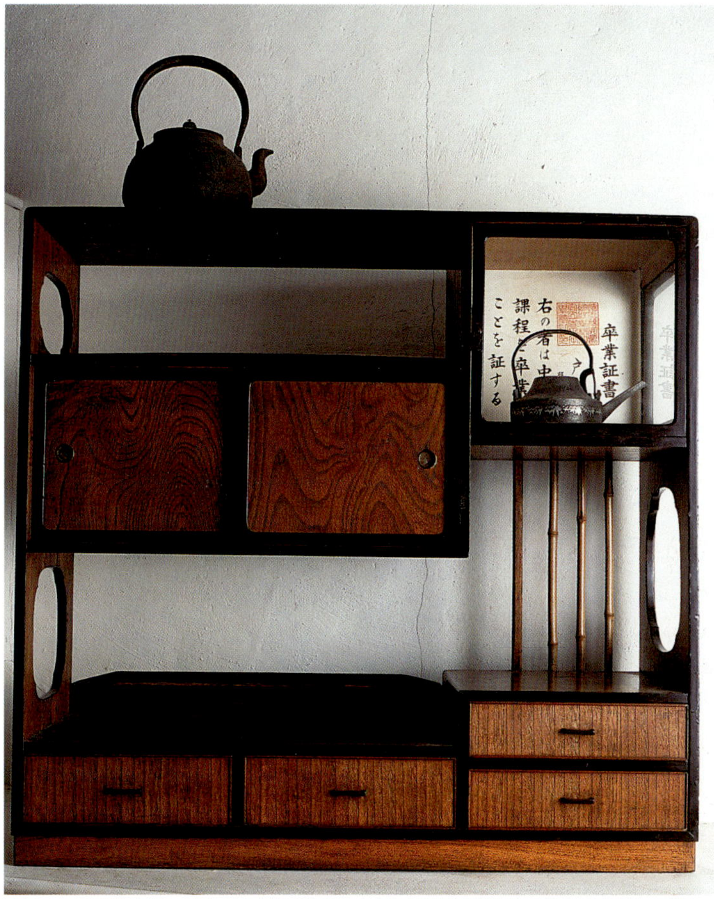

3

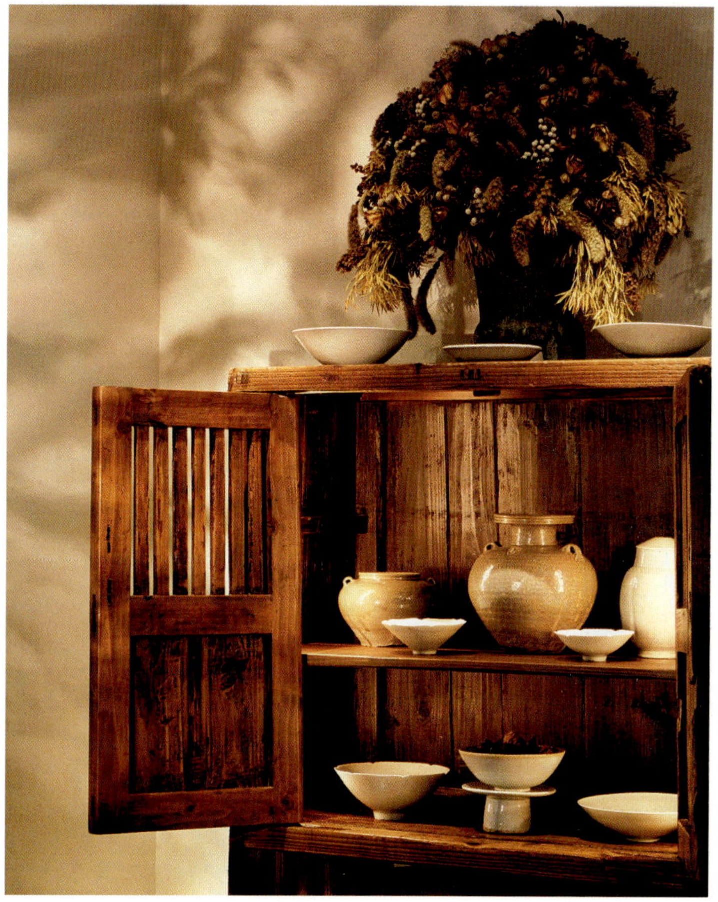

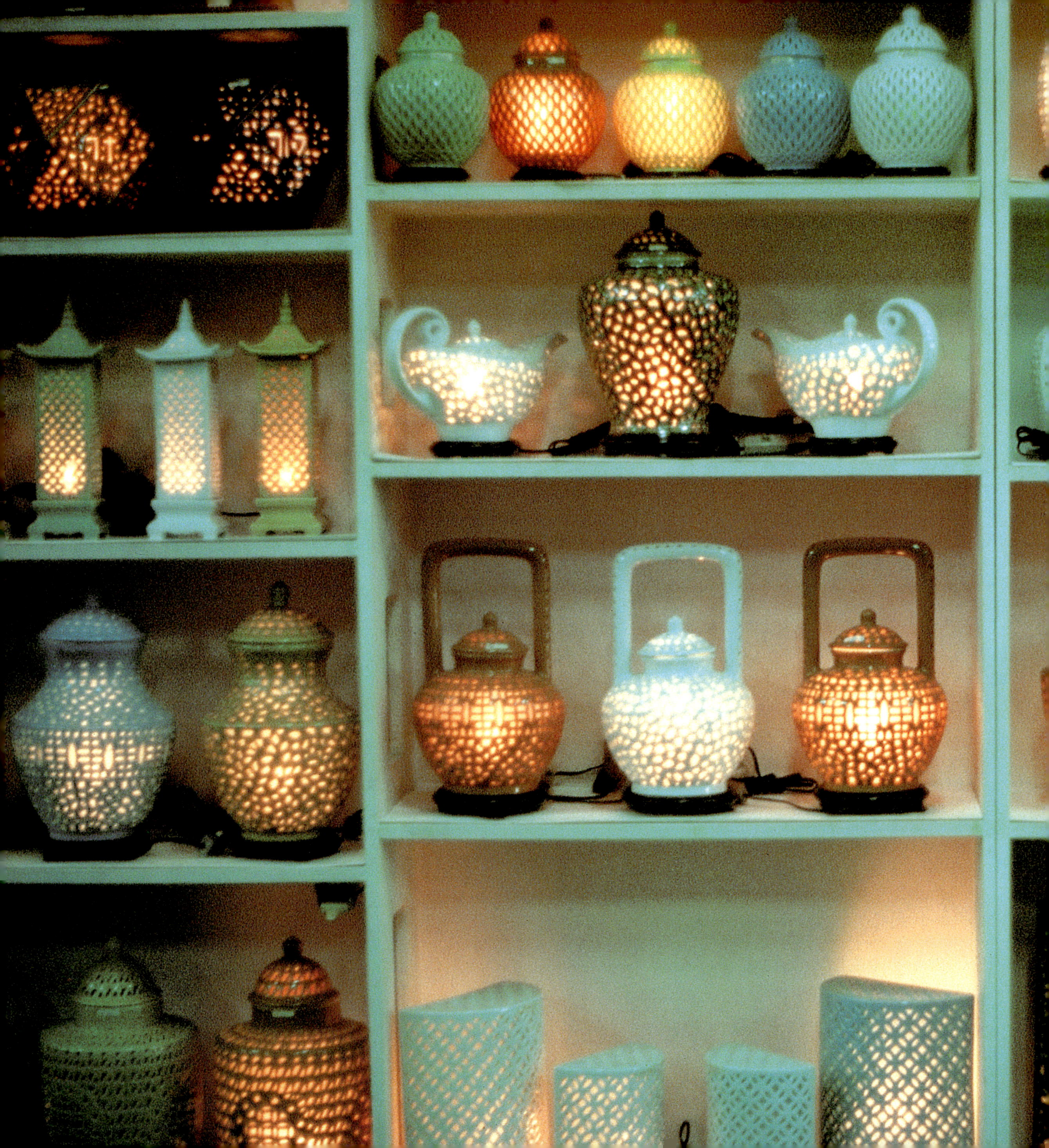

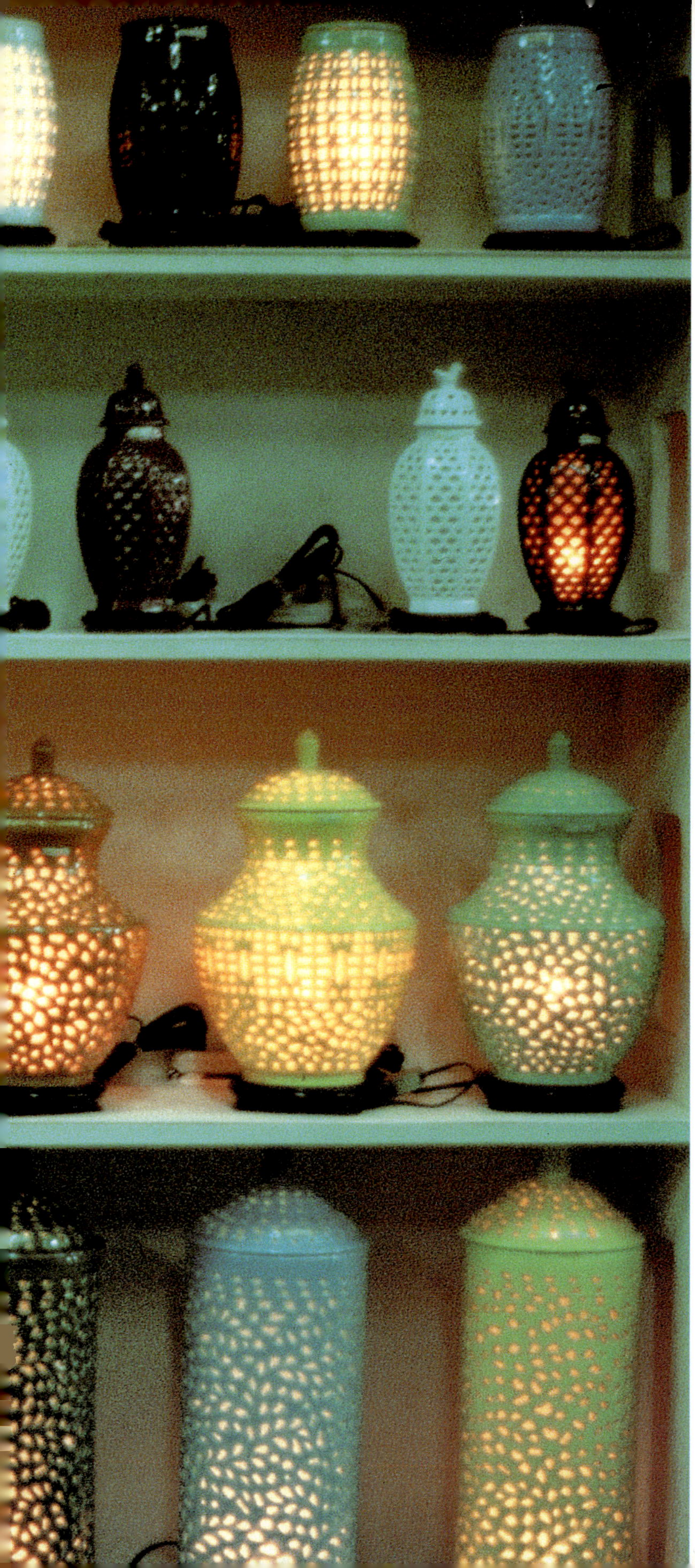

lighting

Lighting is recognized as one of the essential elements of contemporary interior design. Subtle variations and combinations of lighting can dramatically alter the appearance and atmosphere of a room. Recent trends in the West for diffuse, non-directional lighting effects are in tune with the East Asian use of paper and bamboo. Lamps made in East Asia, or modeled on classical Japanese and Chinese models, are now found in design shops all over the Western world.

Chinese and Japanese light fittings employ similar materials and techniques, but there are important differences in execution and decoration. In keeping with the tonal restraint of traditional interiors, Japanese paper lanterns tend to be plain and unadorned, although Chinese characters painted in black ink are sometimes used; free-standing lamps are square or rectangular wood or lacquer frames, covered in rice paper. In contrast, Chinese lanterns are more highly decorated, with animal, symbolic, and floral motifs in vibrant colors. Lanterns are also made in the shapes of dragons, lions, and auspicious animals.

A display of ceramic lamps in the form of pagodas, teapots, and classical Chinese perforated shapes in pale and darker celadon green, white, turquoise, and black create a magic-lantern effect in a Japanese shop.

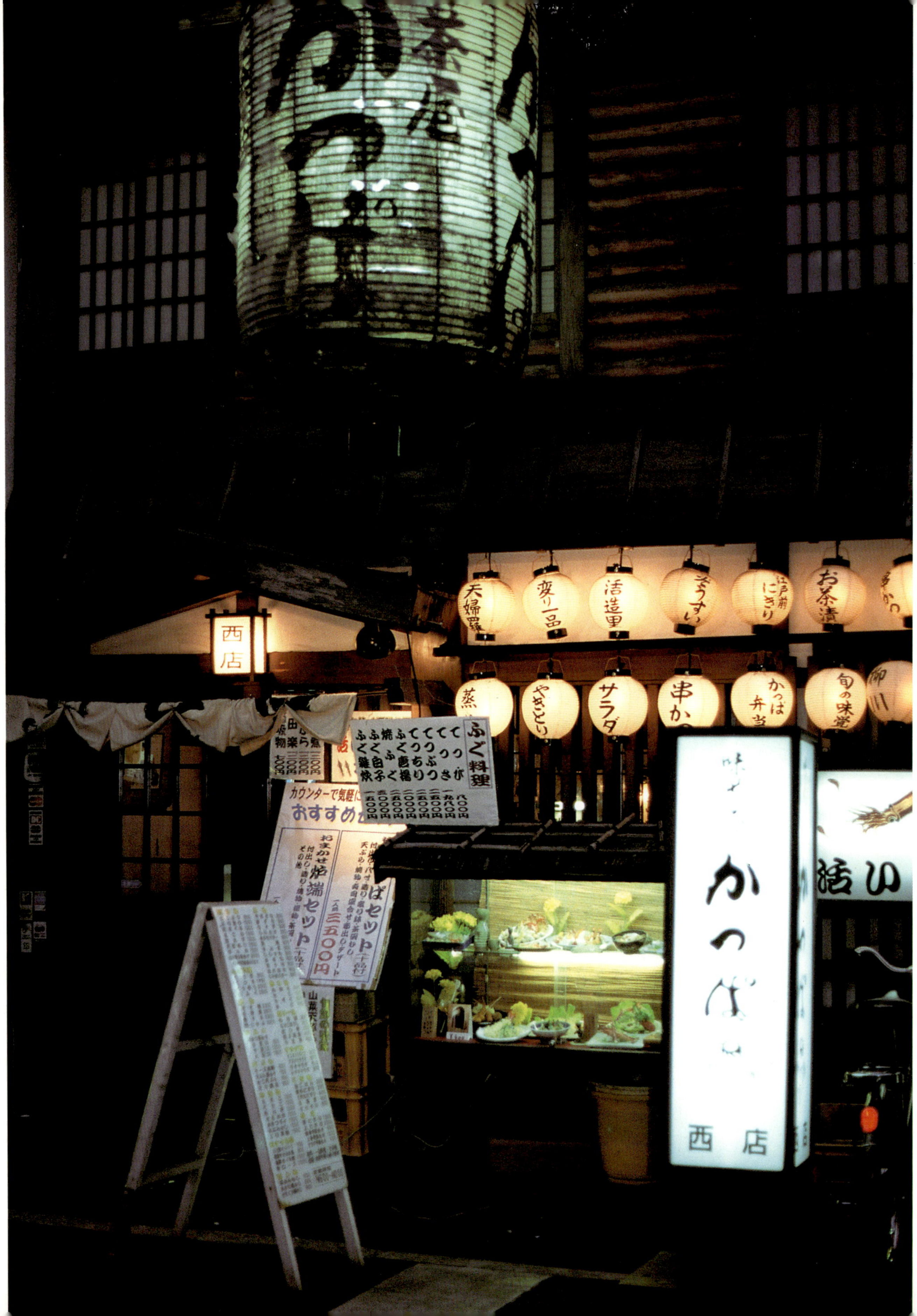
西店
天婦羅
変り一品
活造里
ぞうすい
江戸前 にぎり
お茶漬
やきとり
サラダ
かっぱ 弁当
旬の味覚
ふぐ料理
カウンターで気軽に
おすすめ
炉端セット
かっぱ
西店

1

Traditional lantern styles, which originated in China or Japan, are now made all over Asia, but the basic design remains the same. Popular in the West are the circular globes, made in a variety of colors and sizes, often with exotic tassel pendants, that can be hung from ceiling roses. Floor lamps are made in triangular, concertina, serpentine, and sail shapes, mounted on metal bases. Smaller versions are sold in the West as free-standing table and bedside lamps.

The Chinese display large red balloon-shaped lanterns during festivals, and smaller lanterns decorate Chinese businesses worldwide. In Japan, small *chochin* lanterns, made of thin bamboo cane wound into a spiral and covered in paper, are hung in front of shops and restaurants.

2

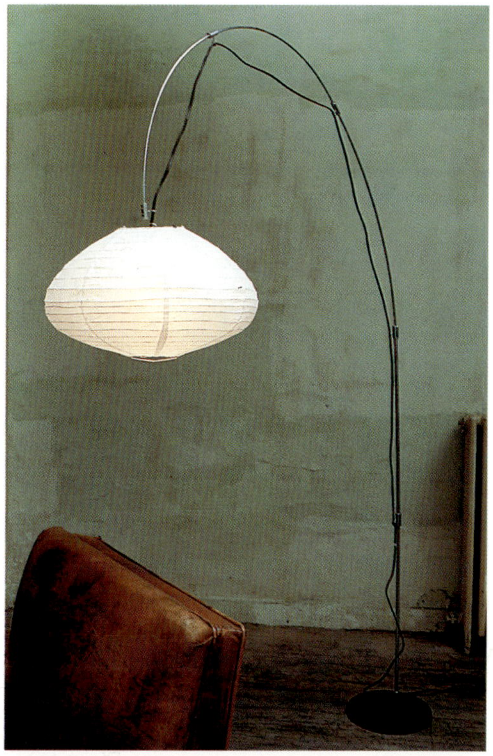

3

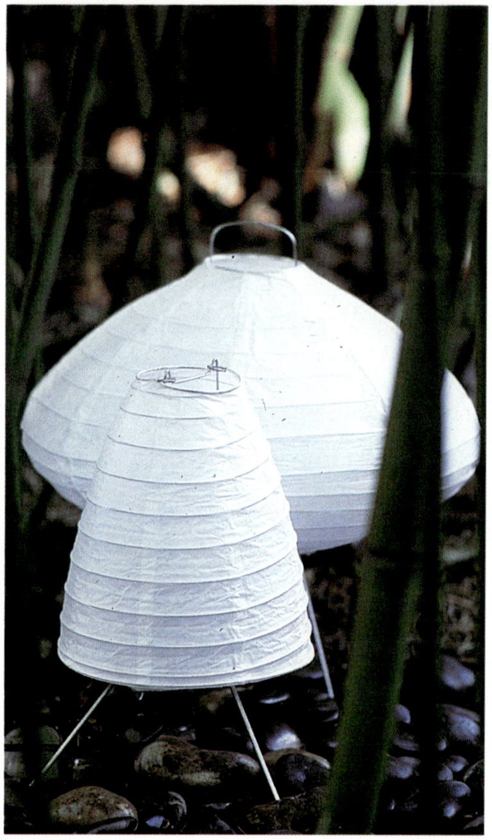

1 Decorative paper lanterns in a Japanese restaurant contrast with the oblong free-standing lamp and the square hanging lantern. The juxtaposition of bright white light and black calligraphy creates a highly dramatic effect.

2 A free-standing modern interpretation of a standard lamp: the overhead light makes it useful for reading, yet it is sufficiently diffuse so as not to be intrusive. This wire-framed paper lantern creates a sculptural shape not unlike a single flower in a vase.

3 Triangular and globular paper lamps, supported by tripod legs. These two lamps are variations on the themes pioneered by Japanese lighting designer Isamu Noguchi.

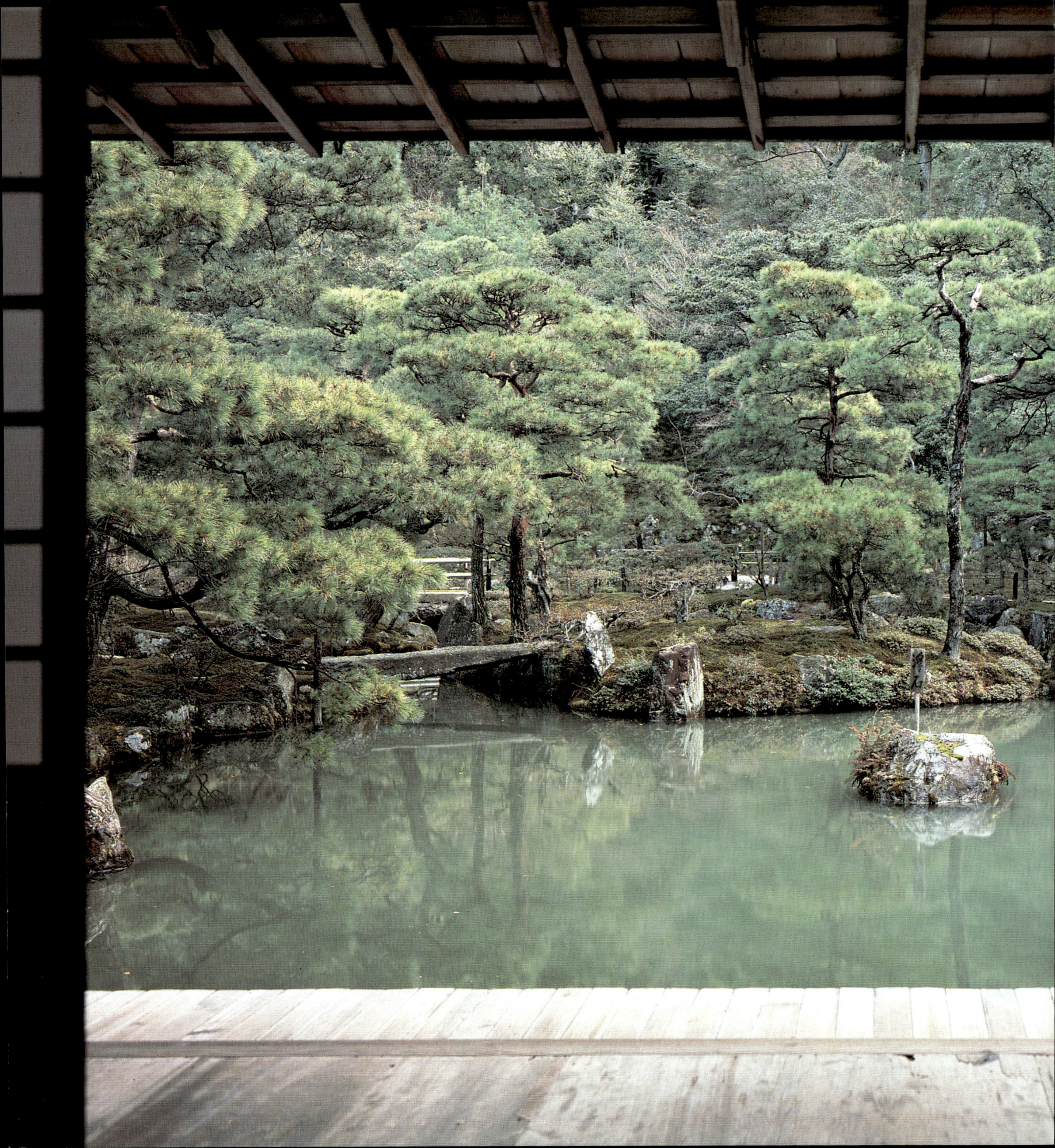

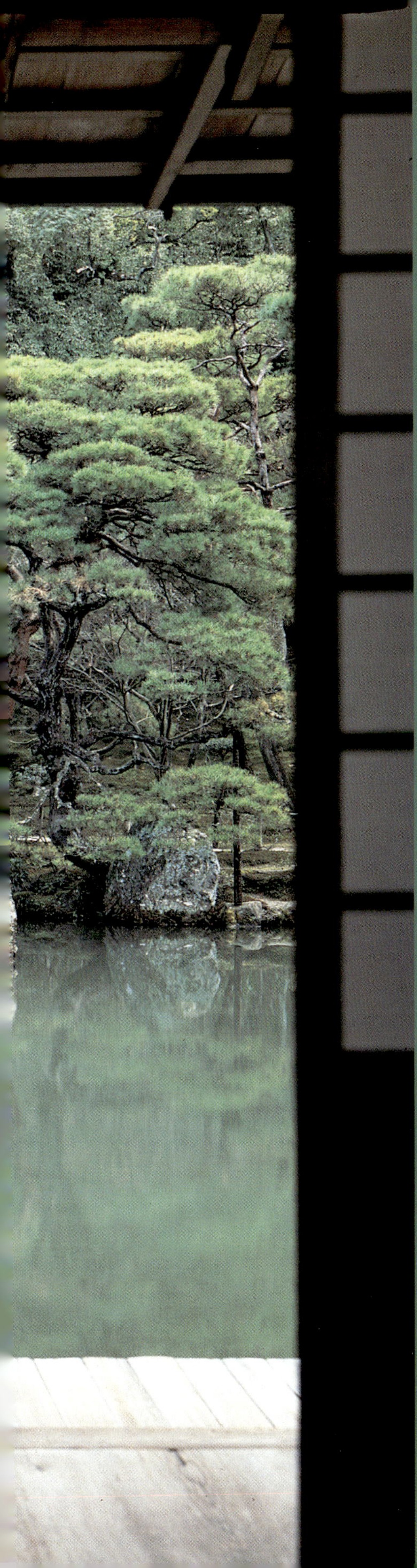

gardens

The gardens of East Asia have a strong spiritual dimension. In both China and Japan, combinations of plants, rockwork, and water transcend the purely simple functions of decoration, display, and recreation, to include symbolic representations of religious concepts. Many of China's classic imperial gardens have been lost through neglect or acts of political vandalism, but a few have survived and are now being restored.

In the twentieth century, the greatest influence on Western garden design has been the gardens of Japan, now familiar for their perfect arrangements of stones and mosses, their pines, and tranquil waters. Chinese ideas about garden design were introduced to Japan as part of the adoption of mainland culture by the Japanese during the late fifth and sixth centuries. Early styles included the "Pure Land," which were earthly representations of the Western Paradise of the Buddha Amida and representations of the Taoist paradise. A central element of these gardens was a stone representing Mount Meru, the sacred mountain believed by Buddhists to be at the center of the universe.

Gardens are designed to bring nature indoors while simultaneously extending the interior into nature, and sliding doors in Japanese houses often open onto a particularly pleasing garden view.

1

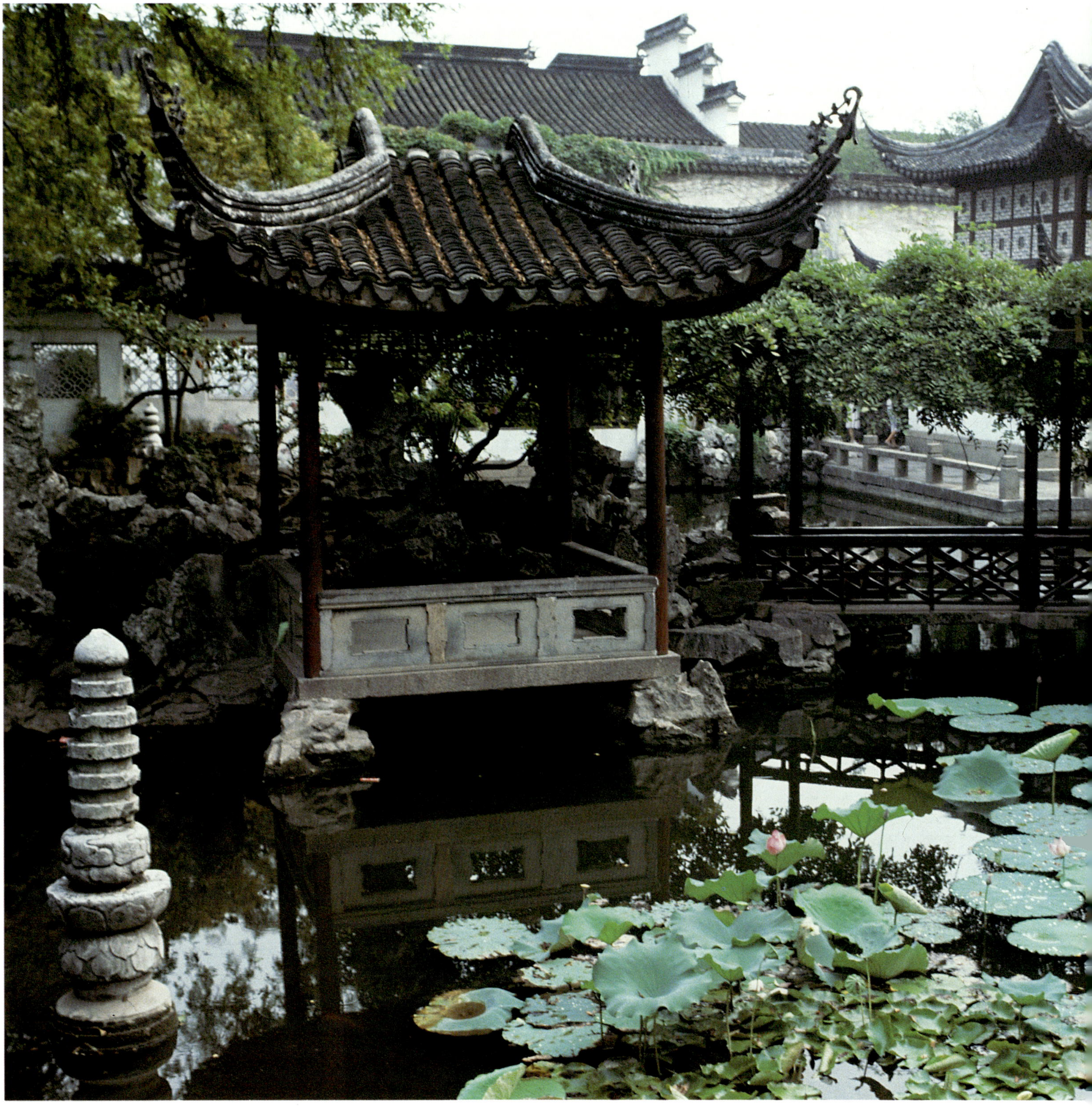

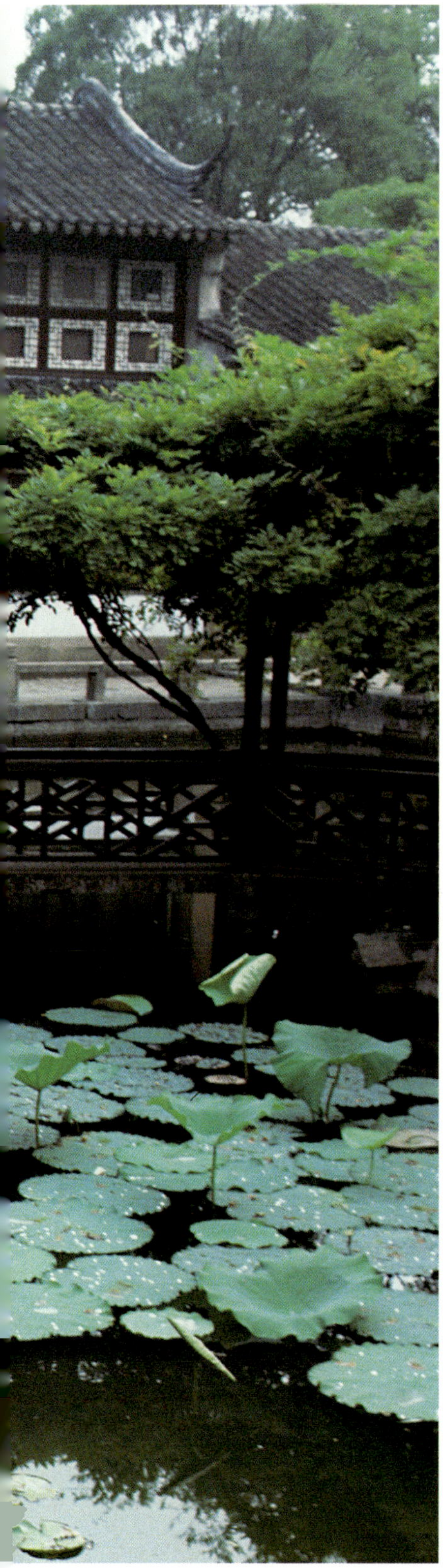

old chinese gardens

2

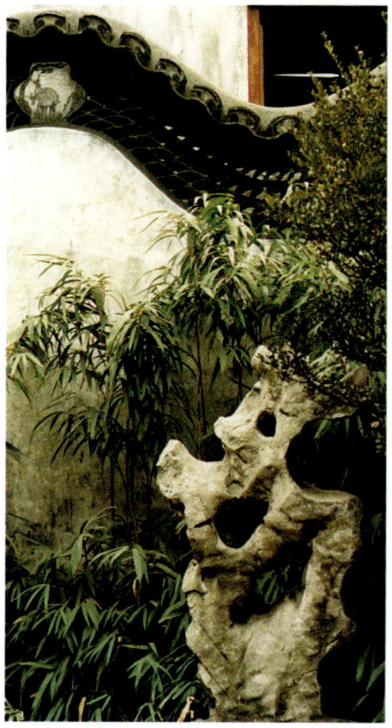

Chinese gardens are cosmological diagrams that represent the universe and reveal man's place within the Taoist world view. The Chinese term for landscape, *shan shui*, literally means mountains and water—a combination that evokes the Isles of the Immortals, and also suggests the opposition of elemental forces, such as in *yin* and *yang.* The classical gardens of China were also frequented by poets and painters, who met and worked in their tranquil surroundings.

Only a few of the ancient gardens of China have survived. But in their heyday, in the seventeenth and eighteenth centuries, when the first descriptions of Chinese landscape gardens were sent to the West by Jesuit missionaries, they inspired a revolution in garden design.

3

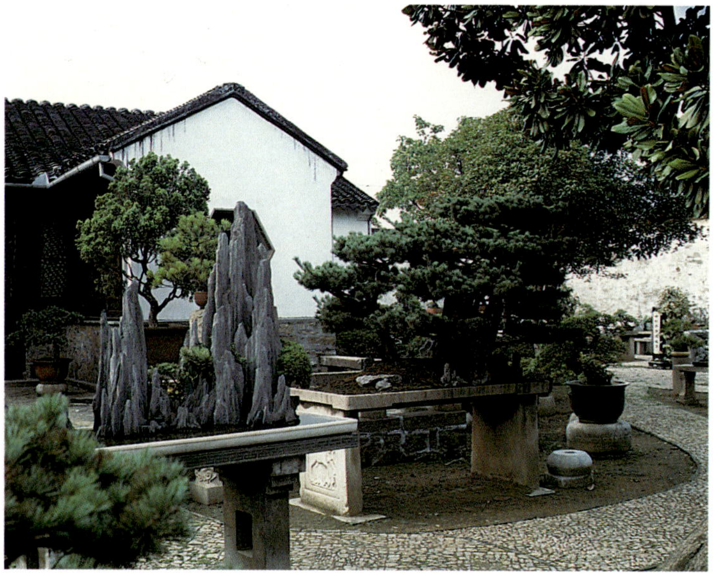

1 Part of the *Liu Yuan,* or "Garden for Lingering," one of the the largest of the gardens at Suzhou. Among ten acres of garden arranged in four main sections, bridges link decorative pavilions over a winding lotus lake.

2 The *Yo Yuan* or "Garden to Please" in Shanghai, created in the sixteenth century. The extraordinary craggy rocks, sculptural in form, are modeled by the action of water grinding pebbles into the stone.

3 These stones at Suzhou represent the five holy mountains.

stone

The dry stone gardens attached to Zen Buddhist temples are the physical expression of the ascetic, transcendent Zen world view. There are three main types of stone gardens: the first, known as *shumizen*, is a symbolic representation of the universe, in which the sun, moon, and planets circle a stone representing the holy Buddhist mountain; the second is the rockwork surrounding a Buddhist image; and the third symbolizes the stages of Zen enlightenment. The followers of Japanese Shinto believe that the gods, or *kami,* are present in all kinds of natural phenomena. *Kami* are said to reside in high places, such as mountains, and are called down to Earth to share in special rituals held in shrines built around sacred stones, trees, or natural springs. This act of communion with the natural world gives believers a direct connection with the larger environment. By honoring natural elements such as stones, which symbolize the many facets of nature, the whole of creation is honored.

1 The famous stone garden at Ryoan-ji in Kyoto was designed in the early seventeenth century. The *shumizen* rockwork symbolizes the Buddhist cosmos, representing the nine mountains and eight seas ruled by the Buddha. The stones are arranged in groups, creating a visual *koan,* or Zen riddle.

2 Stones are symbols of harmony and respect for the natural world. They are used in gardens for their spiritual properties. Their placement is more important than the positioning of plants, assuming a role that we would associate with statuary in a Western garden.

2

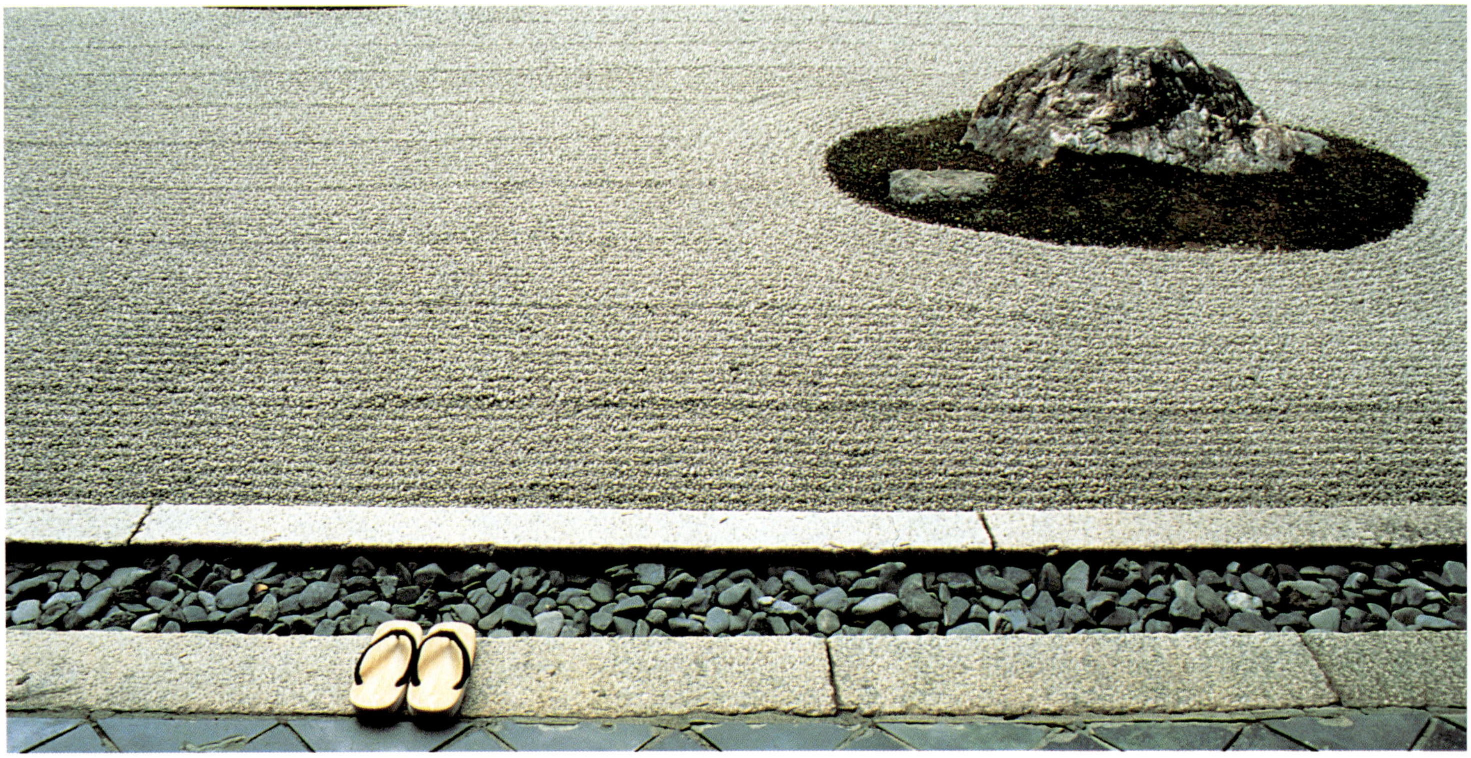

1

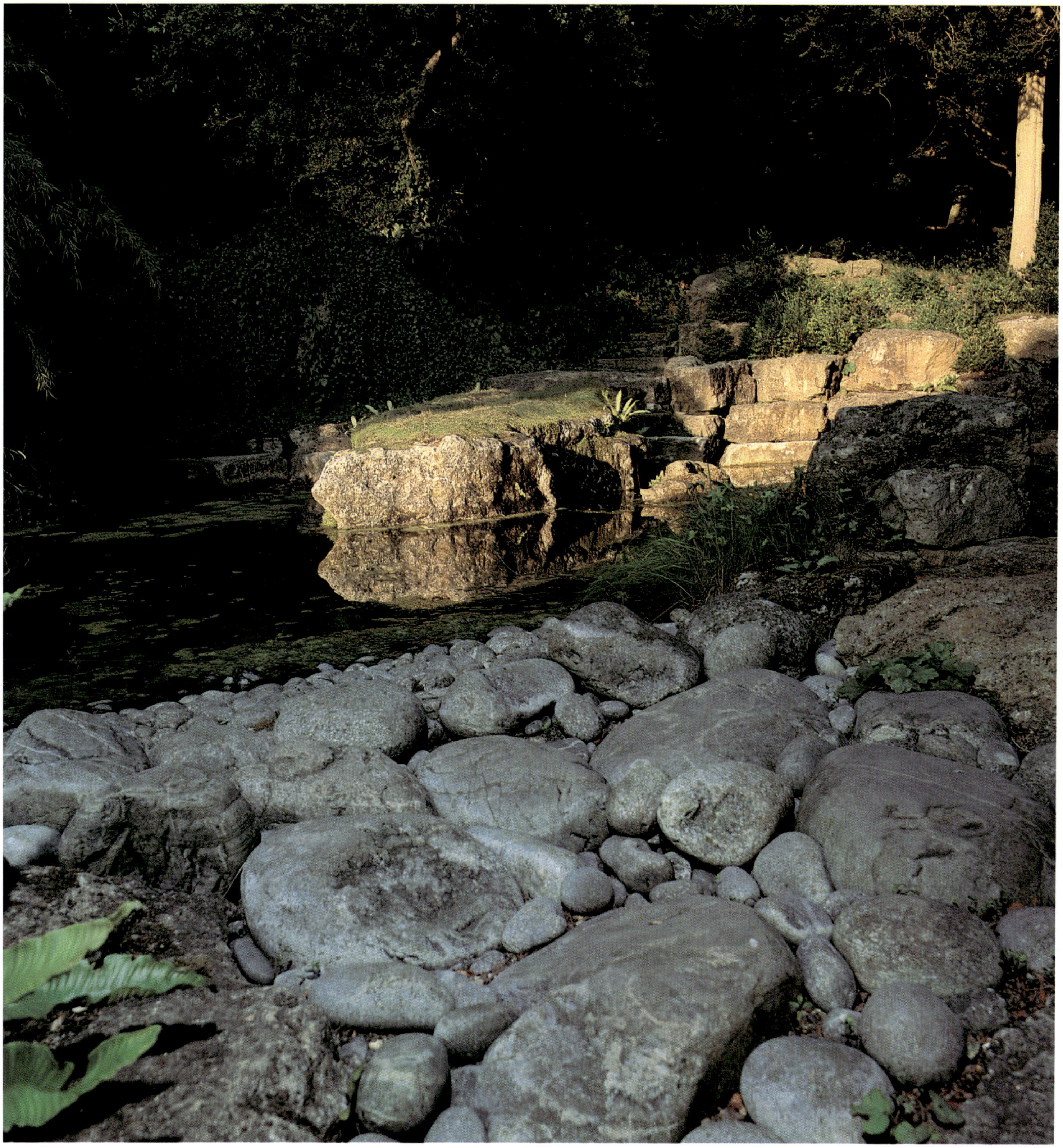

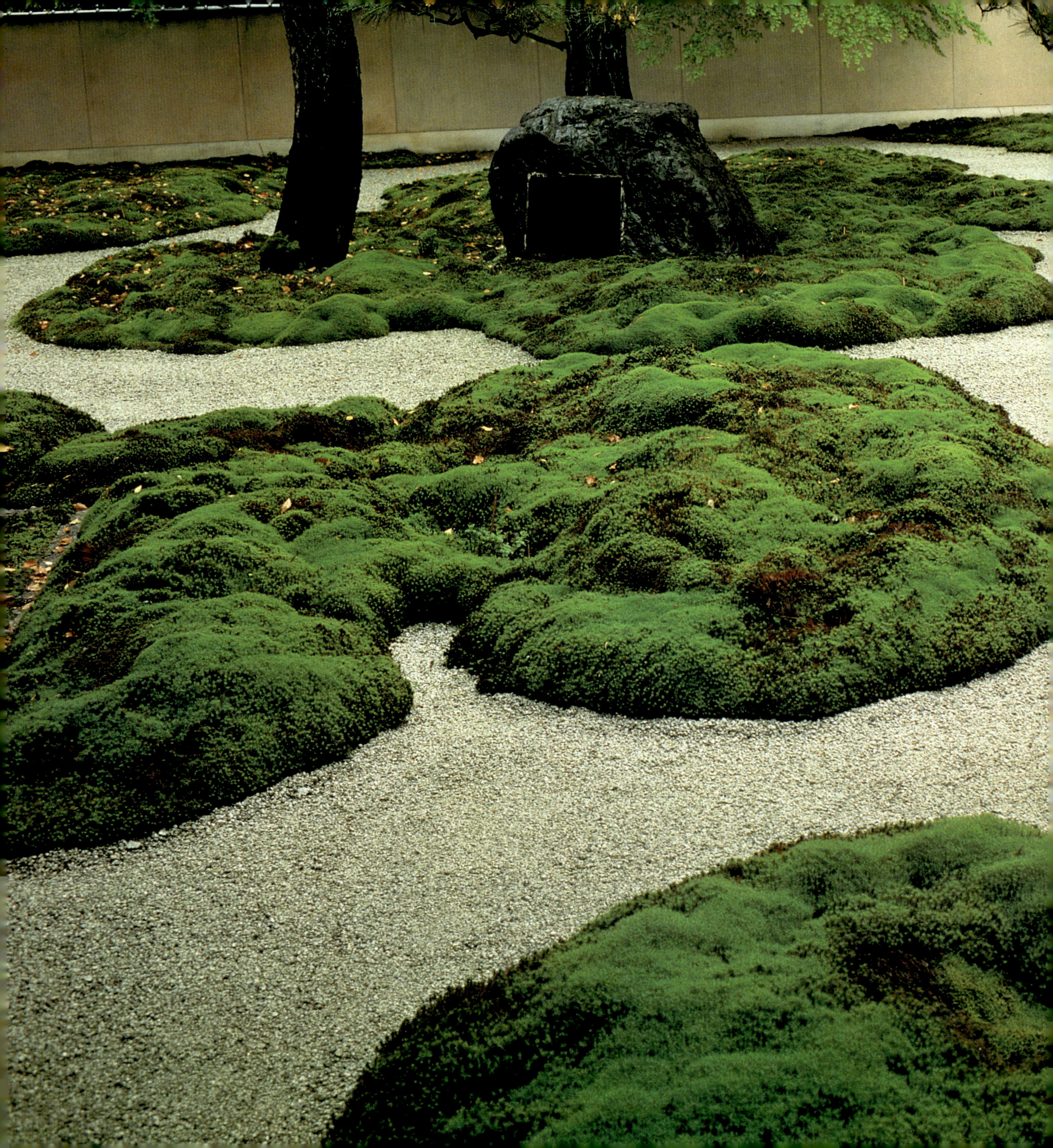

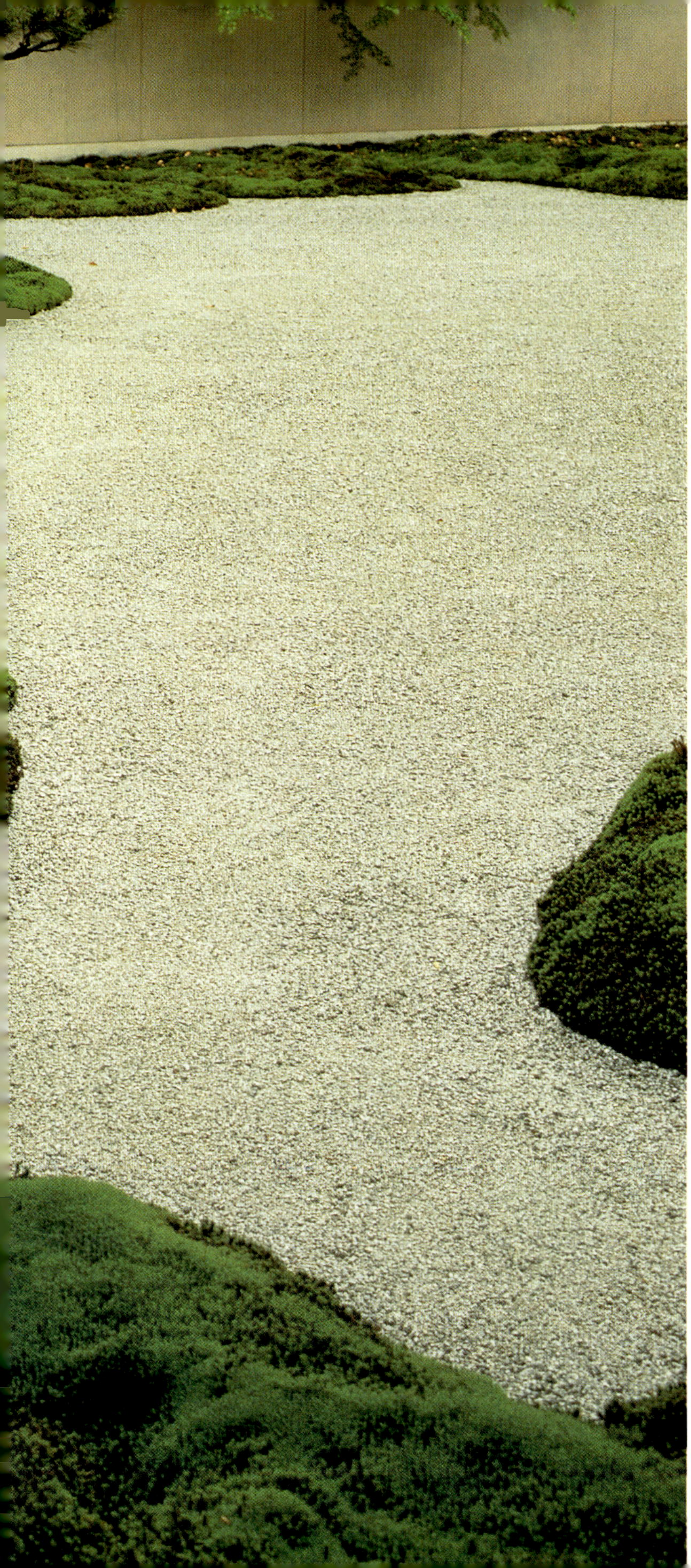

moss

While in many areas of the world, moss is seen as a pest to be rooted out or controlled by fungicides, in Japan, this humble plant is given pride of place in moss gardens. In dry stone gardens, mosses are often used to break up areas of gravel, sand, or stones, and to create visual interest. The damp, humid climate of Kyoto in western Japan is ideal for mosses, which need little encouragement to cover wide expanses of ground. *Sugikoke* (*polytrichum juniperninum*) is grown for its velvety texture, and it is so abundant at Saiho-ji in Kyoto, that this Buddhist temple is also known as the "Moss Temple."

Mosses prefer shady, damp places, and grow well even in areas heavily shaded by evergreen trees, creating lush, soft carpets. Their water-retentive qualities help to preserve the soil, but they need constant watering. As moss requires untreated water, gardeners have sunk wells especially to water their moss gardens. Japan's most famous moss garden at Tofuku-ji in Kyoto, designed by Shigemori Mirei in 1939, has granite slabs inset into cushions of bright green springy moss. The spacing between the slabs is deliberately irregular—in linc with thc Japanese ideals of asymmetry in design.

The softness and striking green color of the islands of moss in a traditional Japanese moss garden create a strong graphic contrast to the sea of neutral gravel and carefully placed granite rocks.

water

The Japanese garden has evolved from the hill and pond gardens depicted in early Heian-period (794–1185) scroll-paintings into spacious and elaborate landscaped parks designed for strolling and recreation. The basic elements, however—stone, water, and plants—have remained the same.

Providing much-needed refreshment during the hot, humid Japanese summer, water is instrumental in creating the atmosphere of the garden. Although it is a fast, free-flowing element, water's calming qualities encourage contemplation and meditation. Still and deep in tree-lined ponds and lakes or combined with rocks in a waterfall, it creates dramatic effects of light, motion, and sound.

1

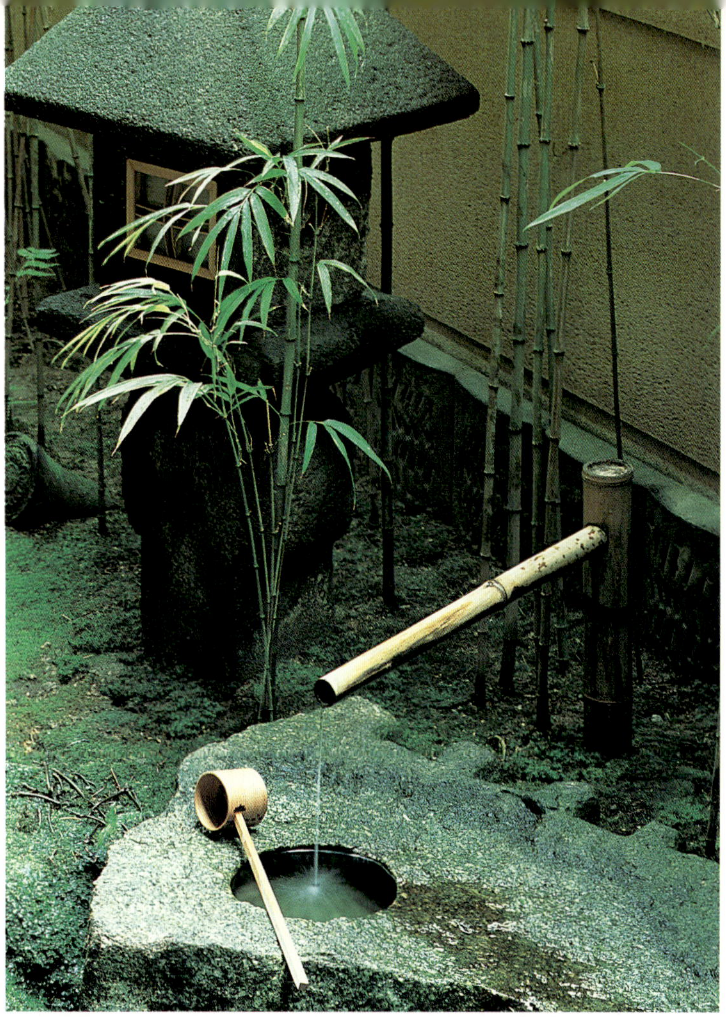

2

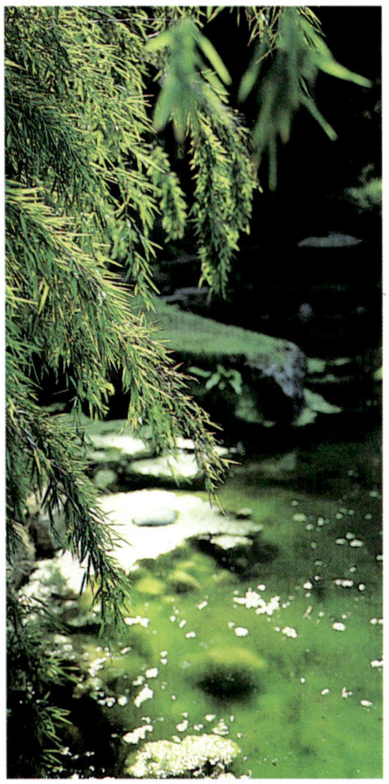

3

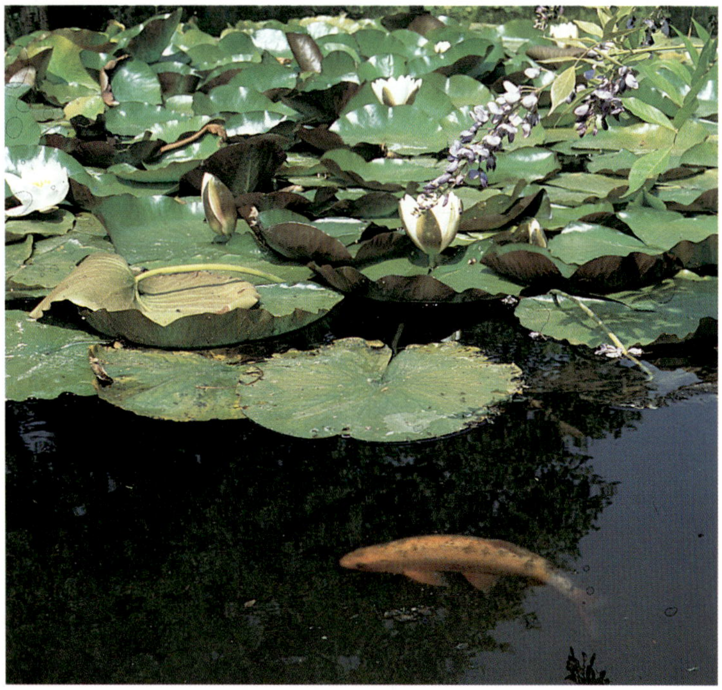

1 Water is an important feature of the Japanese garden, providing sound, motion, and fluidity. If a garden is too small for a pond, a small bamboo or stone fountain can create water sounds and effects.

2 Bamboo grows abundantly beside the water's edge, and a stone lantern's feet are firmly planted in the water.

3 In a scene reminiscent of a Japanese woodblock print, koi carp laze in the sunlight in a pond fringed with waterlilies.

4 In the grounds of this modern spa hotel built around natural hot springs in the foothills of Mount Fuji, Japan, rocks are carefully landscaped around a pool.

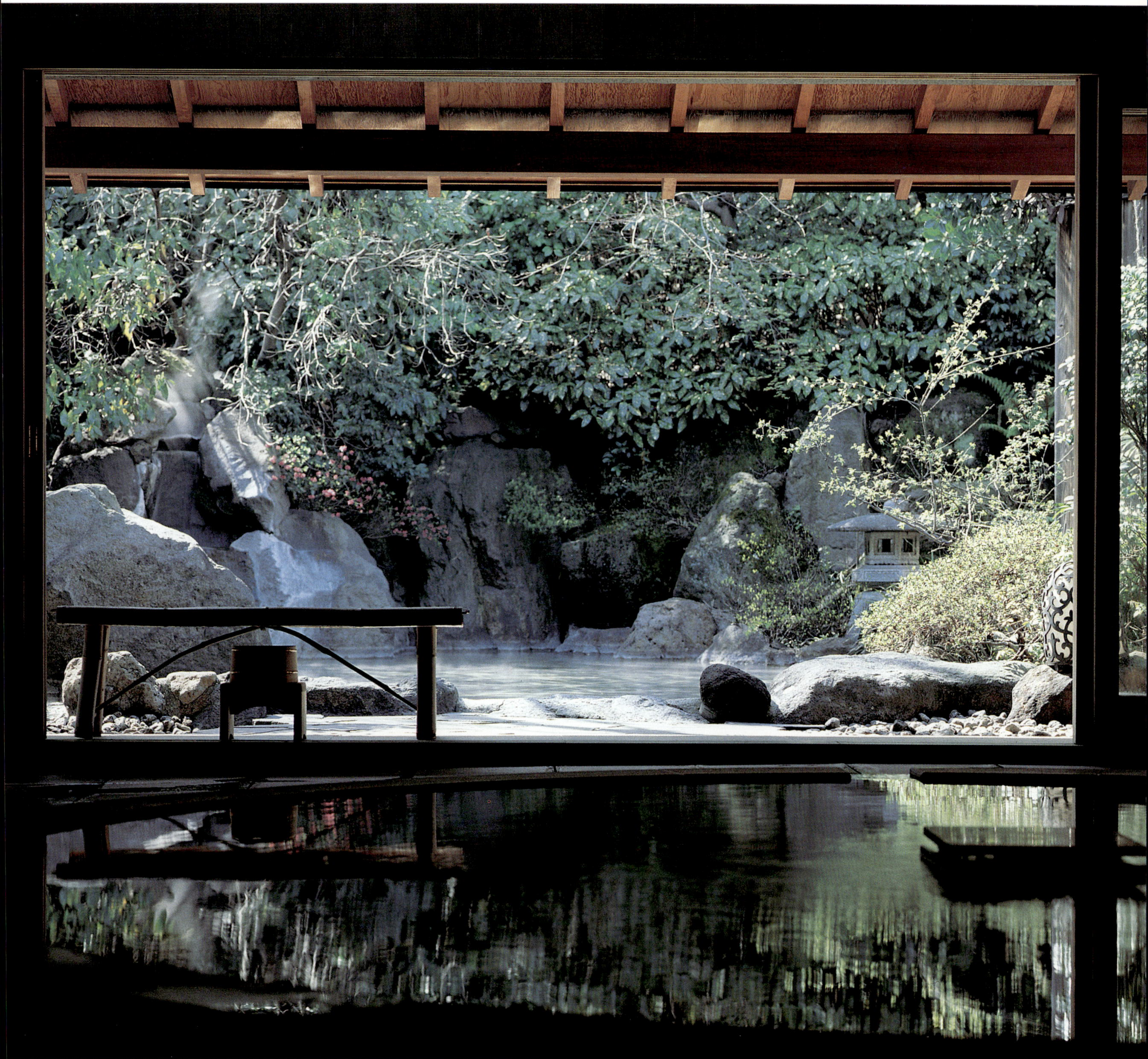

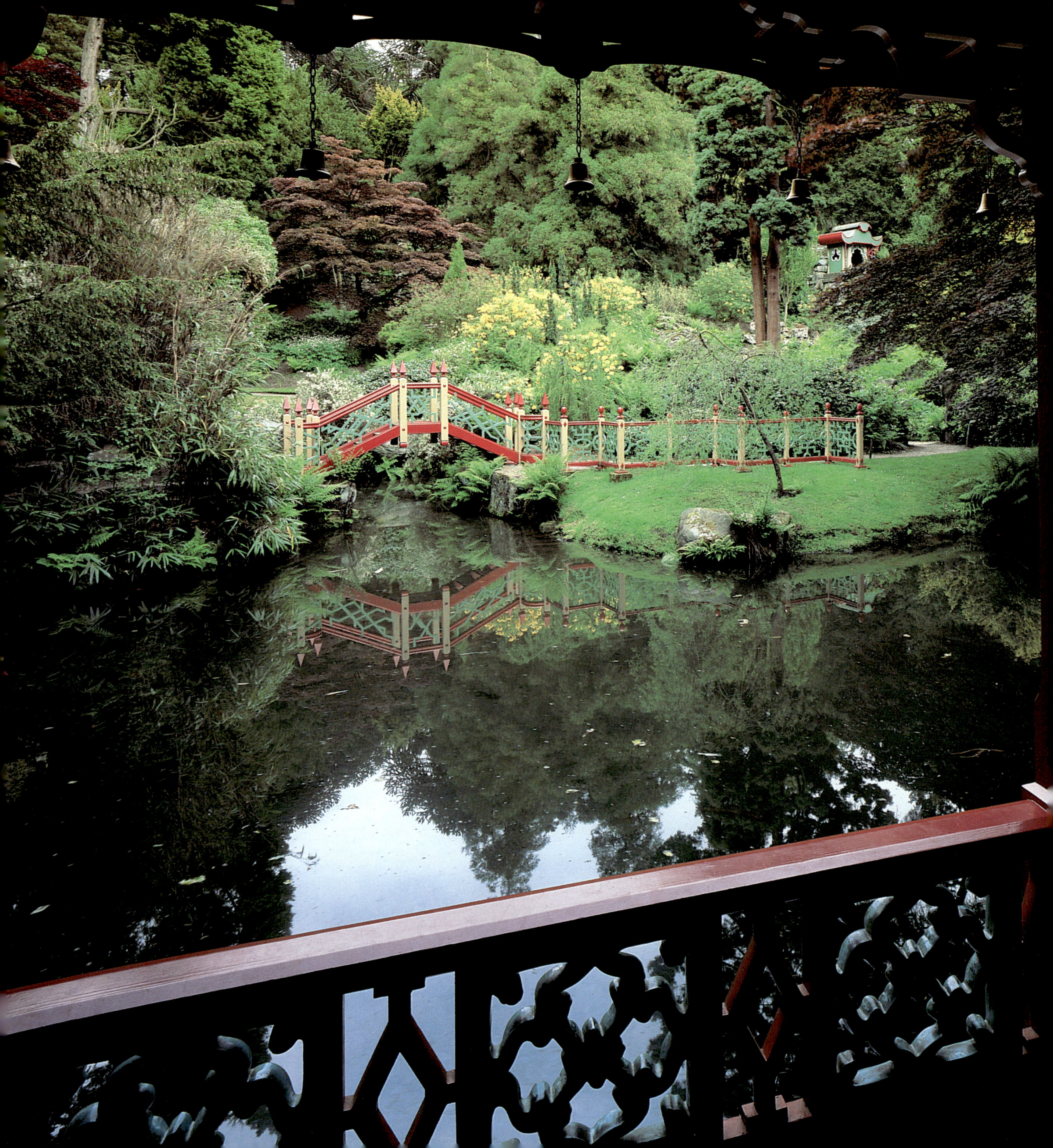

bridges

1 Bridges are functional links within gardens, but they can also be appreciated for their aesthetic and architectural qualities. The Chinese preferred highly ornate decorative bridges, while the Japanese often used unworked natural materials, such as stone slabs and unfinished wooden planks.

Japanese designers are masters of the art of bridging water. They create dramatic visual effects by suspending stone slabs on larger rock bases, or throwing a line of stepping stones across a stretch of water. Wood is another favored material, to make raised-log bridges of arched wood, or arranged in linear patterns to make L-shaped features over the water. Wooden slats or planks in zigzag patterns are often used over marshy ground.

2

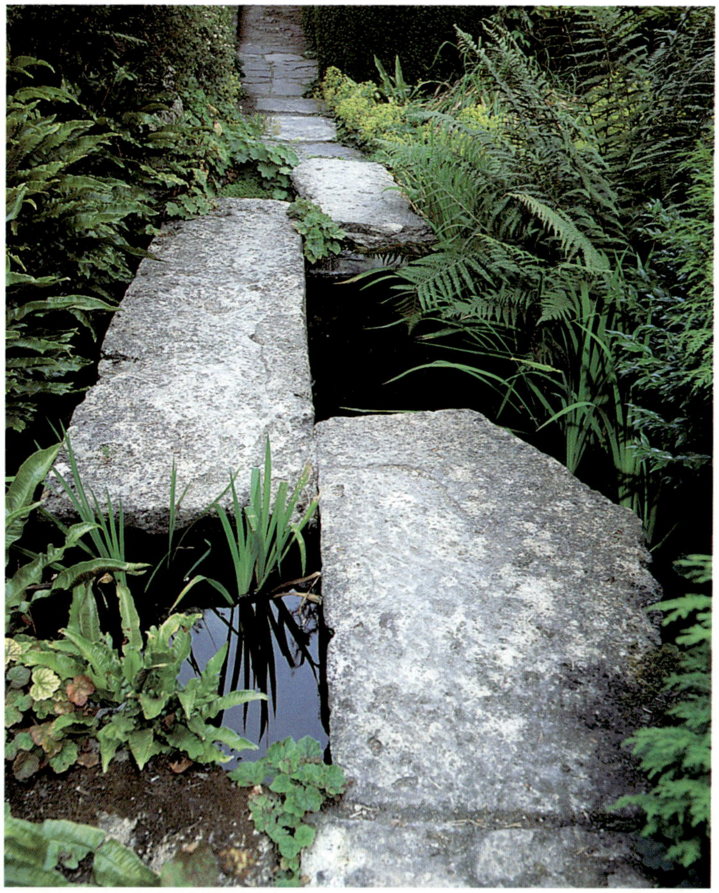

3

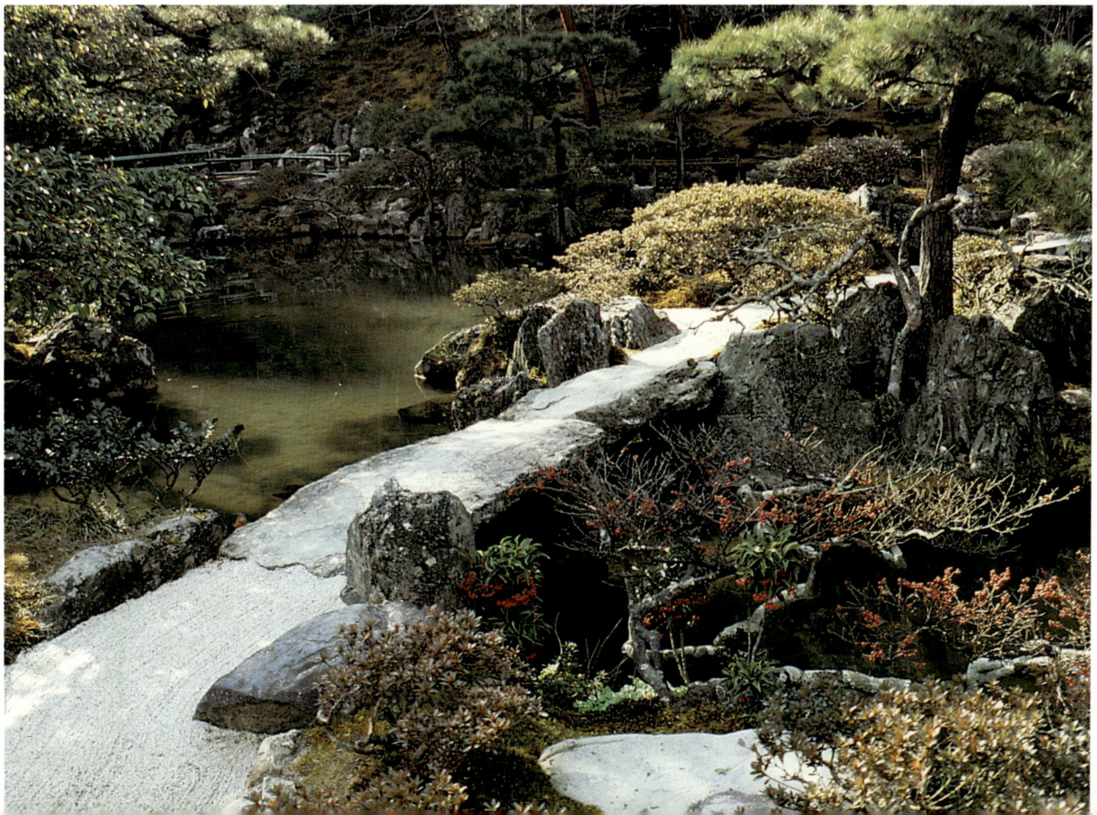

1 A view from the Chinese temple across the water toward the ornate wooden footbridge and the "Joss House" at Biddulph Grange, Staffordshire, England.

2 A stone bridge, along with plants, bamboos, trees, and ornaments, are key Asian elements introduced into a garden at Iford Manor, near Bath, England, by designer Harold Peto, who was influenced and enthused by a visit to Japan in the 1890s.

3 The soft greens of trees in spring combined with water and cherry blossoms make the stroll garden a supremely peaceful place. Here in winter, the stark shapes offset the graphic design of the stone slab bridge, set amidst rocks at Ginkaku-ji in Kyoto.

ornament

1

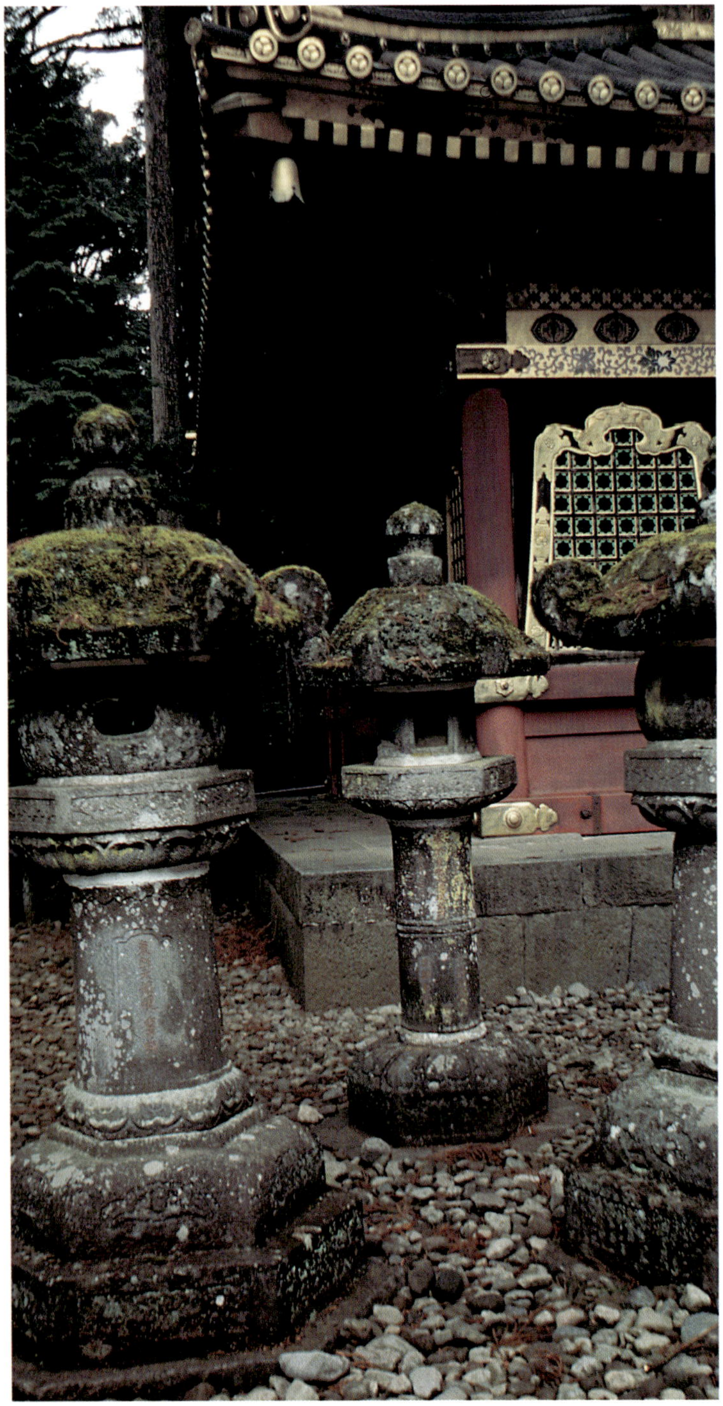

Stone ornaments, such as pagodas, statuary, and lanterns, introduce a human dimension into the garden landscape. Subtly positioned, they can enhance a view, while at the same time serving a practical purpose, by providing light or a quiet corner for meditation or prayer.

Stone lanterns were originally erected in front of Buddhist temples and Shinto shrines as votive offerings. In the sixteenth century they lost these religious associations, when tea masters brought them into their tea gardens to provide lighting for evening tea ceremonies, and decoration, when grouped with stones or reflected in ponds and lakes.

2

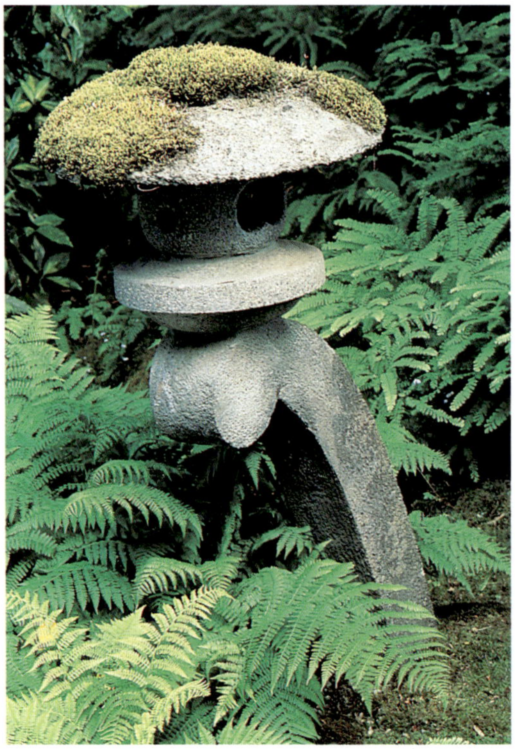

3

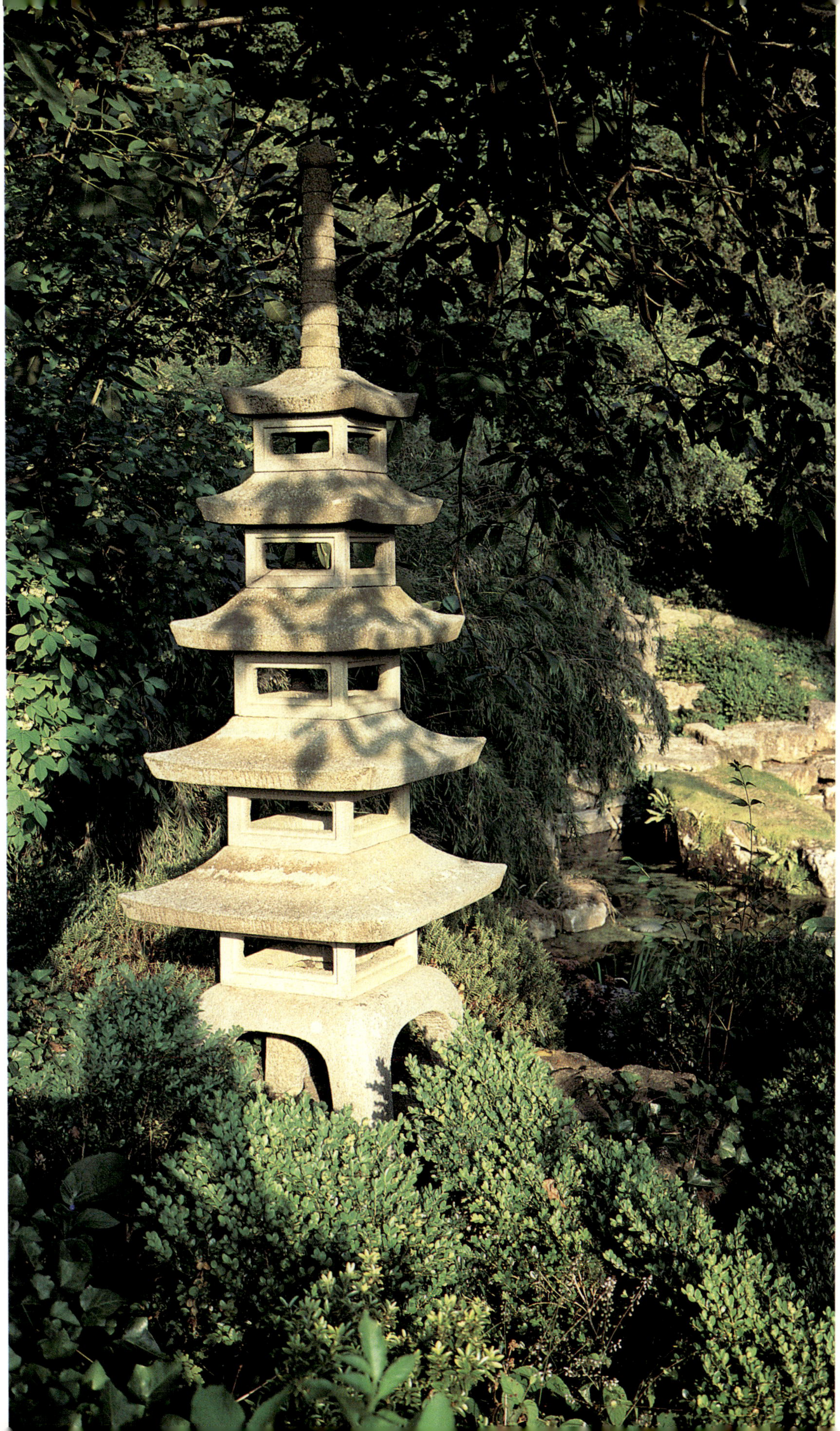

1 Stone lanterns often line ceremonial avenues in front of important shrines and palaces, such as these at the Toshu-gu shrine at Nikko. This extraordinary complex of shrines and temples was built in the early seventeenth century by Tokugawa Iemetsu to honor his grandfather Ieyasu, the first Tokugawa shogun. The natural lichens and mosses enhance the appearance of the weathered granite of the lantern's surface.

2 A stone *yukimi-gata* lantern. Stone lanterns were introduced into gardens by tea masters to illuminate the path through the tea garden to the teahouse.

3 Miniature stone pagodas are now purely decorative, but they are modeled on Indian Buddhist *stupas.* They always have an odd number of stories—five were thought sufficient for a small garden. They are positioned like stone lanterns, near ponds, bridges, and streams, to create a contrast between the vertical and horizontal planes, and to be reflected in water. This small pagoda was brought back from Japan to England by Harold Peto in 1898 for his own garden.

asian gardens in the west

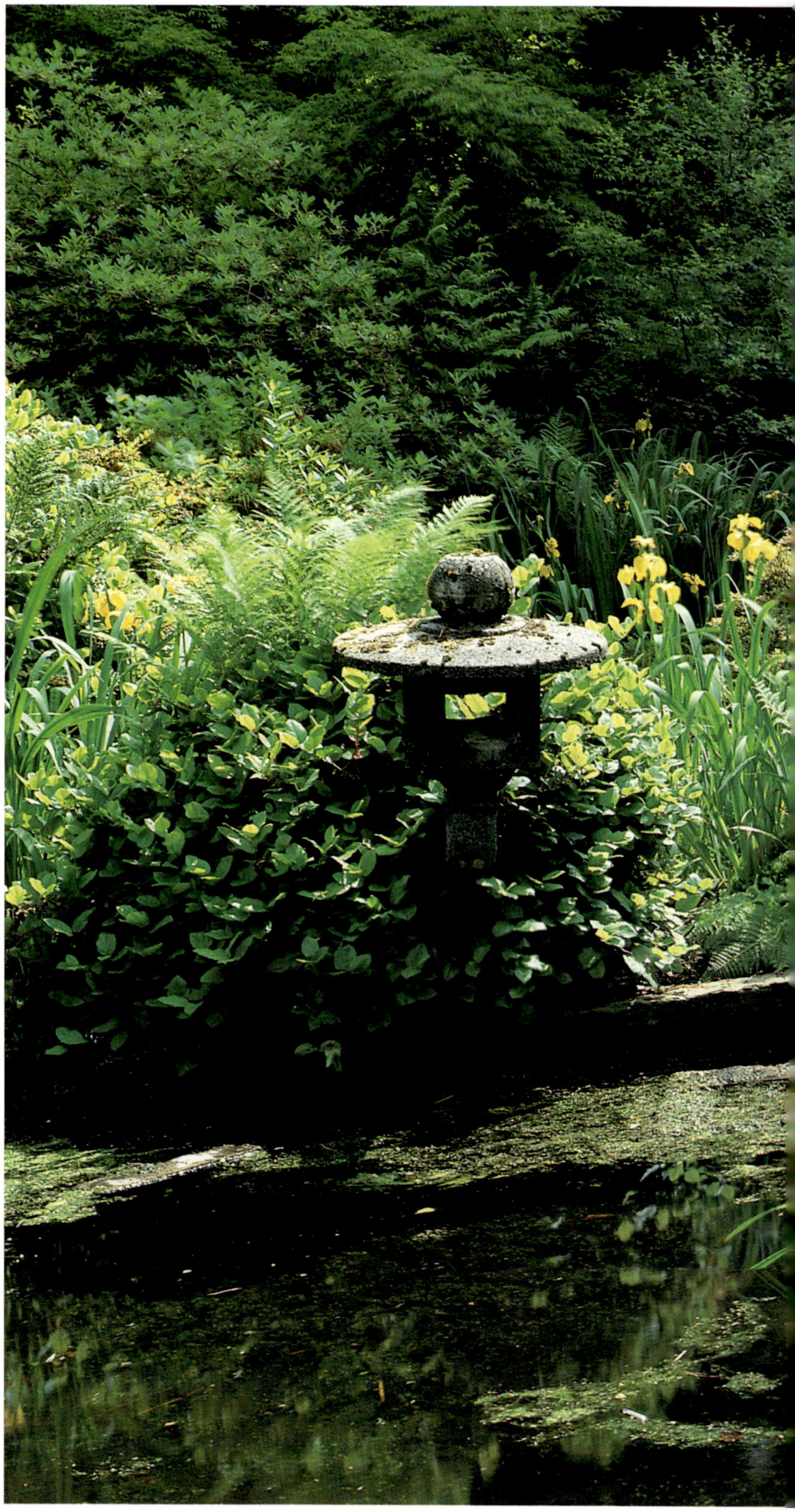

Both China and Japan have experienced long periods of cultural isolation. The Chinese closed their doors to foreigners from the fourteenth to the sixteenth century, and the Japanese, from the seventeenth to the late nineteenth century. It was only in the nineteenth century that the first authentic Chinese gardens were created in Europe. Few of these early gardens have survived, but one example of the genre is "China," which forms part of the gardens at Biddulph Grange, Staffordshire, England (see page 132). The garden reproduces the design of a willow-pattern plate, complete with bridges and pagodas. The fashion for Japanese gardens began even more recently, at the end of the nineteenth century, and is currently enjoying a revival of interest.

The garden created c. 1910 for the third Lord Egerton at Tatton Park, Cheshire, England by Japanese gardeners. A walkway of stepping stones leads the visitor over the tranquil waters of a pond fringed with flag irises and past stone lanterns to a small thatched teahouse hidden amid the trees.

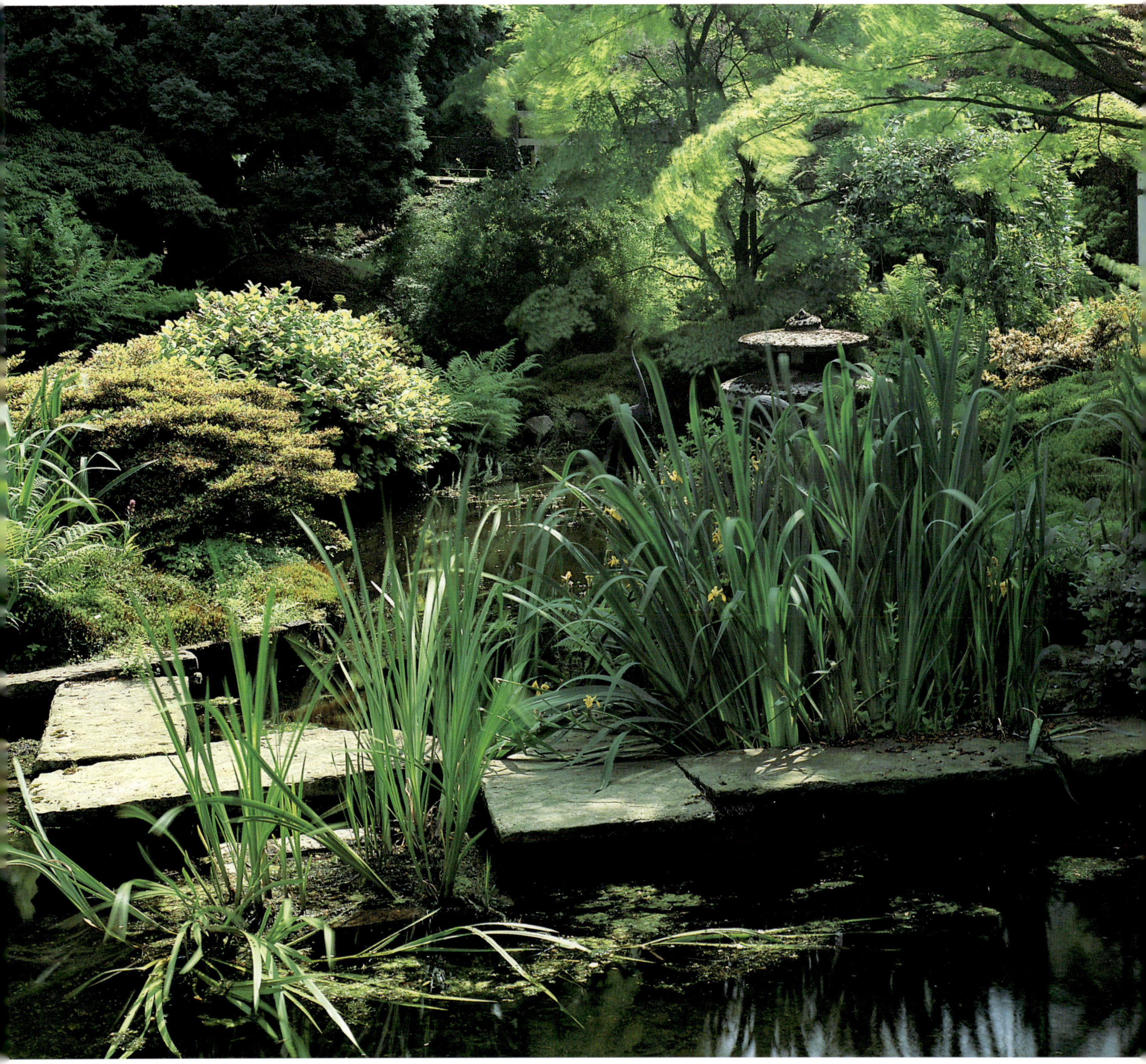

1

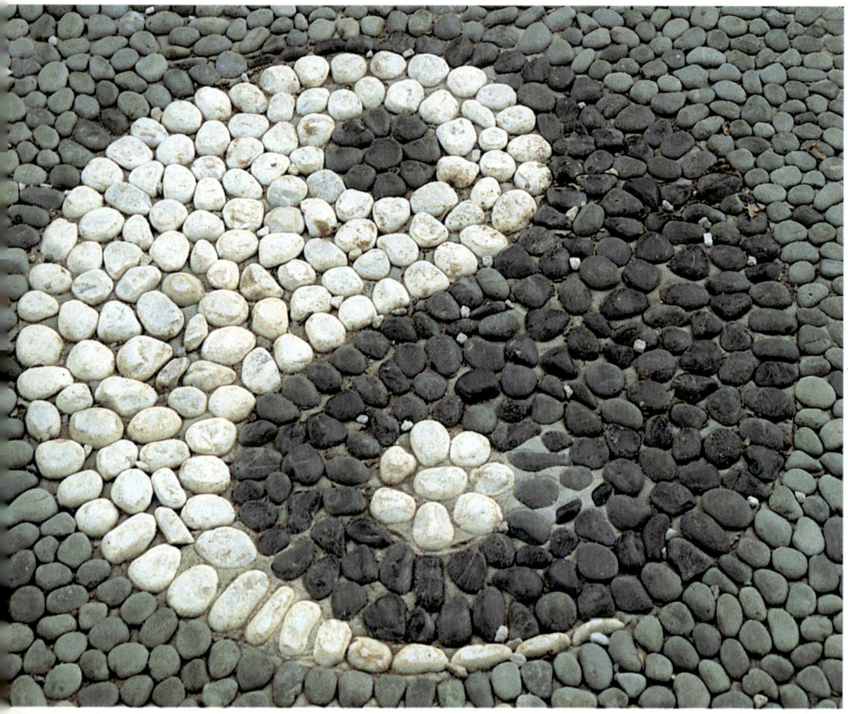

2

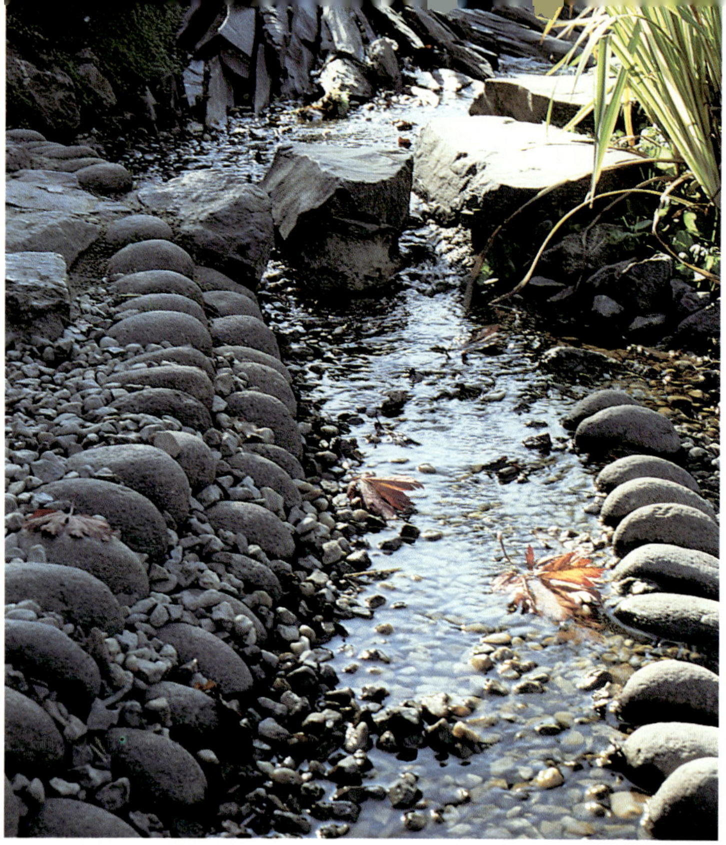

3

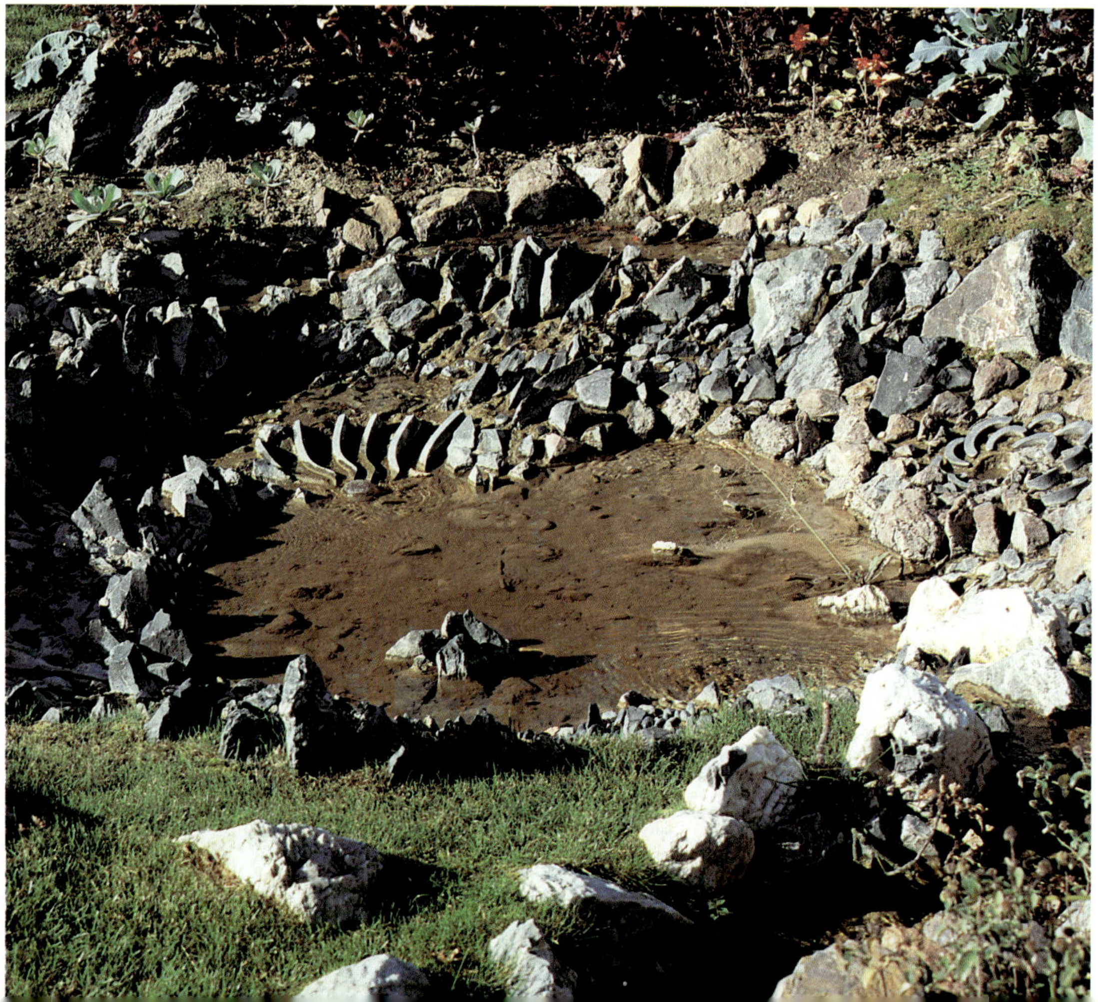

1 This *yin-yang* symbol executed in pebbles is part of a Chinese imperial garden designed by Du Shun-Bao, professor of traditional architecture at the University of Hangzhou, for the 8th Festival International des Jardins at Chaumont in France. It is based on the eight trigrams of *yin* and *yang,* and modeled on the imperial gardens of seventeenth- and eighteenth-century China.

2 & 3 "From sky to earth": three spirals collect water from the earth and sky in a constant cycle. In East Asia, the fundamental energy of a garden, *chi*, is guarded by four gods: *Genbu*, the black tortoise, for the north, *Sieryu*, the blue dragon, for the east, *Sujaku*, the red phoenix for the south, and *Byokki*, the white tiger, for the west. This tranquil garden was designed by Fumiyaki Takano, a Japanese landscape architect working in France.

modern interpretations

Whether by conscious imitation or unconscious borrowing, contemporary garden design in the West is deeply indebted to Japan. The display of stones, the gentle or dramatic uses of water, and the creation of gravel and sand spaces, have traveled far from their original temple and palace settings in imperial Kyoto. Japanese-themed ornamental gardens have been built in North American city parks, complete with native Japanese flora and architectural elements. Private gardeners are also experimenting with Japanese elements, reproducing *torii* shrine gateways in bright red steel girders, camouflaging children's bicycles and garden implements with sliding *shoji* screens, or lighting suburban gardens with stone lanterns.

4

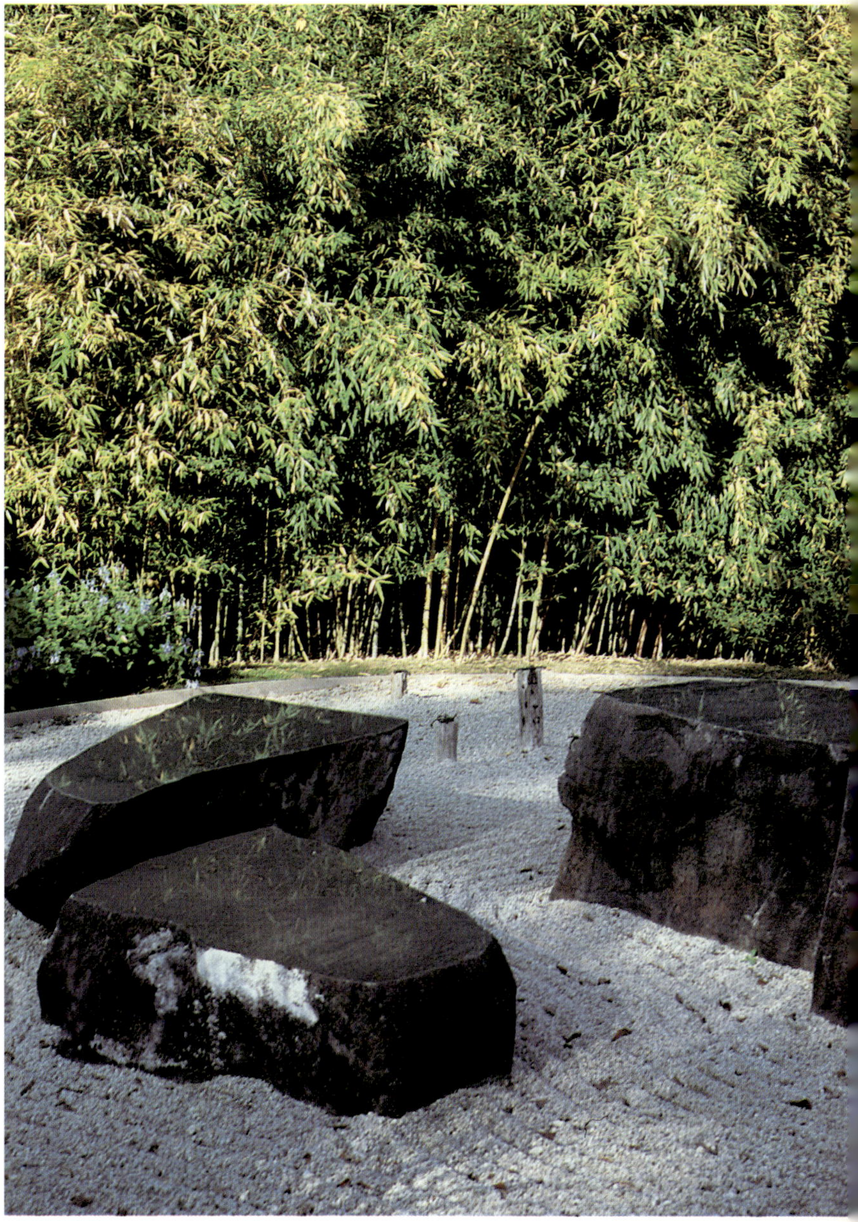

4. "The Archipelago": three polished black stone fragments in a sea of gravel symbolize the Japanese islands. Situated next to the river Loire, they symbolize the constant flow of time. This is the only work outside Japan designed by landscape architect Shodo Suzuki for the Festival International des Jardins at Chaumont. The circle is an intimation of Zen *satori* (enlightenment). The plantings of chrysanthemums, hera, hypericum, millepertuis, and salvia represent the desire for peace and hope.

time line

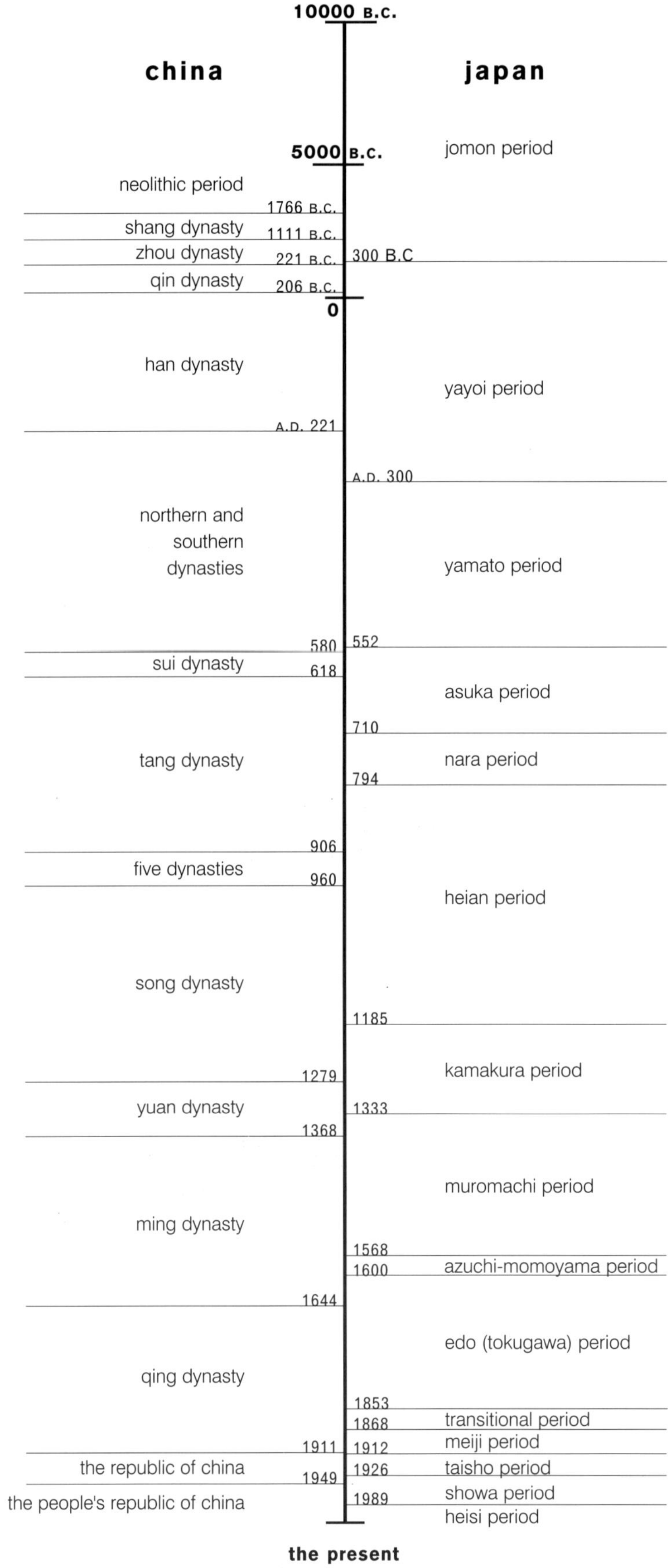

10000 B.C.
china
japan
5000 B.C.
jomon period
neolithic period
1766 B.C.
shang dynasty
1111 B.C.
zhou dynasty
221 B.C.
300 B.C
qin dynasty
206 B.C.
0
han dynasty
yayoi period
A.D. 221
A.D. 300
northern and southern dynasties
yamato period
580
552
sui dynasty
618
asuka period
710
tang dynasty
nara period
794
906
five dynasties
960
heian period
song dynasty
1185
1279
kamakura period
yuan dynasty
1333
1368
muromachi period
ming dynasty
1568
1600
azuchi-momoyama period
1644
edo (tokugawa) period
qing dynasty
1853
1868
transitional period
1911
1912
meiji period
the republic of china
1949
1926
taisho period
showa period
the people's republic of china
1989
heisi period
the present

acknowledgments

Grateful thanks to the many people who have helped so generously with expert advice, information, or cooperation with the loan of items from their collections or the granting of permission for photography. Special thanks are due to Michelle Morgan, Curator at the Museum of East Asian Art in Bath, England, and to Jacqueline Simcox for setting me on what I hope was the right path through such a complex world. As picture editor I should like to thank all at Katie Jones Oriental Art, Ki Design, Snap Dragon, Gong, and Neal Street East. Thanks also to Hilly Cansdale, Elizabeth & John Cartwright-Hignett, Winkie McPherson, Deborah Nash, Olivia and Robert Temple and to Roger Vlitos and Philip de Bay for special photography, in addition to the commercial sources listed below.

Museum of East Asian Art
12 Bennett Street
Bath BA1 2QL, UK
tel 01225 464640
fax 01225 461718
e-mail: museum@east-asian-art.freeserve.co.uk
www.east-asian-art.co.uk

Gregg Baker Oriental Art
132 Kensington Church Street
London W8 4BH, UK
tel 020 7221 3533
fax 020 7221 4410
e-mail: gbakerart@aol.com

Katie Jones Oriental Art
195 Westbourne Grove
London W11 2SB, UK
tel 020 7243 5600
fax 020 7243 4653
e-mail: kjoriental@lineone.net

Ki Design
594 King's Road
London SW6 2DX, UK
tel 020 7736 5999
fax 020 7384 3192

Jacqueline Simcox Ltd
54 Linton Street
London N1 7AS, UK
tel 020 7359 8939
fax 020 7359 8976

Snap Dragon
247 Fulham Road
London SW3 6HY, UK
tel 020 7376 8889
fax 020 7376 5889

The Conran Shop
Michelin House
81 Fulham Road
London SW3 6RD, UK
tel 020 7589 7401
fax 020 7823 7015
e-mail: conranshop@dial.pipex.com

The Futon Co.
138 Notting Hill Gate
London W11 4QG, UK
Tel 020 7727 9252

Gong
182 Portobello Road
London W11 2EB, UK
tel 020 7565 4162
fax 020 7565 4225
e-mail: joplismy@hotmail.com

Graham & Green
4-10 Elgin Crescent
London W11 2JA, UK
tel 020 7727 4594

Habitat UK Ltd
Heal's Building
196 Tottenham Court Road
London W1P 9LD, UK
tel 020 7255 2545

Japan Centre
212 Piccadilly
London W1V 9LD, UK
tel 020 7439 8035

Minamoto Kitchoan Ltd.
44 Piccadilly
London W1V 9AJ, UK
tel 020 7437 3135
fax 020 7437 3191

Monsoon Home
33c King's Road
London SW3 4LX, UK
tel 020 7313 3081

Muji
39 Shelton Street
London WC2H 9HJ, UK
tel 020 7379 1331

Neal Street East
5–7 Neal Street
London WC2H 9PU, UK
tel 020 7240 0135
fax 020 7836 4769

Sala Design Ltd.
The Works
Martock
Somerset TA12 6LG, UK
tel 01935 827050
fax 01935 825556

Biddulph Grange
Stoke-on-Trent
Staffordshire ST8 7SD, UK
tel 01782 517999

Iford Manor
Iford
Bradford-on-Avon
Wiltshire BA15 2BA, UK
tel 01225 863146
fax 01225 862364

Tatton Park
Knutsford
Cheshire
WA16 6QN, UK
tel 01565 654822
fax 01565 650179

Festival International des Jardins
Conservatoire International des
Parcs et Jardins
et du Paysage
Ferme du Chateau
41150 Chaumont-sur-Loire
France
tel 00 33 (0)2 54 20 99 22
fax 00 33 (0)2 54 20 99 24

Gina Corrigan
(specialist study tours to China)
Hoe Barn
Hoe Lane
Bognor Regis
West Sussex PO22 8NS, UK
tel 01243 582178
fax 01243 587239

credits

The publishers would like to thank the following for their permission to reproduce photographs:

Gregg Baker Oriental Art, London 25 (2,3), 38 (3), 50 (2)
Jan Baldwin/Narratives/Peter Ting 98 (1), 113 (3)
Jan Baldwin/Narratives/Andrew Mortada 115 (3)
© Christie's Images Ltd., London 2000 29 (2)
The Conran Shop Ltd. 63 (2)
Gina Corrigan 35 (2)
Dartington Hall Trust/ © Shinsaku Hamada 62 (1)
Jenny de Gex 130 (3)
Jenny de Gex/8th Festival International des Parcs et Jardins, Chaumont-sur-Loire, France 138 (1, 2, 3), 139 (4)
Edifice/Darley 133 (3),134 (1)
Edifice/Hart Davis 32 (1)
Gakken Co. Ltd., Japan/Gin 80 (1)
Gakken Co. Ltd., Japan/Jisho-Ji 122–123
Gakken Co. Ltd., Japan/Mitsuihouse 31 (2), 99 (2), 100 (1) 106–107
Gakken Co. Ltd., Japan/Nijo-Jo 24 (1)
Gakken Co. Ltd., Japan/Nikko Toshougu 89 (3)
Gakken Co. Ltd., Japan/ Ryozan-Ji 128-129
Habitat UK Ltd. 15 (4), 17 (3), 112 (2), 114 (1), 121 (2,3)
Image Bank/China Tourism Press 23 (3), 90 (1)
Image Bank/Andy Caulfield 20–21
Image Bank/Giuliano Colliva 16 (1)
Image Bank/Jean-Claude Comminges 19 (3)
Image Bank/Gary Cralle 45 (2)
Image Bank/Grant V. Faint 12–13, 23 (4), 73 (3)
Image Bank/Kodansha Ltd. 93 (2)
Image Bank/Joanna McCarthy 86 (1)
Image Bank/Yiu Chun Ma 28 (1)
Image Bank/Mahaux Photography 34 (1), 91 (2), 94 (1)
Image Bank/Kaz Mori 19 (2), 92 (1), 126 (1)
Image Bank/Carlos Navajas 46 (1), 78 (1), 95 (3), 130 (1)
Image Bank/Steve Niedorf 19 (4) 48 (2)
Image Bank/Zhen Ge Peng 86–87 (2)
Image Bank/Andrea Pistolesi 88 (1)
Image Bank/P. Redfearn 88 (2)
Image Bank/Don Allen Sparks 68 (1)
Image Bank/Harald Sund 58 (2), 84–85, 134 (2)
Image Bank/Toyofumi Mori 40 (1), 52 (1)
Image Bank/Nevada Wier 45 (3)
Image Bank/Jules Zalon 118–119
Interior Archive/Fritz von der Schulenburg/Grace Wu Bruce, Hong Kong 30 (1), 102–103
Interior Archive/Fritz von der Schulenburg/Kai-Yin Lo, Hong Kong 47 (2), 81 (2)
Interior Archive/Fritz von der Schulenburg/Mimi O'Connell 108 (1)
Interior Archive/Andrew Wood 6, 11, 29 (3), 54-55, 57 (2), 79 (2), 96–97 (1), 101 (3),117 (3), 131 (4)
M Q Publications/Philip de Bay (Neal Street East, London) 49 (4), 73 (2)
MQ Publications/Lucy Mason 83 (4), 109 (3), 114 (2)
MQ Publications/Roger Vlitos (RV):
R V (Katie Jones Oriental Art, London) 39 (4) 56 (1), 75 (3), 82 (2), 110 (3)
R V (Ki Design, London) 42 (2), 74 (2), 83 (3), 101 (2), 110 (1), 117 (2)
R V (Minamoto Kitchoan) 69 (2)
R V (Snap Dragon, London) 14 (1), 48 (1), 74 (1), 111 (4)
R V (courtesy Iford Manor) 127 (2), 130 (2), 133 (2), 135 (3)
R V (Private Collections) 1, 22 (1), 27 (3), 36–37, 50 (3), 64 (1), 66 (1), 70 (1, 2, 3, 4, 5), 82 (1), 105 (2)
Museum of East Asian Art, Bath/Arthur Kan 14 (2), 15 (3), 26 (1, 2), 33 (2, 3, 4), 41 (4), 44 (1), 50 (1), 58 (1), 59 (3), 60 (1, 2), 61 (3), 67 (4, 5), 77 (2, 3)
Deborah Nash 49 (3), 67 (2,3), 116 (1), 120 (1), 125 (2)
National Trust Photo Library/Derek Harris 136–137
National Trust Photo Library/Nick Meers 132 (1)
Neil Setchfield 18 (1), 53 (2), 64–65 (2), 91 (3)
Jacqueline Simcox Ltd, London 2–3, 40 (2), 41 (3), 42 (1), 43 (4), 45 (4)
Snap Dragon, London 109 (2), 110 (2)
Spink, London 76 (1), 104 (1), 105 (3)
Christopher Tadgell 23 (2), 94 (2), 97 (2), 124 (1), 125 (3)
V&A Picture Library 17 (2), 38 (1,2), 42 (3), 72 (1), 112 (1)

index

archways *94*
Arts and Crafts Movement 9

bamboo *10, 14, 47, 68, 74, 78–81, 83, 110, 112, 114, 119, 121, 130*
banners *16, 19, 49, 52*
baskets *14, 14, 64, 77, 78, 78, 82, 83, 110*
bathrooms *114–15*
bats *42, 43, 71*
bird cages *82*
birds *25, 82*
blinds *97, 106*
bottles *63*
bowls *26, 33, 60, 116*
boxes *14, 68, 74, 77*
brick *56*
bronze *59, 59, 74*
Buddhism *26, 47, 67, 73, 88, 92, 92, 123, 126, 126, 134*

cabinets *77, 78, 106, 106, 111, 113, 116*
calligraphy *16, 19, 49, 49, 52, 68, 119, 121*
cane *14, 78, 82, 83, 112*
celadon *33*
ceramics *7, 8, 9, 60, 63*
chair covers *42*
chairs *78, 105*
cherry-blossom viewing parties *40*
chests *14, 43, 49, 74, 110, 110, 111, 113*
chi *138*
China and the West *7–8*
Chinese characters *19, 29, 37, 49, 49, 119*
chinoiserie *8, 78, 103*
clay *55, 60*
cloisonné *44*
colors *14–35*
  black *16-17*
  blue and white *26–7*
  gold *24–5*
  green *32–3*
  multi-colored *34–5*
  naturals *14–15*
  red *18–21*
  red and gold *22–3*
  yellow *28–31*

copper *59*
courtship *50*
cranes *25, 43, 73, 77*
cupboards *110*
cushions *31, 106, 106*

dancers *34*
daybeds *104*
dish carriers *74*
doors *95, 95, 103, 110*
dragons *26, 28, 29, 37, 44, 44, 71, 77, 85, 88, 94, 138*
ducks *43*

earthenware *64*
embroidery *29, 39, 40, 70, 71, 73*

fencing *78*
feng shui 9, *18, 41, 85, 86*
ferns *82*
fire buckets *19*
fireworks *22*
flowers *38–41, 73, 74, 112*
flutes *74*
fly whisks *74*
fountains *10, 130*
fretwork *86, 105*
futons *106*

gardens *32, 47, 55, 56, 94, 95, 97, 122–39*
  Asian gardens in the West *136–7*
  bridges *125, 133, 133, 135, 136*
  modern interpretations *138–9*
  moss *129, 129*
  old Chinese *124–5*
  ornament *134, 135*
  stone *125, 126, 126, 133, 134, 139, 139*
  water *125, 130, 130, 138, 139*
gates *88, 94, 95*
ghost money *67*
gold *16, 59, 59, 77*
gold leaf *22, 25, 43*
grasses *82*
grave goods *60*

hair pins *71*
hats *71, 78*
headdresses *71*
"Hell Money" *67*
hemp *82*
hot spring (*onsen*) *56, 114*
house, model *14, 60*

ikebana *74, 74, 83*
imperial halls *22*
incense burners *22, 59*
inro *77*
interiors, Japan *98–9*
iron *59, 60, 77*

jade *47*
Japan and the West *8–9*
Japanese language *49*
jars *26, 41, 60, 116*
jute *82*

kabuki theatre *16, 51, 52*
kettles *106, 116*
kimonos *39, 43, 49, 73, 73, 117*
kitchens *114*
knots *39, 47*
koto *74*

lacquerwork *8, 16, 22, 55, 74, 76–7, 103, 109, 111, 113*
ladles *60*
lamps *31, 111, 119, 119, 121, 121*
lanterns *16, 18, 17, 119, 121, 121, 134, 135, 136, 139*
lead *59, 60*
lichens *135*
lighting *118–21*

manga *50*
metal *58–9, 110*
Mingei (folk craft) movement *63, 116*
mirrors *32, 59, 78*
modern influences *10*
mosses *123, 129, 129, 135*
mother-of-pearl *16, 77*

netsuke *77*
noh theatre *16*

obi (kimono sash) *39, 77*
origami *68*

pagodas *92, 92, 135, 136*
palaces *34, 85, 85, 86, 99*
panels *25, 44, 83*
paper *119*
China *66–7*
Japan *68–9*
paperweights *44*
patterns
  abstract *46–7*
  calligraphy *48–9*
  dragons *44–5*
  fauna *42–3*
  flora *38–41*
  narrative *50–51*
pavilions *86, 97*
phoenixes *41, 71, 88, 138*
pillows *33*
plates *63, 74*
porcelain *26, 60*
pots *116*
pottery *15, 17, 31*
  contemporary *62–3*
  early *60–61*
purses *71*

quilting *73*

reed *14, 82*
robes *26, 28, 29, 37, 37, 43, 73*
roofs *28, 85, 86, 86, 88, 90–91, 92, 92, 94, 99*
rope *82*

saké casks *49*
screens *14, 25, 37, 39, 44, 50, 51, 68, 81, 83, 97, 99, 99, 100–101, 106, 110, 139*
scrolls *16, 31, 50, 99, 112, 130*
seating
  China *104–5*
  Japan *106–7*

shan shui 125
Shinto *18, 19, 56, 82, 92, 126, 134*
shoes *70, 71, 106*
shrines *19, 22, 49, 52, 56, 68, 88, 135*
silks *7, 26, 29, 39, 42, 44, 70, 70, 71, 105*
silver *16, 25, 59, 77*
skirts *70*
spoons *41*
steel *59*
stenciling, resist *43*
stone *55, 56–7, 81, 86, 114, 123*
  see also under gardens
storage *110–13*
suitcases *110*

tables *31, 47, 78, 103, 106, 109, 109*
The Tale of Genji 50, 51
Taoism *18*
tapestry *41*
tatami mats *14, 83, 99, 99, 106, 106*
tea ceremony *10, 55, 64–5, 116–17, 134*
teabowls *17, 112, 116*
teahouses *88, 117, 135, 136*
teapots *64, 116*
temples *28, 47, 52, 85, 85, 88, 92–3, 92, 95, 134, 135*
textiles *8, 16, 34*
  China *70–71*
  Japan *72–3*
tin *59*
torii (shrine gates) *18, 20, 139*
trunks *110*
tsuba (sword guards) *16*

ukiyo-e woodblock prints *9, 51, 53*

vases *15, 51, 74, 112*

wall hangings *40, 99*
wardrobes *78*
washi (handmade paper) *68*
windows *86, 95, 96–7, 114*
wood *55, 56, 74–5, 109, 109, 114, 116, 133*

yang 9, 26, 47, 125, 138
yin 9, 47, 125, 138

Zen style *10*